GW00599586

RWE Thames Water is pleased to sponsor Reading Ornithological Club's Annual Bird Report. The occurrence and distribution of birds is a vital component of biodiversity and the information gained from bird records, such as those reported here, is a key element of understanding where to target protection. Many of our operational sites across the Thames Water region are recognised as internationally, nationally or locally important for birds whether for breeding, wintering or migration. The compilation and reporting of bird statistics can be used as indicators of the health of the countryside and to reflect other issues such as climate change which itself has important implications for water resources management. The compilation of bird records requires a great deal of effort on the part of birdwatchers and we endeavour to support birdwatching activity on our sites wherever possible. To this end we are planning to increase the opportunities for access to sites across our region. We have enhanced numerous sites to improve habitats for birds. Recently we planted reedbed habitat at Bracknell Millpond and Slough STW and continued sponsorship of the RSPB Wessex Downs and Chilterns Farmlands Birds project, which covers much of Berkshire."

Dr Brian Crathorne
Head of Environment.
Thames Water Utilities Limited

THE READING ORNITHOLOGICAL CLUB (ROC) was founded in 1947. Its objects are to promote education and study of wild birds, their habitats and conservation in Berkshire. Membership is open to anyone interested in birds and bird-watching, beginner or expert, local patch enthusiast or international twitcher. The Club organises a full programme of events with indoor evening meetings and outdoor excursions. It publishes a quarterly Newsletter and *The Birds of Berkshire* annual report, which are free to members.

INDOOR MEETINGS are held during the winter season at the University of Reading on fortnightly Wednesday evenings. These are usually illustrated lectures by visiting speakers drawn from the UK's best-known ornithologists.

The Club holds a popular annual **PHOTOGRAPHIC COMPETITION** with film and digital sections; it attracts outstanding work, which is judged by experts including the President, Gordon Langsbury.

SOCIAL EVENINGS are held at Christmas and occasionally during the year.

FIELD EXCURSIONS, held throughout the year, range from short walks to weekend visits to many top bird-watching sites locally and further afield. Recent trips have included weekends in Norfolk, Cornwall, Anglesey and the Lake District as well as many day trips in southern England. Regular midweek walks are arranged to many of the best bird-watching sites in the county. All members are welcome – beginners or experts. Suggestions of places to visit and volunteers to arrange or lead are always welcome. Joining an ROC field excursion can be an excellent way to discover new sites, meet other birders and improve your bird-watching skills.

CONSERVATION of important local habitats and species is important to us: the Reading area contains a growing number of excellent reserves and projects that enhance the diversity of the region. Many ROC members are involved in practical conservation work with groups such as Friends of Lavell's Lake, the Theale Area Bird Conservation Group and Moor Green Lakes. The Club manages *The Birds of Berkshire Conservation Fund*, which supports local bird conservation projects.

SURVEYS AND RECORDING. The Club organises local bird surveys and is affiliated to the British Trust for Ornithology, in whose surveys members are encouraged to participate, to assist conservation nationally. Members are encouraged to keep records of local observations and submit them, electronically or in writing, to the County Recorder for collation and analysis.

The Birds of Berkshire, published in 1996, is available to Club members while stocks last at £5. This excellent atlas and avifauna is the authoritative book on the status of birds in the county and is lavishly illustrated by Robert Gillmor and others. Work on a new atlas will start in 2007, for publication in about five years time.

For more information and the current programme visit
www.theroc.org.uk
or contact the Secretary
Renton Righelato,
63 Hamilton Road, Reading, RG1 5RA
renton.righelato@theroc.org.uk
telephone 0787 981 2564.

The Birds of Berkshire

Annual Report for the year 2003

Contents

Page

Edited by Colin Wilson and Peter Standley.
Published 2006 by
READING ORNITHOLOGICAL CLUB
© Reading Ornithological Club
ISBN 978-0-9553497-0-6
Price £6.00

Introduction

We are pleased to be able to publish a new style county report this year with more colour and a better overall finish. This report has been a long time in coming but since we produced Birds of Berkshire 2002 we have also caught up with some of our arrears and published the 1998/99 report. Work on the 2000/2001 report is also well advanced and once this has been published all our resources will be focused on producing an annual report every year in good time.

For the time being I shall remain as Managing Editor of the Birds of Berkshire but the technical editing, basically the enormous responsibility of ensuring a high quality interpretation of the 40,000 records received, will come from the recording team of Chris Heard and Derek Barker. This report is the last Peter Standley will complete as Technical Editor and it is my pleasure to record the considerable appreciation of the Reading Ornithological Club and I am sure, the whole birdwatching fraternity in Berkshire who have all benefited from his wise counsel and contributions to the ornithological scene over so many years.

This year the order of species accounts has changed. Following over 26 phylogenetic studies, many using DNA analysis published in recent years, a large body of evidence showed that the order of birds in the British list (reflected in Voous Order, (BOU 1977)) did not properly reflect their evolution. The BOU have accepted the recommendations of their Taxonomic Sub-Committee and changed the order which they urge report editors and publishers to adopt for their reports from 2003 onwards. Accordingly, this report has followed this new Order.

The thousands of bird records collected in Berkshire come from many sources and are combined in a database administered for us by Marek Walford. Work is currently under way to allow these records to be shared with Thames Valley Environmental Records Centre to enable them to provide quality data to Councils and Developers so planning decisions can be made in an informed way. This follows a national trend and should ensure birdwatchers records have high value in the years ahead, fighting inappropriate development and protecting important habitats.

Finally, in this introduction I wish to mention the Berkshire Atlas Group, a team who are planning a new County Atlas and Avifauna to follow the previous Birds of Berkshire published in 1996. Discussions are at an early stage but fieldwork will be linked to the British Trust for Ornithology (BTO) national atlas project for which some experimental pilot survey work was recently undertaken. Enthusiastic surveyors will be recruited soon to help with this project which is intended to combine both breeding and winter atlas data, making the most comprehensive atlas ever published for the County.

Colin Wilson
Managing Editor
June 2006

Acknowledgements

The production of a report of this nature requires the input of many people and none more than the contributors of bird records, a detailed list of those whose records have been used to compile this report is shown at the end of the systematic list.

The writing of the species accounts requires considerable commitment from a team of experienced ornithologists and we thank Derek Barker, Paul Bright-Thomas, Keith Chard, Brian Clews, Bill Nicoll, Chris Robinson, Ted Rogers and Marek Walford for their hard work in drafting accounts from the many thousands of records reviewed. The detailed editing of the accounts by Derek Barker is an enormous task requiring skill and diligence and we are very grateful for the dedication and knowledge of Berkshire's birds and geography he brings to this task. Peter Standley has completed final reviews and adjustments to the systematic list along with the Summary of Weather and Bird Highlights and the Report of the Berkshire Records Committee. Chris Heard has undertaken a final reading to ensure no technical errors remain. Keith Chard has undertaken a considerable amount of work in analysing, formatting and checking large volumes of typed text so the final article is of a high standard and special thanks go to him for this work.

This Report consists of much more than just the systematic list and we thank the writers and providers of articles for the work and time that went into providing them often involving considerable fieldwork or desk based study. Each article is listed on the Index page with their names alongside.

We are very grateful once again to Robert Gillmor for his beautiful painting on the cover of the Report. Other artists showing their considerable talent include Martin Hallam who has provided outstanding drawings for many years, and newcomers, Andrew Cowdell for his lovely Siskin family, Andrew Brooks, Tony Keene and Helen Chadburn for their much appreciated contributions.

Photography is now a widespread hobby not least for birdwatchers and we are very lucky to have some photographers in the County who have managed to capture superb images of rare birds seen in 2003. We thank Jerry O'Brien, Mike McKee, Dave Rimes and Gary Randall for allowing us to use their images on our pages.

Of course, the matter of sponsorship and advertising is vital to production of this Report. We are fortunate to have the continued support of RWE Thames Water and, for the first time, Thames Valley Environmental Records Centre about which an article appears later. Another valuable sponsor this year is Lafarge Group and we appreciate their contribution. The advertisers are often long term supporters including members who very generously assist us with meeting ever increasing production costs. We thank them and urge all readers to use their services and to mention this Report when they do so.

Finally, to anyone inadvertently omitted we apologise and offer our thanks to you and all those who have helped in ways large or small to produce this publication.

Colin Wilson
Blakeney, St Catherine's Road
Frimley Green, Camberley, Surrey
GU16 9NP
Tel: 01252 837411

County Directory

COUNTY RECORDER

Recorder tasks are divided between the County Recorder and Assistant Recorder as follows:

Recorder: Chris Heard, specialisation in bird identification. Chairman of the Berkshire Rarities Committee. 3, Waterside Lodge, Ray Mead Road, Maidenhead, Berks SL6 8NP. Telephone 01628 633828.

Assistant Recorder: Derek Barker, specialising in breeding birds in Berkshire. Secretary to the Berkshire Rarities Committee. 40, Heywood Gardens, Woodlands Park, Maidenhead, SL6 3LZ.

READING ORNITHOLOGICAL CLUB

www.theroc.org.uk

A Club for birdwatchers throughout Berkshire, with indoor and outdoor meetings, surveys and publications, including Birds of Berkshire annual reports – see page 2 for details. Collects bird records for the county and is responsible for the county database.

Secretary, Renton Righelato, 63 Hamilton Road, Reading, Berks RG1 5RA

Telephone 0118 926 4513
Email: **renton.righelato@theroc.org.uk**

NEWBURY DISTRICT ORNITHOLOGICAL CLUB

www.ndoc.org.uk

A Club for birdwatchers in the Newbury area with a recording area of 10 miles radius of the town. Offers indoor and outdoor meetings, surveys and publications.

Secretary, Trevor Maynard, 15 Kempstone Close, Newbury, Berks, RG14 7RS

Telephone 01635 36752
Email **info@ndoc.org.uk**

BERKSHIRE BIRD BULLETIN

Publisher of monthly newsletters of birds reported in the County with a news summary and detailed listings of sightings. Records are welcome for publication.

County Ornithological Services. Contact Brian Clews, Telephone 07071 202000 or email **brian.clews@btconnect.com**

www.berksbirds.co.uk

An independent website devoted to offering a free resource to birdwatchers in Berkshire and providing news, photographs and records of birds with additional optional information services.

BRITISH TRUST FOR ORNITHOLOGY (BTO)

Local representative for BTO matters including organising surveys: Chris Robinson, 2, Beckfords, Upper Basildon, Reading, Berks, RG8 8PB

Telephone 01491 671420

Email **berks_bto_rep@btinternet.com**

FRIENDS OF LAVELL'S LAKE

Conservation volunteers managing Lavell's Lake local nature reserve near Dinton Pastures Country Park, Wokingham. Bird walks, occasional meetings and newsletters. Contact Chairman Fraser Cottington at **Fraser1947@hotmail.com or see**
www.friendsoflavells.freeola.com/index.shtml

MOOR GREEN LAKES GROUP

Conservation volunteers who manage Moor Green Lakes Nature Reserve near Eversley. Newsletters an annual report and access to bird hides. Contact Membership Secretary:

Keith Littler, 316 Yorktown Road, College Town, Sandhurst, Berks, GU47 0PZ

THEALE AREA BIRD CONSERVATION GROUP

A local Club devoted to the conservation of birds in the Theale area, west of Reading. Indoor and outdoor meetings, annual bird race and survey work.

http://tabcg.mysite.wanadoo-members.co.uk/

Contact Cath McEwan, Secretary,

Email **Catherine@cmcewan.fsnet..co.uk**

LOCAL RSPB GROUPS

Groups promote and represent the RSPB in the local community. Activities include indoor and outdoor meetings and fund raising events.

Further details from the RSPB or directly from:

East Berks Local Group
www.eastberksrspb.org.uk/

Reading Local Group
www.reading-rspb.org.uk/

Wokingham and Bracknell Local Group
www.wbrspb.btinternet.co.uk/

The Thames Valley Environmental Records Centre in Berkshire

By Adrian Hutchings

What do we really know about the wildlife of Berkshire? There are some places in the County that are well known for the wildlife they contain, but when we look at the wider countryside we find that a large proportion of our wildlife is under recorded. For much of the wildlife in Berkshire we have very little idea where it is and whether it is increasing, decreasing or staying the same.

It's true that there are lots of us out and about recording wildlife and many enthusiasts, particularly ornithologists, take the trouble to make a written record of what they see – but are we making the most of all this information?

Information can be an extremely powerful tool in nature conservation. Some groups and individuals in the County have done, and continue to do, excellent work collecting valuable data about wildlife and making that data work. Many environmental groups are using this data to assist them in managing land and habitats for wildlife, and increasingly Local Authorities are recognising the need for up to date and accurate information to help inform the decision and policy-making processes.

But it has long been recognised that more resources need to go into supporting and co-ordinating the collection, management and supply of wildlife information locally. With this in mind the Thames Valley Environmental Records Centre (TV ERC) was set up in 2003 covering Oxfordshire and Berkshire. With funding from English Nature and all the Local Authorities in the two Counties the Records Centre acts to help people collect information and make good quality wildlife information more easily available.

TV ERC manages a large database of information and is a secure centre where groups and individuals can lodge copies of their own data and get access to data collected by others. Security of sensitive data is paramount to TV ERC. The Records Centre only uses data in ways which will benefit wildlife and for the purposes agreed by the owners of that data. The ultimate goal of TVERC is to see more wildlife information being used by a greater number of people and thereby enabling sensible and informed decisions about wildlife.

More details about TV ERC can be found on their website: www.tverc.org

The TV ERC Berkshire staff – Adrian Hutchings and Sarah Gorman – can be contacted at ahutchings@westberks.gov.uk, sgorman@westberks.gov.uk

or

C/o Planning,
Council Offices
Market Street
Newbury
RG14 5LD
Tel. 01635 519179

The Reading Ornithological Club gratefully acknowledges the financial contribution made by TV ERC towards the publication of this report.

A SPRING FLOCK OF POMARINE SKUAS IN BERKSHIRE

By Chris Heard

The up-channel movement of Pomarine Skua flocks is one of the highlights of Spring migration along Britain's South coast. One would not expect to witness any part of this in Berkshire but in April 2003 a migrant flock overflew Queen Mother Reservoir and disappeared into the gloom...

On Friday 25th April I was manning Birdline South East, while my birdline partner Jerry Warne got an early start for the drive down to Dungeness - in the hope of seeing some Pom' Skuas! The morning was quite bright, with a blustery South-easterly wind, but a solid band of rain spread into East Berkshire during the afternoon (from around 2pm onwards). By early evening I fancied a break from the birdline and, hoping for a Whimbrel or other rain-induced wader, I visited Queen Mother Reservoir. It was still raining when I arrived - so I stayed in the car for another 20 minutes-or-so until it eased - and it didn't rain again for another 50 minutes.

Long-range visibility wasn't good (there was complete overcast) and halfway around the reservoir I'd noted nothing apart from an increase in Common Sandpipers when, casually looking upwards, my eye was attracted by a rapid movement almost directly overhead. A flock of gull-like birds, about 200 feet up, had made a sudden 'whiffling' descent - disturbed by an outward-bound jet from Heathrow - and, with the naked eye, their buoyant flight brought Little Gulls to mind. I put down my telescope and raised my binoculars... and found myself uttering some prime Anglo-Saxon! Almost directly overhead was an unquestionable flock of *thirteen* skuas - all of them with tail-streamers.

To be honest, I wasn't thinking about their actual identity at this point - I was too stunned - and the first thing I noted was the variation: 1 wholly dark bird, 1 barred and 11 light morphs. The light morphs had variable breast-bands but those with the whitest underparts had a clean cut-off between the belly and the dark undertail-coverts. They were clearly Common Gull-sized and had quite broad, but pointed, wings and as they circled and briefly hung on the wind I noted that the outer part of the wing (the 'hand') was held slightly depressed, recalling Hobby. There were magical moments as they evidently eyed the reservoir (and me?!) but then they quickly regrouped and continued overhead. Although I was looking straight up, these were quite good views and I could see that the tail-streamers were rounded at the tip - in fact none of them had sharp points to the streamers - and as they went over the tail projections looked more blob-shaped. They were now flying steadily away, in formation, and I realised it was time to get my telescope on them. They maintained a northerly heading with regular wingbeats and the tail-projections - which now looked more like the classic 'spoons' - actually appeared to bob on the downstrokes (making the body appear to undulate). I did wonder why the 'spoons' had not been obvious earlier and it was a while before I realised that the twisted tail projections, which are popularly compared to spoons when seen in a profile view, would not in fact be obvious from directly below.

There was still an hours light left but my mind was so preoccupied that I knew I had to head home. I kept replaying the sighting in my head - everything was right for Pomarine Skua (size, structure, plumage, flight action, even flock-size) but I had never heard of an inland sighting of a whole flock before! I had to speak to the UK's top skua expert, Dave Davenport... but it was a while before he returned home. When I did get through I said "I've had a flock of 13 skuas over my local reservoir: 11 light morphs, 1 dark morph...." and before

I could say anymore he said "They were Poms then". He explained that the size of the flock and the balance of the plumage morphs "would be impossible for Arctic Skua" and that since the barred birds also had tail projections, they were just more heavily marked individuals [which also fits the probabilities - since 2nd-3rd summers are apparently unlikely before mid May]. He went on to confirm that a passage of Pomarine Skuas had been expected along the South coast that day but that very few had been sighted further East than the Isle of Wight - the rain had presumeably impeded further up-channel movement. On a more philosophical note, I complained to Dave that I wished I'd had longer to enjoy such an amazing sight but he countered that I should be content with whatever views I got - I was very lucky to have seen this at all.

In fact, Pomarine Skuas may regularly overfly large continental land-masses (eg many sightings from the Black and Aral seas in Spring) and it has been suggested that much of the passage up the English Channel may continue overland across the European mainland (Davenport, 1975). In Scotland, Pomarine Skua flocks regularly head off overland from the Solway Firth but, to date (June 2006), I can find no other English sighting of an inland flock in Spring (but note that several small groups were seen inland during the late autumn influx in 1985; see Fox & Aspinall, 1987).

It is characteristic for Pomarine Skuas to pass rapidly through UK waters in the Spring - rarely resting or stopping to feed. The Queen Mother flock appeared to have come over from the South-east and they continued northwards without delay. They did not appear to be attracted down by the reservoir or the roosting gulls and, had they not manoevered because of the overhead plane, they might well have passed over unnoticed by me against the dull grey sky. Of course, such weather conditions are not uncommon but inland skua occurrences are notoriously unpredictable, especially in Spring: my last Spring sighting was of an Arctic Skua circling over Windsor Forest on a sunny May morning!

References
Davenport, D.L. 1975. Brit.Birds 68: 461.
Fox, A.D. & Aspinall S.J. 1987. Brit.Birds 80: 404-421.

Pomarine Skuas (Martin Hallam)

SNELSMORE COMMON – A REPORT

By Jonathan Wilding

Snelsmore Common comprises of 100 hectares (250 acres) of heathland, mire valleys, scrub and fringe woodland. The common is the largest tract of heathland remaining in Berkshire and accounts for one sixth of the total of this sort of habitat in the county. Because of its nature conservation importance, Snelsmore is designated a SSSI (Site of Special Scientific Interest). As well as the heathland the country park also has areas of grassland set by for picnics, bar-b-q's and family games. The site is managed by the West Berkshire Council who provide a range of organised activities throughout the year aimed at educating users of the site about its importance in the area.

Snelsmore Common (SU4670) is located 1.25miles (2 km) to the north of Newbury along the B4494 road from Donnington to Wantage. There are good car parking areas set back from the main entrance, but well sign posted from the road. The car parks are locked at night, but signs give clear warning of when the locking times are, so it is worth checking these. There are toilet facilities by the main entrance, including a disabled facility accessed with a RADAR key.

The surviving original heathland at Snelsmore is of great value, containing as it does the most comprehensive and extensive examples of heathland vegetation in West Berkshire. Heathland is an ancient landscape, and a valuable part of our natural heritage. Its sweeping expanses of heather creates a beautiful wilderness which supports a richly diverse range of plants and animals including birds such as the Nightjar and Woodlark, the Green Hairstreak butterfly, the Emperor moth and Adders and Lizards.

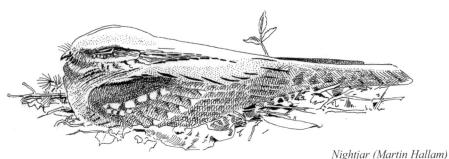

Nightjar (Martin Hallam)

Without management Snelsmore Common would decline, as birch and bracken invade and kill off the heather. Of the 100 Hectares some 67 Hectares has been fenced to allow for grazing by cattle and ponies. As well as grazing there are a number of volunteer organisations which work on the site clearing birch, pulling bracken and helping to restore pathways and ponds. The objectives are to conserve and enhance features of the greatest conservation value by using a variety of different management techniques as close to those which originally created the habitat ie. grazing, cutting and controlled burning.

Purpose of Survey

Following his appointment in January 2003 the council's Countryside Ranger for Snelsmore Common, Keith Toomey was keen to establish a list of species for the common. He managed to enlist a whole army of naturalists in his quest and has built an impressive and very comprehensive list to date. In order to assist in this task the Newbury District Ornithological Club (NDOC) organised a team of four willing volunteers in order to perform a survey over the common. The survey comprised of one visit early in the breeding season and another later in order to record the visiting migrants. The results of this survey are detailed below. The NDOC are keen to continue this survey in order to build a detailed picture of the value of the site for breeding birds in West Berkshire.

Recorded below are details of the bird species seen or heard across Snelsmore Common, south of the Winterbourne road. All the records relate to two " BTO - Breeding Bird Survey" method visits made during the 2003 breeding season (March till June), by Jim Burnett, Pam Niblock, John Dellow and Jonathan Wilding. The total number of species recorded was 41 (34 resident and 7 migrant), plus two further species listed below from an evening visit, but excluded from the statistics.

Blackbird	R	Greenfinch	R	Robin	R
Blackcap	S	Green Woodpecker	R	Rook	R
Blue Tit	R	Jackdaw	R	Skylark	R
Buzzard	R	Jay	R	Song Thrush	R
Carrion Crow	R	Lesser Black–backed Gull	R	Stock Dove	R
Chaffinch	R	Lesser Redpoll	R	Tree Pipit	S
Chiffchaff	S	Linnet	R	Treecreeper	R
Coal Tit	R	Long–tailed Tit	R	Willow Tit	R
Cuckoo	S	Magpie	R	Willow Warbler	S
Dunnock	R	Mallard	R	Wood Pigeon	R
Garden Warbler	S	Meadow Pipit	R	Woodcock	R*
Goldcrest	R	Nightjar	S*	Woodlark	S
Goldfinch	R	Nuthatch	R	Wren	R
Great Spotted Woodpecker	R	Pheasant	R	Yellowhammer	R
Great Tit	R	R = resident species; S = summer migrant; * = recorded on separate evening visit			

Visit dates when the surveys were performed were Sunday 5th April, Sunday 18th May. An evening walk, specifically to search for Nightjars and Woodcocks took place on Thursday 22nd May.

Findings

Percentage comparison between resident and summer migrant species expressed as singing or displaying males;

Resident Species	=	209 Plots	71%
Migrant Species	=	86 Plots	29%
Total	=	295 Plots	100%

Percentage comparison between resident and summer migrant species expressed as territories held;

Resident Species	=	101 Territories	81%
Migrant Species	=	24 Territories	19%
Total	=	125 Territories	100%

League table of breeding birds within the recording area

Resident Species	Territories	Summer migrants	Territories
Wren	20	Chiffchaff	10
Robin	17	Willow Warbler	7
Blackbird	13	Tree Pipit	5
Blue Tit	8		
Great Tit	7		
Song Thrush	7		
Chaffinch	5		
Wood Pigeon	5		
Dunnock	4		

The table confirms the most common resident species as Wren and Robin but the least common resident species were Stock Dove and Goldfinch where no territories were found. Amongst the migrant species, most common was Chiffchaff and least common was Garden Warbler, which despite being found on both visits appeared not to hold a territory.

A34 Newbury By-Pass and it's effect on the birdlife of Snelsmore Common

Since opening the Newbury By-Pass in November 1998 it has had only a small impact on the birdlife of Snelsmore Common. Due to nature of the habitat at Snelsmore, with woodland running along it's southern edge, noise generated from the road is deadened – although not eliminated completely. Research carried out by Jim Burnett and myself in 2001 showed that by the roadside, peak noise levels reached 78dB, but only 100m back within the trees and the peak noise level had dropped to 58dB. Moving out of the trees and onto the heath proper, a distance of around 400m, and the peak noise level had dropped again to circa 45dB. In a control habitat to the north of the site, and in another woodland fringe the peak noise levels were recorded at between 41dB and 50dB.

The most noticeable impact on the birdlife was seen in the Treecreeper population. Birds that had previously been recorded on the southern edge of the common were, after opening the by-pass, no longer recorded. At no time since 1998 has Treecreeper been recorded in this location, although other locations on the common, away from the by-pass still have a healthy population. The only explanation that I can offer for this translocation of the population would be related to the bird's very thin and high pitched song and calls. With the increase in traffic noise from 45dB to, up to 78dB it would make the females task of locating singing males difficult, if not almost impossible.

Most other species seem to be unaffected by the road, with one presumably juvenile male Tree Pipit, actually trying to establish a territory (unsuccessfully) on the roadside bank during the spring of 2000. This record relates to a yearly national high of Tree Pipits in 2000, as noted by the BTO.

THE GROWTH OF HERONS IN BERKSHIRE 1992-2003

By Chris Robinson (Berkshire BTO Rep)

2003 was the 75th anniversary of the world's longest running single species survey – the British Trust for Ornithology's Heronry Census and to mark the occasion, the BTO attempted to make a full count of all heronries in the UK. As well as arranging for counts from all their regularly counted heronries (there are about 500 of these in the UK) Reps were encouraged to seek out new or previously uncounted ones in order to maximise the coverage. Up until now I thought we had a fairly complete knowledge of heronries in Berkshire but some extra research plus a couple of tip-offs revealed one new and one rediscovered heronry!

The nett result is that we now know of eleven heronries in Berkshire varying in size from 2 to 23 nests and giving a grand total of at least 71 occupied nests in the county during 2003 although, in reality, this figure is known to be low as the eleventh heronry is in the grounds of Windsor Castle which it has not been possible to count in recent years.

As well as these traditional heronry counts, the anniversary effort also targeted a number of randomly selected tetrads (2km squares) which volunteers were asked to scour for any signs of hitherto undiscovered heronries. Of the four tetrads allocated to Berkshire, nothing new was discovered; in fact in the one I did, which was nearly 100% farmland, I never even saw a heron let alone a nest! Nevertheless, taken at a national level this was an essential exercise to measure how complete a knowledge we have of the UK's heronries.

In the period 1992 – 2003 and during which I have been BTO Rep, four of the eleven heronries within Berkshire have been continuously monitored. Another six have been monitored for shorter periods of time due to their being either new or previously undiscovered. In the new category are the two small heronries on Theale Main Pit and the even smaller one at Heath Lake, while previously undiscovered ones have been found at Donnington (Newbury) and Bray Lock; the latter being one of the 2003 discoveries. Both these have up to six nests and according to local sources have been there for some time. The rediscovered heronry was the one at Wraysbury which has been there for many years but had eluded my early attempts to locate it either by searching or interrogation of birders who might have known its whereabouts.

The picture presented by the four regularly censused heronries is slightly mixed, as over the twelve year period, two have declined in size and two have increased. Taken together

13

however, there has been an overall increase of around 40%, somewhat higher than the national trend for England and Wales which for the 10-year period 1992-2002 was +15% *[Marchant et al. 2004]*. The reasons cited for the general (UK) increase include reduced persecution, improvements in water quality, increased feeding opportunities at freshwater fisheries and the provision of new habitat as new lakes and gravel pits mature. It seems likely that the latter may well be a major factor in Berkshire as the county is well endowed with such sites and this is probably the main reason for any increases above and beyond the national figures. It is significant that the two heronries which have had the largest increase in size over twelve years (Twyford and Searles Farm) are both situated on gravel pits which are now well matured.

The graph below shows the changes over twelve years in the combined total of occupied nests at the four sites (Aldermaston GPs, Englefield, Searles Lane and Twyford GPs):-

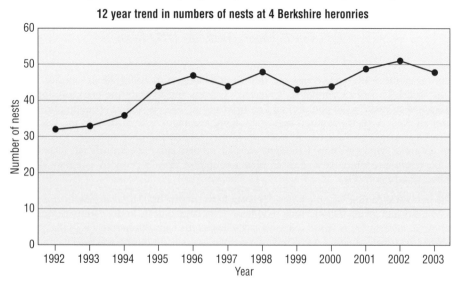

BERKSHIRE BIRD INDEX 2003

by Chris Robinson, with acknowledgment to Patrick Crowley

The Berkshire Bird Index (BBI) survey uses a similar method to that used by the BTO Breeding Bird Survey (BBS). Surveyors walk two 1km transects across randomly selected one kilometre squares, recording all birds seen or heard during two visits during the breeding season. This survey method has been kept deliberately simple in order to attract a large number of participants and although it is relatively unsophisticated, it is possible to determine accurate population trends of many bird species over time provided there is a sufficiently large number of squares covered.

2003 was the fourth year of the Berkshire Bird Index (BBI) survey and, once again, there was an increase in the number of 1km squares which were surveyed. The previous year's

Distribution of squares covered in 2003

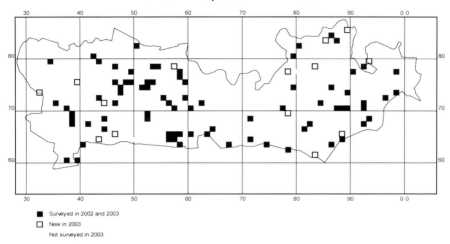

■ Surveyed in 2002 and 2003
□ New in 2003
Not surveyed in 2003

total of 84 squares increased by eleven to give a coverage of 95, a very satisfactory number and representing about 8% of the county's land area. The distribution of these squares is shown in the map above. Fourteen new squares were covered (shown as white squares) but three of the previous year's squares were not surveyed in 2003. This sort of change is inevitable, with some surveyors dropping out and new ones coming in to take on different squares but, as the survey uses randomly selected squares and coverage is fairly even across the county, these changes should have little effect on the results. The overall coverage of the county was good, and it is gratifying that four of the new squares surveyed were in the far west of the county, which in past years has suffered from a slightly lower coverage than the rest of Berkshire.

As the BBI had been going for 4 years it was thought that there might now be sufficient data for a trend analysis to be attempted so 2003 saw the first attempt to assess recent population changes for the commoner species. The same techniques and tools as are used for the BTO's Breeding Bird Survey were adopted for this analysis as these are capable of making allowance for missing visits/years and (for example) the fact that the data set for the Foot and Mouth year 2001 is much smaller than for the other three years. More detailed discussion of the method and results is given below.

The detailed numbers for all the species in the 2003 survey are shown in Appendix 1. These include the total number of birds seen/heard, the percentage of squares occupied and the percentage of 200 metre transect segments where the species were found. The 2003 survey recorded 119 species, the highest number in the four years of the BBI (c.f: 107 in 2002 and 106 in 2000). Birds recorded in 2003 but not in 2002 were Grasshopper Warbler, Nightjar, Ringed Plover, Teal, Water Rail, Wood Warbler and Common Gull, of which the first five were recorded for the first time. Birds not recorded in 2003, but which have been seen in at least one of the previous years, were Wigeon, Long-eared Owl, Snipe, Tree Sparrow and Shoveler.

The results from the last 4 years were analysed by the author (with much help from the BTO). The analysis is given in the form of percentage population changes from the previous year (2002-2003) and the 4-year trend over the period 2000-2003. The results are shown in the table overleaf.

Berkshire Four Year vs UK SouthEast Region Ten Year Trends

Species	Berkshire 4–year Change (2000–2003)			Berkshire 1–year Change (2002–2003)	National SE Region 10–year Change (1994–2003)
		LCL	UCL		
Goldfinch	**+76%**	21%	131%	**+49%**	+5%
Chiffchaff	**+68%**	23%	112%	+19%	**+34%**
Greenfinch	**+29%**	0%	58%	+24%	−1%
Great Spotted Woodpecker	+27%	−7%	61%	**+65%**	**+76%**
Woodpigeon	**+24%**	7%	40%	**+26%**	**+12%**
Dunnock	+22%	−3%	47%	+23%	+1%
Blue Tit	**+18%**	2%	34%	+14%	**+8%**
House Sparrow	+16%	−9%	40%	+16%	**-29%**
Pheasant	+16%	−8%	40%	+17%	**+30%**
Blackbird	**+15%**	3%	27%	+10%	**+6%**
Collared Dove	+14%	−17%	46%	+7%	**+35%**
Mistle Thrush	+12%	−26%	50%	+1%	**-27%**
Chaffinch	**+12%**	1%	23%	+10%	**+11%**
Whitethroat	+8%	−23%	39%	**-25%**	**+44%**
Blackcap	+5%	−15%	25%	+3%	**+22%**
Starling	+2%	−29%	33%	+2%	**-46%**
Song Thrush	No change	−18%	18%	+10%	**+10%**
Robin	No change	−12%	11%	−2%	**+19%**
Long–tailed Tit	−1%	−34%	33%	**+75%**	**-20%**
Wren	−1%	−12%	11%	+2%	−3%
Skylark	−2%	−18%	14%	+1%	−23%
Pied Wagtail	−5%	−39%	29%	+15%	**+33%**
Mallard	−5%	−34%	24%	−15%	**+30%**
Great Tit	−10%	−25%	5%	+6%	+7%
Jackdaw	−11%	−31%	9%	+2%	**+16%**
Swallow	−15%	−38%	8%	+14%	+5%
Magpie	**-21%**	−36%	−6%	No change	−2%
Yellowhammer	**-22%**	−40%	−4%	−10%	**-36%**
Carrion Crow	**-24%**	−39%	−8%	+23%	+2%
Green Woodpecker	**-39%**	−57%	−22%	−20%	**+22%**

Bold indicates statistically significant change.
LCL = Lower 95% Confidence Level, UCL = Upper 95% Confidence Level.

For the mathematically minded the population changes were assessed using a loglinear model with a Poisson regression, using the higher count from the early and late visit for each species on each square as our best estimate of the abundance of that species. The 30 species shown in the table all occurred in at least 49 squares; around 50 squares being considered the minimum requirement for statistical robustness.

As can be seen there have been a number of statistically significant changes (at the 95% level, shown in bold) but the margins of error are quite wide due to the short survey period so far and the relatively small sample size during the early years. These margins are shown as upper and lower confidence levels (UCL and LCL, respectively) in the table. Put simply, "95% confidence level" means that we can be 95% certain that the percentage change in population size is true, within the margins of error given. With time, the impact of any single year will be less apparent on the overall trend and confidence levels should increase.

So what conclusions can be drawn from these data?

- Firstly it is important to remember that our dataset is still a relatively small and somewhat patchy sample, gathered over a short time period and with one year's data (2001) significantly reduced by the FMD outbreak. Some caution must therefore be applied in interpreting the numbers but it does not mean that they cannot be believed. Note that trends for all but the commonest species have very wide margins of error which reflects the current limitations of our dataset. Even one of our commonest species (Chaffinch) which shows a 4-year upward trend of 12% ±11 which means that it could be up by nearly a quarter or virtually unchanged! Our data are therefore best viewed (as they are presented in the table) alongside the national trends which, being taken from a larger sample over a longer period, are likely to be more robust. The one obvious limitation in doing this is that, due to the difference in survey periods care needs to be taken in making direct comparisons.

- There is a marked difference in changes for some species over one year (2002-2003) and over four years (2000-2003), highlighting the importance of looking at changes over a reasonable period of time and the danger of reading too much into results from any single year. These sorts of differences are usually explainable by seasonal factors such as good (or poor) breeding success rates in the preceding year, weather patterns or food shortages.

- For 2000-2003 there has been a large, statistically significant, increase in populations of seven species. These are Woodpigeon, Blackbird, Chiffchaff, Blue Tit, Chaffinch, Goldfinch and Greenfinch. National trends for the same period are not available but if we compare with the 10-year trend for the SE Region we can see that all the increases bar one are of similar proportion to Berkshire's (once margins of error are taken into account). The apparent exception in Berkshire is Goldfinch which, with at least a 21% increase, is well in excess of any change in the rest of this region. The reasons for this are not yet clear but may be linked to the increases which have occurred in winter gardens or, possibly, the adoption of more bird-friendly farming practices

- On the minus side Green Woodpecker, Carrion Crow, Magpie and Yellowhammer have suffered the most marked reduction. However, when one looks at the trends for the whole of the UK for 1994-2002 (the duration of the Breeding Bird Survey), the former three species are doing well. Two of them are so-called pest species and may have been the victims of perfectly legal control but it is difficult to suggest why Green Woodpecker appears to be faring so badly in our county. The plight of the Yellowhammer nationally is well known so perhaps we should not be surprised to see the decline in Berkshire's population but at least one other farmland species, the Skylark, does appear to be doing slightly better here than in the rest of the Southeast. It is to be hoped that with the introduction in 2005 of the new agri-environment schemes we will start to see an improvement in these birds' fortunes.

Appendix 1: BBI Survey data for 2003.

Table showing all species recorded, in order of abundance

No.	Species	No. of Birds	% 1 km Squares Occupied	% 200 m Sections Occupied	No.	Species	No. of Birds	% 1 km Squares Occupied	% 200 m Sections Occupied
1	Woodpigeon	3336	100.0	74.4	61	Grey Wagtail	16	11.7	1.4
2	Chaffinch	1392	100.0	69.6	62	Little Owl	14	11.7	1.4
3	Blackbird	1256	100.0	62.0	63	Marsh Tit	24	10.6	1.6
4	Blue Tit	1093	96.8	53.6	64	Lesser B-b Gull	40	9.6	1.1
5	Robin	799	96.8	52.6	65	Grey Partridge	17	9.6	1.1
6	Wren	790	95.7	53.4	66	Spot. Flycatcher	11	9.6	1.2
7	Great Tit	576	95.7	36.2	67	R-n Parakeet	43	8.5	2.1
8	Carrion Crow	847	93.6	40.5	68	Little Grebe	12	8.5	1.0
9	Dunnock	355	89.4	26.0	69	Blk-headed Gull	16	7.4	1.3
10	Song Thrush	310	88.3	25.4	70	Hobby	7	7.4	0.7
11	Pheasant	503	84.0	29.5	71	Common Tern	20	6.4	1.3
12	Chiffchaff	244	79.8	22.0	72	Sand Martin	14	6.4	0.6
13	Greenfinch	483	78.7	21.8	73	Reed Warbler	11	6.4	1.0
14	Magpie	375	77.7	24.7	74	Herring Gull	9	6.4	0.6
15	Blackcap	249	77.7	21.3	75	Sedge Warbler	38	5.3	1.4
16	Jackdaw	715	71.3	25.1	76	Greylag Goose	29	5.3	1.0
17	Skylark	484	69.1	28.5	77	Gt. Crested Grebe	22	5.3	1.2
18	Starling	901	67.0	19.3	78	Corn Bunting	16	5.3	1.1
19	Gt. Sp. Woodpecker	158	67.0	14.8	79	Fieldfare	408	4.3	0.6
20	Goldfinch	278	62.8	11.6	80	Crossbill	148	4.3	1.3
21	Swallow	303	61.7	12.7	81	Yellow Wagtail	19	4.3	0.7
22	Mistle Thrush	115	58.5	9.3	82	Redpoll	13	4.3	0.4
23	Green W'oodpecker	88	57.4	8.5	83	Meadow Pipit	12	4.3	0.9
24	Whitethroat	135	56.4	10.4	84	Willow Tit	6	4.3	0.4
25	House Sparrow	580	55.3	14.7	85	Nightingale	4	4.3	0.4
26	Long-Tailed Tit	228	55.3	9.0	86	Shelduck	9	3.2	0.4
27	Yellowhammer	176	54.3	13.7	87	Gadwall	6	3.2	0.4
28	Mallard	360	52.1	11.5	88	Redshank	6	3.2	0.4
29	Collared Dove	221	52.1	12.3	89	Turtle Dove	5	3.2	0.4
30	Pied Wagtail	91	52.1	7.1	90	Redstart	5	3.2	0.5
31	Jay	98	51.1	8.1	91	Tree Pipit	5	3.2	0.5
32	Swift	239	47.9	7.1	92	Kingfisher	3	3.2	0.3
33	Linnet	332	45.7	9.1	93	Tawny Owl	3	3.2	0.3
34	Rook	1579	44.7	14.9	94	Golden Plover	71	2.1	0.2
35	Lapwing	237	44.7	8.6	95	Egyptian Goose	9	2.1	0.2
36	Nuthatch	97	44.7	8.5	96	L R Plover	7	2.1	0.3
37	House Martin	297	43.6	7.0	97	Mandarin	5	2.1	0.3
38	Goldcrest	153	42.6	10.4	98	Brambling	5	2.1	0.3
39	Kestrel	51	42.6	5.1	99	Ls. Sp. W'dpecker	3	2.1	0.2
40	Stock Dove	107	40.4	5.5	100	Common Sandpiper	3	2.1	0.2
41	Willow Warbler	103	40.4	8.5	101	Quail	3	2.1	0.3
42	R-L Partridge	102	38.3	6.6	102	Teal	8	1.1	0.2
43	Buzzard	51	37.2	4.9	103	Siskin	4	1.1	0.1
44	Coal Tit	116	36.2	8.0	104	Whinchat	4	1.1	0.1
45	Cuckoo	42	33.0	4.3	105	Cetti's Warbler	2	1.1	0.2
46	Canada Goose	234	27.7	4.7	106	Stonechat	2	1.1	0.1
47	Moorhen	59	27.7	4.6	107	Curlew	2	1.1	0.1
48	Grey Heron	43	26.6	3.7	108	Nightjar	1	1.1	0.1
49	Treecreeper	35	24.5	2.9	109	Wood Warbler	1	1.1	0.1
50	Garden Warbler	46	22.3	3.8	110	Woodlark	1	1.1	0.1
51	Bullfinch	46	22.3	3.5	111	G'hopper Warbler	1	1.1	0.1
52	Coot	103	18.1	4.3	112	Woodcock	1	1.1	0.1
53	Feral Pigeon	152	17.0	2.2	113	Water Rail	1	1.1	0.1
54	Lesser Whitethroat	20	17.0	2.0	114	Ringed Plover	1	1.1	0.1
55	Mute Swan	62	16.0	2.9	115	Gt. B-b Gull	1	1.1	0.1
56	Sparrowhawk	16	16.0	1.7	116	Pochard	1	1.1	0.1
57	Cormorant	27	14.9	1.8	117	Firecrest	1	1.1	0.1
58	Reed Bunting	32	13.8	2.8	118	Common Gull	1	1.1	0.1
59	Tufted Duck	88	12.8	2.3	119	Wheatear	1	1.1	0.1
60	Red Kite	16	12.8	1.5					

RINGING HIGHLIGHTS 2003

By Brian Clews

NEWBURY RINGING GROUP

A slight increase over 2002 saw 3664 birds ringed, involving 47 species, none of which were new. However, the first Common Sandpiper since 1989, first Fieldfare since 1994 and 10 Barn Owl pulli were of note.

Top six species were Blue Tit (855 – 16% down), Great Tit (572 – 7% up), Chiffchaff (293 – 62% up), Reed Warbler (284 – 20% down), Greenfinch (207 – 47% down), and Blackcap (134 – 3% down).

Other interesting species included 11 Cuckoos, 12 Kingfishers, 21 Cettis Warbler and 1 Willow Tit.

Recoveries of interest included:-
Cormorant – Ventjagersplaten, Holland, 10/6/97 – Lower Farm GP 18/10/03 (392km, 6 years)
Herring Gull – Bristol 2/7/99 – Lower Farm GP 13/10/03 (89km, 4 years)
Reed Warbler – Thatcham 14/8/99 – Dinton Pastures 28/5/03 (27km, 3 years)
Reed Warbler – Guildford 18/7/01 – Woolhampton GP 8/7/03 (46km, 2 years)
Reed Warbler – Tring 28/7/01 – Thatcham 3/5/03 (59km, 279 days)
Reed Bunting – Icklesham, E Sussex 7/10/02 – Brimpton GP 24/2/03 (140km, 140 days)
Reed Bunting – Litlington, E Sussex 4/10/03 – Brimpton GP 17/12/03 (114km, 74 days).

The last two items indicate an interesting community of interest between East Sussex and Berks for this species. The total number of birds ringed since 1967 stood at 183205 at the end of 2003, a significant effort.

DINTON PASTURES

A total of 250 birds were ringed at Dinton Pastures, the top 5 species being:-

Long-tailed Tit (47), Blackcap (27), Chiffchaff (22), Bullfinch (21), Dunnock (20) and Blue Tit (17).

Highlights included 2 Cetti's Warblers, 2 Treecreepers and a Siskin.

HUGHENDEN RINGING GROUP

Work continued at Jealott's Hill with 419 pulli of 22 species being ringed. Top six species were:-

Chaffinch (142), Yellowhammer (56), Blue Tit (40), Reed Bunting (37), Great Tit (28) and Greenfinch & Dunnock (each on 20).

Interesting species caught were 2 Water Rail and 10 Brambling. In addition, 91 birds were re-trapped or recovered, including 19 Blue Tits, 17 Chaffinch, 17 Reed Bunting and 4 Yellowhammer.

Thanks to Mick McQuaid and Jan Legg for the information summarised above.

Footnote: Regrettably on this occasion Runnymede Ringing Group were unable to offer all their data but propose to make this available for future reports. Some details for individual species appear in the species accounts

WINTERING GULLS IN THE THAMES VALLEY

By Paul Cropper

Between July 2003 and December 2004 a study of wintering gulls in the lower Thames valley was undertaken. The main aim of the project was to evaluate any changes in risk to air traffic from gulls, should non-lethal bird deterrence be enforced on the landfill at Wapsey's Wood, near Gerrard's Cross, Buckinghamshire (known to birders as 'Hedgerley Tip').

To this end I set out to study all of the major gull feeding sites within 30 miles of Queen Mother Reservoir (the main roost for gulls from Hedgerley), 30 miles being the maximum range that gulls will travel each day in search of food. We were particularly interested in landfills for domestic or commercial/industrial waste which provide ample food for gulls, and thirteen of these were identified in the study area. Four of these were in Berkshire, at Sutton Lane (Colnbrook), Lea Farm (Reading), Burghfield (Reading) and Hermitage. The location of these landfills, and reservoirs that support the main gull roosts, are shown in Fig.1 below:

During the study gulls were observed exploiting many new sources of food including urban refuse, bread put out for other birds, sewage works, and searching for worms on playing fields, as well as more natural food sources such as live fish, shadowing diving duck to pick up disturbed particles, and invertebrates such as swarming ants.

However three food sources appeared to be most significant: the tidal mud of the Thames, which attracts many thousands of Black-headed Gulls; worms from agricultural land, particularly during ploughing which may occur anytime from autumn to spring; and landfill sites, which offer very easy pickings.

To study the birds' movements we trapped, ringed and dye-marked a total of 1,175 gulls at Hedgerley as well as attaching radio-tags to the tails of 10 Herring Gulls. The main flightlines between feeding and roosting sites were identified and counted. The ringing results showed a very rapid dispersal of all species around the region, but with a particularly strong link between Hedgerley and the tips at Lea Farm and Burghfield.

The radio-tracking was a great success and we followed the signals from eight of the Herring Gulls at Hedgerley for several weeks after the release in November, reducing to two by the following February.

During the first week after release, two of the radio-tagged birds roosted at Queen Mother Reservoir, and three at Broadwater (5 miles east of the tip), while one bird alternated between both roosts. However the final week of November 2004 saw dramatic changes as Queen Mother Reservoir dried out almost completely, and Broadwater became the main Herring Gull roost; unsurprisingly, six of our radio-tagged birds now roosted there. The next change came in the third week of December when night-time temperatures dropped below freezing and Broadwater was threatened by ice. Three of our six remaining tagged birds now 'disappeared', with no signals from either Hedgerley or any of the usual roosts (although one of them returned in January). The other three continued feeding at the landfill but abandoned the diminishing Broadwater roost in favour of Wraysbury and KGVI Rsvrs.. Curiously they did not go back to using Queen Mother Rsvr until January, despite the fact that it had largely refilled by mid December and they were presumably flying over it every day on their route between Wraysbury and Hedgerley.

Fig.1 The landfills studied, showing maximum gull counts

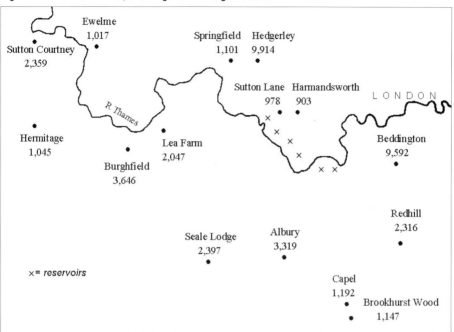

The peak in gull numbers in the Thames valley came in late December / early January. During February birds began to depart for their breeding grounds, some of the most obvious movers being Common Gulls which formed huge flocks before departing en masse. The most dramatic changes occurred over the weekend of 13th – 14th March 2004, when gull numbers of all species at Hedgerley crashed from 6,300 on 12th to 1,600 on 19th, a change reflected around the region. The reason for this mass departure was probably that the winds between 12th Feb – 11th March had been chiefly easterly, but then switched to westerly for the next fortnight, making it easier for gulls to depart towards their main breeding grounds on the east coast and in Scandinavia.

Unexplained Phenomena

Perhaps the most curious phenomenon was the geographical distribution of large gull species in the Thames valley over the winter. During August-September, the Lesser Black-backs were the commonest large gull species, dominating on 9 of the 13 landfills. They then went into a steep decline between October and December, while at the same time Herring Gulls increased in number. The evidence points to a gradual westerly drift of the Lesser Black-backs during autumn and winter; this movement is quite often visible on autumn evenings, when lone Lesser Black-backs can be spotted circling steadily westward, regardless of the direction of other birds heading to roost.

By November, the pattern for the winter had been established: west of a line running north-south through Reading, Lesser Black-backed was the dominant large gull. At Burghfield at least 75% of large gulls were Lesser Black-backs, while on the five landfills west of here they comprised 89-100% of all large gulls over the winter. By contrast, on eleven landfills east of this line, Herring Gull was the dominant large gull species, comprising 45-100% of all large gulls (with the exception of Seale Lodge landfill where the figure was 20-38%). There is no obvious explanation for this east-west divide.

Another puzzle is why Black-headed Gulls do not take more advantage of the easy pickings at sewage and water treatment works. The works were only popular when they happened to be underneath flightlines, or during severe weather, when gulls that normally fed on nearby fields move in seeking food (observed at Bracknell and Sandhurst works). Even works such as Chertsey, a mere 5 miles from the largest gull roost of all (Queen Mary Resvr), were shunned by the gulls. The reason may lie with the algal bloom that periodically covers the surface of the tanks, preventing the Black-headed Gulls from picking food off the surface. The algae thrive during times of peak flow at the works, which usually occur during the winter. Thus it tends to appear just at the time of year when the gulls are most in need of food.

The Future of Gulls in Berkshire

In 2003, within a 40-mile radius of Queen Mother Rsvr., there were twenty-two landfills that supported gulls. Between the beginning of the study in 2003 and writing this article in 2005, seven have closed for domestic waste tipping and no longer provide food for gulls. A further three have upgraded their bird deterrence procedures, thus reducing the amount of food available for gulls, whilst there is increasing pressure to reduce and eliminate food waste going to landfill.

All these changes will certainly have an impact in our county. The central importance of landfills was highlighted by an extensive study of the gull population around E Berks and W Surrey by Horton, Brough & Rochard (1983). They discovered that whenever a landfill closes, there is an immediate reduction in gull numbers at other nearby foraging and loafing sites. Thus we should expect a general decline in gull numbers, and particularly in the larger species which have fewer alternative food sources.

It is interesting to examine what happened at Burghfield, which used to be the third busiest landfill for gulls within my study area. In October 2004, bird deterrence by falconry was imposed here. Over the next few days, there were reports of a sudden increase in gull numbers at other sites – Springfield, Hedgerley and Sutton Lane, possibly displaced from Burghfield. However, two weeks later, everything seemed to have returned to normal; numbers at the nearest alternative landfills (Lea Farm, Hermitage, Hedgerley) were comparable with the same date the previous year. Roughly one third of the original landfill flock remains in the area, outside the tip on Smallmead gravel pit.

This paper has been written to provide a 'snapshot' of the gull situation in the Thames valley and as a thank you to all those who submitted ringing data and counts during our study.

A full version of this document with ringing recovery data and flightline map is available on: www.birdmanagement.co.uk

Paul Cropper,
WEMD,
Central Science Laboratory,
Sand Hutton,
York YO41 1LX

ROC GARDEN BIRD SURVEY
The First Ten Years (Winter 1994/5 – Summer 2004)

By John Farnsworth

In the mid nineties the ROC decided to introduce an annual Winter (October – March) Garden Bird Feeding Survey not only to complement its other data collection activities but also for the benefit and interest of those Club members not easily able to attend indoor meetings or participate in Club outdoor events. Birds present and feeding in gardens were recorded on a weekly basis using two quarterly forms hence providing data over the chosen 6 month winter period.

The survey method was modified from the winter of 98/99 by using a single 6 month recording form and bird species present but not necessarily feeding were also recorded, the survey subsequently being simply referred to as the ROC Garden Bird Survey. Following members' interest in GBS winter recording, starting in 2000 the survey was extended to also cover the intervening summer periods (April – September). The 6 month forms make provision also for notes including garden type (urban/suburban, rural), size (large/small), presence of pond, supplementary food/water provided, nearby presence of a significant water body, presence of trees/shrubs if garden generally organic and (optionally) the maximum number of any one species occurring at any time during the recording week.

Gardens surveyed are not limited to those in the county of Berkshire nor exclusively to Club members, although they do reflect generally the geographic location of members. Being centred on Reading, most gardens surveyed are in fact within Berkshire.

The ROC GBS completed its tenth winter period in March 2004 and its fifth summer period in September 2004 during which time 101 bird species have been recorded. Details of the earlier winter surveys were reported at Club indoor meetings. More recent summary results have been published in Club Newsletters. The following Table recapitulates for the first ten years the occurrence of the 58 species recorded in 10% or more of gardens (all garden types combined) in any of the winter or summer periods, expressed as a percentage of the total number of gardens surveyed during the relevant 6 month periods. This (non-dimensional) number is a fairly broad indicator of the status of garden birds and can be used e.g. for seasonal comparisons. By looking across the Table for a given species, trends in percentage occurrence (the "O" figures) over the years can be appreciated. The order of the species in the Table is initially that reported for the first winter (94/95) survey, the more commonly occurring species at the top of the Table tending to the generally less common further down, additional species being added as they first occurred during the subsequent surveys. Species in **bold** in lines tinted ▨ are of high conservation concern (Red-listed)*, species in *italic* in lines tinted ▨ are of medium conservation concern (Amber-listed)*.

Garden species in the Table whose occurrence appears to have declined in recent years taking into account both winter and summer periods include 4 Red-listed, 3 Amber-listed and 2 Green-listed species. Using as an example for comparitive purposes the BTO/JNCC/RSPB population trends 1994-2004* for the South East region (includes Berkshire), the apparent ROC GBS declines in occurrence for Red-listed **Starling, Bullfinch** and **Marsh Tit** reflect the SE regional population declines; that for **Lesser Spotted Woodpecker** is in line with the earlier suggested decline for Berkshire*. The apparent ROC GBS decline for Amber-listed *Mistle Thrush* reflects also the regional decline; *Goldcrest* and *Swallow* were increasing regionally, the reasons for the (modest) GBS apparent downward trend may be more complex.

23

Period	Winter (Oct – Mar)						
	1994/5	1995/6		1996/7		1997/8	
Coefficient	O	O	L	O	L	O	L
Urban/suburban Gardens	34	19		16		15	
Rural Gardens	23	11		7		8	
Total no. of gardens	57	30		23		23	
Total no. of species	39	58		56		53	
Blue Tit	100	100	97	100	98	100	95
Blackbird	100	100	92	100	93	100	90
Robin	100	100	95	100	91	100	87
Greenfinch	100	97	69	100	96	96	69
Chaffinch	100	97	79	100	89	96	87
Collared Dove	100	100	66	100	81	91	74
Great Tit	98	100	82	100	89	91	82
Dunnock	97	97	83	100	79	96	74
Magpie	97	93	62	100	74	91	69
Woodpigeon	97	100	63	100	73	87	66
Starling	95	97	76	100	75	96	70
Long-tailed Tit	95	100	41	78	39	78	33
Wren	93	87	38	83	19	78	29
Coal Tit	93	70	39	91	55	74	42
House Sparrow	90	100	89	96	84	91	77
Song Thrush	81	97	39	100	33	74	25
Jay	79	50	14	70	24	39	12
Siskin	77	40	4	57	18	78	31
Nuthatch	68	43	22	61	30	52	24
Goldfinch	68	47	17	78	35	65	28
Great Spotted Woodpecker	65	87	21	83	30	65	36
Goldcrest	56	57	11	17	2	57	13
Carrion Crow	54	60	18	70	19	52	19
Sparrowhawk	52	40	6	43	6	57	7
Mistle Thrush	51	57	6	52	11	43	4
Bullfinch	49	33	5	35	5	30	5
Pied Wagtail	44	57	16	52	17	35	7
Redwing	39	87	19	78	19	52	12
Blackcap	37	50	16	49	12	70	7
Jackdaw	28	17	4	13	3	17	2
Treecreeper	23	27	3	13	5	35	4
Rook	23	20	5	13	3	17	2
Pheasant	19	27	-	22	8	22	6
Feral Pigeon	18	17	10	22	9	17	9
Fieldfare	14	47	7	30	4	22	3
Marsh Tit	14	17	6	17	8	9	4
(Lesser) Redpoll	11	3	-	4	-	-	-
Lesser Spotted Woodpecker	9	10	-	-	-	13	1
Reed Bunting	5	20	2	9	1	13	2
Green Woodpecker		33	5	35	6	39	6
Black-headed Gull		30	5	13	2	-	-
Brambling		13	1	17	3	48	9
Linnet		13	1	4	-	4	-
Grey Heron		10	-	9	2	22	3
Chiffchaff		10	1	9	-	13	2
Kestrel		7	1	4	2	-	-
Mallard		3		13		4	
Grey Wagtail		3		-		4	
Buzzard		3		-			
Little Owl		3		4		4	
Stock Dove		3		4		4	
Red Kite		-		4		-	
House Martin							
Garden Warbler							
Whitethroat							
Willow Warbler							
Swallow							
Swift							

Note: ■ = **Species of high conservation concern**. ▧ = *Species of medium conservation concern*

	Winter (Oct – Mar)					Summer (Apr – Sep)				
	1999/00	2000/1	2001/2	2002/3	2003/4	2000	2001	2002	2003	2004
32	32	35	35	30	32	22	29	23	27	29
6	16	15	14	12	15	12	17	13	13	9
48	48	50	49	42	47	34	46	36	40	38
52	65	64	67	60	64	65	67	61	59	65
0	0	0	0	0	0	0	0	0	0	0
00	100	98	100	100	100	100	100	100	100	100
48	100	98	100	100	100	100	100	100	100	100
00	100	98	100	100	100	100	100	100	100	100
94	100	90	96	95	96	100	91	92	98	97
00	100	98	98	98	100	100	96	100	95	97
00	96	94	98	98	80	97	96	97	95	97
00	98	94	100	100	100	100	100	97	100	100
94	100	98	100	100	100	100	100	94	100	97
48	87	96	92	90	91	88	91	92	90	92
48	98	98	100	95	98	97	87	94	100	100
42	98	92	96	98	83	88	93	100	100	87
33	93	94	96	90	94	88	83	75	80	63
90	93	96	94	93	89	82	83	89	88	66
36	83	88	92	90	91	85	76	83	83	74
45	91	94	90	95	81	91	98	100	98	92
45	89	88	90	95	98	85	78	83	98	82
45	61	60	71	50	68	50	52	50	68	53
42	57	40	18	48	60	18	11	28	15	21
50	52	68	54	50	68	53	61	67	58	53
33	83	86	84	79	70	76	65	72	80	71
73	63	68	67	69	70	71	74	75	75	66
76	65	70	49	60	38	50	30	36	43	37
73	67	68	65	74	64	68	76	64	70	63
76	52	62	49	52	66	53	50	47	40	55
42	39	30	41	36	23	41	33	19	15	8
43	39	36	27	31	17	38	39	42	45	26
34	52	40	49	36	30	32	26	19	33	16
58	43	28	43	60	38	-	-	-	-	-
44	61	60	54	60	62	38	48	50	48	42
49	41	30	35	33	30	32	50	42	50	39
8	35	18	35	10	6	15	13	42	5	5
0	15	8	22	21	15	15	20	19	13	11
9	26	24	20	33	30	-	7	14	15	11
2	6	2	6	7	9	9	4	8	5	5
45	33	26	29	29	26	-	2	-	-	-
1	20	20	18	14	4	12	13	6	10	3
4	20	-	4	2	9	-	-	-	-	5
4	2	-	-	5	-	6	4	-	3	3
4	15	10	6	12	6	3	9	8	5	5
23	50	30	41	29	43	44	37	42	48	29
1	13	10	10	7	11	3	2	-	-	-
5	35	8	35	7	23	18	2	6	3	13
6	6	6	2	2	4	12	9	14	10	8
8	26	12	12	14	28	6	22	3	10	13
5	28	22	16	38	28	59	48	67	45	53
4	2	4	4	12	6	-	9	-	3	5
8	4	6	6	2	6	6	4	8	13	16
3	11	12	8	10	13	15	2	3	5	5
-	2	-	10	-	2	-	-	-	-	-
2	2	4	-	-	13	6	4	-	-	-
4	4	8	6	7	6	15	7	8	13	13
-	-	-	4	5	13	-	-	-	10	18
-	2	2	4	5	2	29	39	28	30	21
-	-	-	-	-	-	9	2	11	5	5
-	-	-	-	-	-	15	2	8	5	5
-	-	-	-	-	-	21	17	25	10	18
-	-	2	4	-	2	24	28	20	18	13
-	-	-	-	-	-	35	35	36	33	29

Garden species whose occurrence appears to have increased in recent years include 2 Amber-listed and 1 Green-listed species. The apparent increase for Amber-listed *Green Woodpecker* reflects the regional trend, that for *Red Kite* is probably due to the success of the recent Chilterns reintroduction project. The apparent increase for Chiffchaff (winter periods) reflects the regional trend and may result also from wintering migrants normally summering in continental Europe.

The 43 species recorded in less than 10% of gardens (all gardens types combined) in any of the winter or summer periods are Little Grebe, Great Crested Grebe, *Mute Swan*, Canada Goose, *Shelduck*, Mandarin Duck, *Merlin*, Hobby, Red-legged Partridge, Lady Amherst's Pheasant, Moorhen, Coot, *Lapwing*, *Snipe*, *Woodcock*, *Common Gull*, *Herring Gull*, Ring-necked Parakeet, *Cuckoo*, Tawny Owl, *Kingfisher*, **Wryneck**, *Sand Martin*, *Meadow Pipit*, *Yellow Wagtail*, Waxwing, *Black Redstart*, Whinchat, Wheatear, Sedge Warbler, Reed Warbler, *Dartford Warbler*, Lesser Whitethroat, *Firecrest*, **Spotted Flycatcher**, Pied Flycatcher, **Willow Tit**, **Tree Sparrow**, Crossbill, *Hawfinch*, **Yellowhammer**, Peacock and Pekin Robin.

The data available also allow (amongst others) a measure of the length of occurrence (the "L" figures in the table) to be calculated for any 6 month period (see Appendix), representing the average time for which a species occurred, averaged over all garden types. The table shows the "L" figures for the winter periods 95/96 to 97/98 for Blue Tit down to *Kestrel*. Hence some conclusions on length of occurrence ("L") compared to percentage occurrence ("O") can be drawn:

- the interannual trends in the "L" figures generally follow the trends in the "O" figures;
- the "L" figures are always lower than the "O" figures;
- for high "O" figures (generally the more common species), the "L" figures appear to give a clearer understanding of occurrence;
- a relatively high "O" value coupled with a relatively low "L" value can indicate:
    - feeding method (e.g. Sparrowhawk, Grey Heron);
    - migration/dispersal tendency (e.g. Blackcap, Chiffchaff).

Some examples from the table of particular species are e.g. for winter 96/97:
- Robin occurred in 100% of all gardens, for 91% of the time.
- **Starling** occurred in 100% of all gardens, for 75% of the time.
- **Song Thrush** occurred in 100% of all gardens, for 33% of the time.
- **Bullfinch** occurred in 35% of all gardens, but only for 5% of the time.
- *Green Woodpecker* occurred in 55% of all gardens, but only for 6% of the time.

ROC GBS data collected will also allow weekly variation throughout the year in species occurrence to be calculated. It is intended that future analysis will be carried out on this theme and in particular for species of conservation concern. As the value of such analysis depends on the quality and quantity of garden bird records submitted, please carry on recording. My thanks to all the participants who have contributed to this survey.

Appendix

By adding up the number of weeks in which a species was recorded for each and every garden, then dividing by the total number of recording weeks for the 6 month period for which each and every garden was surveyed, a non-dimensional number is obtained which is less than 1.0 but effectively represents the average time for which that species was recorded, averaged over all gardens. This decimal fraction is then converted into its equivalent percentage value ("L") which can be used for e.g. seasonal comparisons. By being non-dimensional the "L" numbers are better (seasonal) comparators than e.g. simply comparing the number of "bird-weeks" in the different 6 month recording periods.

References *

Gregory R D, Wilkinson N I, Noble D G, Robinson J A, Brown A F, Hughes J, Proctor DA, Gibbons D W and Galbraith C A (2002). British Birds 95 : 410-450.

Raven MJ, Noble DG and Baillie SR (2005) The Breeding Bird Survey 2004. BTO Research Report 403, Thetford.

The Berkshire Atlas Group (1996) The Birds of Berkshire.

ROC Garden Bird Survey (Oct 94 – Sep 04)

APPARENT ATTEMPT BY RAVENS TO BREED IN BERKSHIRE AFTER 143 YEARS OF ABSENCE

By Bruce Archer

For a couple of years prior to 2002 a pair of Ravens had been seen regularly in southwest Berkshire. In 2002 in addition there were several reports of 2 juveniles in the area but to the best of my knowledge no nest site within Berkshire had been reported, the last confirmed record of breeding being in 1860 in Hamstead Park, 4.5km west of Newbury (The Birds of Berkshire, Berkshire Atlas Group 1996).

During reconnaissance for a Breeding Bird Survey in a 1km square near Enbourne on 15 April 2003 I spoke to various landowners and interested parties, including Andy Pocock who has shooting rights to much of the area being surveyed. I also met his sister, Julie Pocock who mentioned that Ravens had bred in Hamstead Park that year. At that stage I was not aware of the status of Raven in Berkshire but made a visit to the Park on 24 May to explore the area. I found a rather run-down area of parkland that held several large pine and cedar trees, which might provide a Raven nest site, and plenty of sheep (Ravens feed their young on sheep carrion and placental remains). After discussing this breeding claim with Chris Robinson (Berks BTO Rep) and Peter Standley (County Recorder) the importance of following up the report became clear.

Julie Pocock had been working with Wendy Maxwell who was the gamekeeper for the Park until late April 2003. I eventually made contact with Wendy on 14 June 2003 and the following report is based on our phone conversation and follow-up visits to Hamstead Park.

There is no doubt that Wendy could recognise Ravens having seen them in Wales. She described the physical features in comparison with Rook and Crow and mentioned the distinctive call and flight "tumble". She had first seen Ravens in the area of the Park in 2002 but with no signs of breeding. They developed a habit of drinking from one of the water troughs (presumably for the sheep), always the same trough. They had also been seen at that time in 'The Wilderness' according to a fellow keeper.

In 2003 Ravens were initially seen in the Park during February. In early March (date not recorded but a very windy day) they were first seen carrying twigs and sticks to the top of an old Cedar tree. This continued for some time until a nest was built with the birds apparently un-perturbed by the presence of people in the Park (the Cedar is the third tree on the right of the drive from the Enbourne church entrance with the nest on a bough at the back of the tree as seen from the drive). However, Wendy did not see any evidence of young present in the nest before leaving the Park in the third week of April (when incubation might still have been in progress?).

On 15 June I visited the Park and inspected the tree concerned. There was an evident nest in the tree described but it did not appear to me to be big enough to have held a clutch of Ravens and it is possible that the nest was never completed for some reason. Pictured below are the nest tree and the nest as seen from beneath.

The evidence available appears to support the attempted breeding of Ravens in Berkshire in 2003, apparently the first such attempt for 143 years and in the same location as the last breeding record in 1860.

Note by Recorder.

Ravens have regularly nested in adjacent Wiltshire for some years and juvenile birds seen in Berkshire may well be from that source. As they are normally an early nester (February to mid March is usually given with a 3-week incubation period) if eggs were indeed laid there might reasonably have been an expectation of some signs of young by mid April. A degree of tolerance by gamekeepers would also be necessary in the presence of breeding Ravens where stock protection might be an issue!

Top: Raven's nest
Below: Raven's nest tree

28

SUMMARY OF WEATHER AND BIRD HIGHLIGHTS IN 2003

By Peter Standley

JANUARY

Weather The month started with local flooding and ended with snow. East and northerly winds from 4th brought overnight frosts and mostly sunny days but culminating in 2cms snow on 8th, which lay until 10th. It remained cold till 13th when dull, wet conditions arrived, 20th being very wet and windy. 24th to 27th were very mild (15C) but north winds returned on 28th and remained to the month end, bringing 4cms snow on 30th. *Birds* Rollovers from 2002 included a wintering Red-necked Grebe, several Med Gulls, Caspian Gull and on the downs Hen Harrier and Short-eared Owl (numbers increasing to 8). New arrivals included 5 Red-breasted Mergansers, Little Gull, the returning Iceland Gull to Queen Mother Reservoir (QMR), Water Pipit and Waxwings. As usual with our now generally mild winters there were several reports of both Chiffchaff (a minimum of 23) and Blackcap (min of 26). Among wintering duck there was a notable count of 576 Wigeon at Moor Green Lakes.

FEBRUARY

Weather A predominately dry, cold month with winds mostly from the east and many grey, raw days. 17th to 21st were bright with overnight frosts and from 22nd it was milder, reaching 13C on several days in the last week. *Birds* First of the more unusual species to be reported was a Red-throated Diver at QMR on 10th but the bulk of such records were concentrated into the period from 17th to 25th following the change in the weather pattern mid-month. These included Great Grey Shrike on 17th, Glaucous Gull on 20th, 17 Bean Geese on 24th and 5 on the 25th when there was also an Avocet at QMR and a Great White Egret at Theale (the first for Berks). A flooded Forbury meadow attracted Caspian Gull and a high count (for Berks) of up to 150 Pintail. In spite of it being a cold month nesting activity by Long-tailed Tits was reported.

MARCH

Weather No statistics were collected in March due to holidays but the dry conditions appear to have continued, with easterly winds bringing cool nights and warm days in the last week. *Birds* Passage migrants included Common Scoter at Lower Fm GP, 9 Cranes entering Berks airspace from Bucks (only 5th county record), two more Avocets, Spotted Redshank and Water Pipit. Ten summer migrants had been reported by the end of the month with early records of Little Ringed Plover (on 3rd), Wheatear (6th), Sand Martin (8th), Tree Pipit (16th, the earliest for Berks), Willow Warbler (23rd), Yellow Wagtail (25th) and Sedge Warbler (29th). The remaining arrivals were Swallow, House Martin and White Wagtail. Also notable was a large influx of Bramblings and good numbers of Crossbills. Long-eared Owls were reported from two sites.

APRIL

Weather A generally warm, dry and sunny month. Unsettled for the first few days but becoming sunny with northerly winds on 7th and snow in the wind early on 10th. By 16th temperatures reached 27C with heathland and woodland fires in Scotland, Wales, Dorset and Surrey. Only 2mm of rain fell between early March and late April but the last few days of the month saw some sharp showers locally. *Birds* A quiet start with few highlights, the only notable passage record in the first ten days being 10 Kittiwakes at QMR on the 3rd and a Ring Ouzel near Lambourn on the 4th. Then after 2 Temminck's Stints at Lower Fm GP on the 11th, another

Glaucous Gull record at QMR also on the 11th and a Little Tern at Dinton Pastures on the 15th, there was an influx in the third week with Eider on 21st, an unprecedented inland passage of 13 Pomarine Skuas at QMR on 25th (4th county record) and a Marsh Harrier at Lower Farm GP on 26th. After Nightingale on 6th there was a surge in summer visitors with Cuckoo, Redstart, Reed Warbler, Garden Warbler and Whitethroat in the three days from 12th to 14th followed by Grasshopper Warbler, Lesser Whitethroat and Wood Warbler in the four days from 21st to 24th after a rise in air temperatures. Spotted Flycatcher on 29th was early. Other April highlights included 3 records of passage Osprey, a passage count of c2500 Golden Plover over Hungerford and strong passage of Little Gull, Sandwich Tern and, surprisingly, Ring Ouzel (with 6 records from 21st to 25th which included a party of 9 at Inkpen Hill). Survey results included 3prs of Black Redstart in Reading and at Thatcham a count on the 6th of 17 Cetti's Warblers (13 in song).

MAY

Weather Nationally a dull and wet month but Berkshire escaped much of the wetness. Only 2nd and 17th were wet but locally heavy showers developed on 11th and 25th. In the final week an anticyclone moved north east to Scandinavia with temperatures reaching 29C on 31st. *Birds* Wader passage included Black-tailed Godwit, Little Stint and Knot (all at Lower Fm GP), Bar-tailed Godwit and Wood Sandpiper. There were two records of late passage Great Northern Divers (on 2nd at Theale and on 17th at QMR), a Marsh Harrier over Wraysbury GPs on 6th and 2 Spoonbills over Finchampstead on 7th (13th county record). Black-headed Gull breeding pairs reached 82 and Common Terns about 70.

JUNE

Weather Mostly warm and dry apart from heavy showers around 22nd. *Birds* Surveys of breeding birds produced population estimates of 50-70 Woodcock, at least 60 Nightjar, over 110 Skylark in the Kennet Valley at Englefield, 92 Reed Buntings in the Theale/Burghfield GP area and on East Berks heaths/woodland 70 Firecrest and 29 Spotted Flycatcher territories. Barn Owl records involved 20 birds at 12 sites, there was evidence of several Siskins having bred and at least 3 pairs of breeding Shelduck. Perhaps a portent for the future, there were several summer records of Herring Gull. Passage migrants included two Mediterranean Gulls and an early Osprey (at Marsh Benham on 17th, perhaps summering in southern England?).

JULY

Weather Another warm and dry month, with temperatures reaching the low 30's C between 13th and 16th. The only appreciable rain was on 25th. *Birds* Early passage movement included 14 Black-tailed Godwits at Eversley GP on 1st and 10 at Lower Fm GP on 6th and there were several Osprey sightings from the 17th. An early cause for some excitement was a Red-footed Falcon at Pingewood GP from the 4th to the 17th (the 7th county record) but a Fulmar escaped live observation being found freshly dead at Newbury on the 9th (the 4th county record). The month ended with an early returning Pied Flycatcher at West Woodhay Down on the 30th.

AUGUST

Weather Another hot, dry and sunny month. No cloud or wind at the start of the month culminated in a temperature of 38C/100F at Heathrow on the afternoon of 10th. The rest of the month was mostly in an East or Northerly airstream, bringing early cloud and sunny afternoons. There was only one day of rain which, although steady, brought little relief to the parched conditions. *Birds* A Red-backed Shrike at Greenham Common from the 3rd to 6th (the first in W Berks since 1978) got August off to a good start. After a Wood Warbler at Dinton Pastures on the 9th, easterly/northerly winds from the 10th produced records of Marsh Harrier (on 10th and 16th), Spotted Redshank (13th) and Long-tailed Skua at QMR (on 17th and only the 2nd county record). Also at QMR there was a total of 70 Yellow-legged Gulls on the 11th. Not too surprisingly Red Kites were suspected of having bred in W Berks and there was a juvenile Raven at Combe on the 30th. The peak 2003 count for Ring-necked Parakeets occurred on the 20th with 227 in the Bray area.

SEPTEMBER

Weather The warm, dry weather continued for much of the month with the only appreciable rain falling on 22nd, with 4mm. Temperatures reached 28C around 17th but a north westerly airstream from 22nd brought a taste of autumn. *Birds* Apart from no less than 3 records of Wryneck (on 11th, 14th and 27th) and a Rock Pipit on 26th this was a quiet month. Counts of note included 67 Egyptian Geese in the Cookham Rise area, a party of 17 Stone Curlew on the downs and a peak of c22,000 Lesser Black-backed Gulls in the Theale roost on 23rd. The long staying Bittern at Lavells Lake was sadly found dead on the 16th wearing a French ring.

OCTOBER

Weather Months of consistently dry and warm weather came to an end with occasional days of heavy showers bringing rainfall to near normal. In between, mild sunny days kept temperatures up and with light winds resulted in one or two frosts. Many trees were still in full leaf at the end of the month with a wonderful display of colour. *Birds* Late passage included 2 Knot at QMR, several Little Gulls, an Arctic Skua at QMR from 18th to 20th (13th for county), Water Pipit at three sites, a Yellow-browed Warbler at Theale GP on 30th (only the 2nd county record) and Lapland Buntings at QMR on the 4th and Widbrook Common on 6th. Low water at QMR resulted in a count of c1480 Cormorants on the 31st. Late departing summer migrants included Sedge Warbler on 5th, Redstart on 10th, Reed Warbler on 11th and Sand Martin on 24th. Winter arrivals included Bramblings from the 11th and the first Caspian Gull of the winter on the 28th.

NOVEMBER

Weather Generally mild and dry early in the month but the last 10 days turned colder as a series of depressions moved north east over SE England, bringing up to 90mm(3½ ins) rain in places between 20th and 23rd. Definitely a washed-out weekend! More rain and strong winds followed on 25th and 26th. *Birds* With the month's top three rarities choosing to prolong their stay observers were provided with the opportunity to extend their county species list. At Eversley GP a Pectoral Sandpiper was present from 1st to 7th (the 13th for Berks), re-appearing at Dorney Wetlands from 12th to 13th, and low water in QMR encouraged first a Spoonbill to stay from the 2nd to the 25th (14th county record and second for the year) and then a Grey Phalarope from 15th to 20th (24th county record). Other highlights included 9 Avocets at QMR on 29th and a roost of 42 Red Kites on the downs. There was a late Swallow on the 16th and an influx of Chiffchaffs (minimum of 34). Now a rarity in Berks there was a report of Tree Sparrow on the 27th in East Berks.

DECEMBER

Weather Rainfall rather above average in the south this month and with several days of strong winds. Otherwise a mixed bag of mild (13th) and frosty (8th) days, with snow showers on 28th. *Birds* QMR continued to figure prominently with a Storm Petrel and a Snow Bunting on the 2nd (the former falling prey to the local Peregrine!). Apart from three records of Kittiwakes the remaining notable records were of passerines with the first December record for Berks of a Yellow Wagtail (at Wokingham Sewage Works on 17th), a Bearded Tit at Theale GP from the 30th and on the last day of the year a count of c200 Corn Buntings at Sheepdrove Farm near Lambourn, the highest since 1979.

Our thanks go to Runnymede Ringing Group for the use of weather information from their monthly Newsletters.

REPORT FOR 2003 BY
THE BERKSHIRE RECORDS COMMITTEE

By Peter Standley

RECORDS COMMITTEE UPDATE

Since publication of the 2002 Berkshire Bird Report Ken Moore has joined the BRC which now comprises Chris Heard, County Recorder and Chairman, Ken Moore, Peter Standley and as Secretary to the Committee, Derek Barker. We continue to examine all descriptions submitted and any other records for which descriptions would normally be required but for which they have not been received. Where the bird will have been seen by a number of observers the record may be found acceptable without the need for details, although this should not be assumed, as if no one provides a report and the sighting has conflicting elements it may not be possible for the BRC to give the record unqualified acceptance. A considerable number of reports of rare or unusual occurrences are still unsupported by descriptions and in most cases the BRC has had no alternative but to omit these until some supporting details are provided on which an assessment can be made.

The list of species for which descriptions/notes are required has been extended by the addition to the Category 3 list of the following species in view of the infrequency with which they are now recorded in Berkshire:

Additions to Category 3 from 2003 -
Wood Warbler
Tree Sparrow

As already reported in the 2002 Bird Report, during 2003 the British Birds Rarities Committee accepted a record of a Great White Egret, a new addition to the County Checklist, bringing that total to 310 species (301 in Category A and 9 in Category C). Including that record a total of 216 species were recorded (including 8 breeding and 2 non-breeding feral/released species). A well above average year.

REVIEW OF 2003 RECORDS

The following report on the outcome of the BRC's consideration of rare or unusual Berkshire records for 2003 follows the pattern of the BRC's report for 2002 except for the omission of a listing of accepted records, the details of which can be found in the Bird Report/systematic list.

2003 Records which the BRC have not been able to accept

In many cases the information provided in support of these records was insufficient for the BRC to reach a judgement as to their acceptability and therefore to be sure of correct identification. All records listed are of single birds unless stated otherwise. An asterisk (*) indicates that no details were received by the BRC. Where a record for a commoner summer or winter visitor has not been accepted because of an unusually early or late date this is indicated by "(date)" after the record. These will include some from Birdtrack which lack observer details.

Red-necked Grebe	QMR 21.1*
Slavonian Grebe	QMR 27.1*
Shag	R Kennet Reading 15.4*
Scaup	1m1f Kindersley Centre 1.5*
Common Scoter	4 Lower Fm GP 8.3*; Thatcham GPs 30.10*
Smew	48 Wraysbury/Horton GPs in Jan, 21 in Feb and 40 in Dec
Honey Buzzard	Woodley 10.5*; Crookham Com 4.6*; Pingewood GPs 31.8
Black Kite	Woodley 25.4*
Marsh Harrier	Lower Farm GP 26.4*; Cockmarsh 25.8*
Goshawk	Burghfield GPs 9.2*; Wokingham 31.3*; Catmore 17.4*, 29.4*, 11.11*
Common Buzzard	34 or 35 over Reading 13.7
Rough-legged Buzzard	Sonning 20.9*
Golden Eagle	Thatcham Marsh 13.4*
Merlin	Theale GPs 12.1* and 13.4*; Mid Berks 22.1.*; Wokingham 10.4*; Greenham Common 4.8 (data error); Charvil 30.11*
Hobby	Snelsmore Common 29.3* (date)
Crane	Dorney Wetland 3.4*
Avocet	4 QMR 25.2 (data error); 10 over Caversham 8.8*
Spotted Redshank	Lower Farm GP 18.4*; Lea Farm 15.5*
Wood Sandpiper	Eversley GP 28.4
Ring-billed Gull	Wraysbury GP 25.1*; R Thames, Henley 29.11*; Lower Farm GP 5.12*
Common Gull	12 Lake End 8.5, 15 on 2.6, 1 on 21.6 (dates); AWE Aldermaston 14.6 (date)
Yellow-legged Gull	9 Lower Farm GP 25.1*
Caspian Gull	QMR 31.1*; Pingewood 19.3; Dinton Pastures 21.4; QMR 31.10* and 19.12*
Kittiwake	Lower Farm GP 30.3* and 14.12*
Little Tern	2 Dinton Pastures 28.6*
Bee Eater	Cookham 20.8*
Swift	Thatcham 1.4 (date)
Swallow	2 Lower Fm GP 8.3 (date)*
House Martin	5 Lower Fm GP 8.3 (date)*
Tree Pipit	Dinton Pastures 3.4*
Water Pipit	QMR 9.3*
White Wagtail	Twyford GP 19.2 (date)*
Wheatear	Sheepdrove 1.2 (date)*
Ring Ouzel	Lake End 20.4*
Garden Warbler	Snelsmore Common 23.3 (date)*; Wraysbury GP 5.4 (date)*
Yellow-browed Warbler	Sandhurst 25.10 and 27.10*; Theale GP 31.10*; Tilehurst 14.12*
Willow Warbler	Dorney Wetland 11.10*; Eversley GP 18.10*
Wood Warbler	Swinley 16.4; Lavells Lake 25.4*
Firecrest	Theale GP 21-22.2*; Cookham Rise Cemetery 8.6*; Winnersh 18.11*
Spotted Flycatcher	Upton Park, Slough 29.4* (date)
Bearded Tit	Thatcham 1.1*
Golden Oriole	Binfield 30.5*
Red-backed Shrike	3 Cockmarsh 21.6
Great Grey Shrike	Wargrave 11.5*
Raven	Eversley GP 2.6*; Lambourn 25.6; Lavells Lake 24.9*
Tree Sparrow	2 Hambridge 28.3*
Serin	Lake End 26.4* and 7.6*
Mealy Redpoll	Dinton Pastures 17.11*

2003 Records still under consideration
None remain under consideration by the BRC

SYSTEMATIC LIST
BIRD REPORT FOR 2003

Edited by Derek Barker and reviewed by Chris Heard and Peter Standley.

See Acknowledgements for a list of those drafting the accounts.

Observers

Please see the list of contributors at the end of this report to whom we extend our thanks.

Abbreviations and place names

The normal abbreviations are shown below in the table. For place names difficulties arise where there are several names for the same sites including where, for example, a gravel pit complex is named but not the individual pit. A map and guide to the main sites is included towards the end of the report to assist with identification.

AGE/SEX		PLACES/ LOCALITIES	
Ad	adult	**Com**	Common
F/s	First summer	**CP**	Country Park
Fw	First winter (plumage)	**Fm**	Farm
Imm	Immature	**GC**	Golf course
Juv	Juvenile	**GP**	Gravel Pit(s)
M	Male	**Res**	Reservoir
Pr	pair	**R.**	River
F or **fem**	Female	**SF**	Sewage Farm
Rh	Redhead	**STW**	Sewage Treatment Works
R/t	Ringtail		
S/p	Summer plumage	**E Berks**	East Berkshire
S/s	Second summer	**M.Berks**	Mid Berkshire
S/w	Second winter	**W Berks**	West Berkshire
W/p	Winter plumage	**Dorney W**	Dorney Wetlands
W	Winter	**QMR**	Queen Mother Reservoir
W/p	Winter plumage		
3/s	Third summer		

Order of species

Game birds now follow ducks, divers to herons follow game birds which are then followed by raptors and rails.

'Channel Wagtail', Cold Harbour
– Dave Rimes

Black Redstart, Dorney Wetlands
– Jerry O'Brien

Water Pipit, Queen Mother Reservoir – Jerry O'Brien

Arctic Skua, Queen Mother Reservoir – Mike McKee

Eider, Lea Farm – Dave Rimes

MUTE SWAN *Cygnus olor*

Locally common resident

Monthly maxima at the main sites were:

	Jan	Feb	Mar	Apr	May	Jun	Jul	Aug	Sep	Oct	Nov	Dec
Dinton Pastures	50	15	12	–	–	–	–	5	–	68	69	60
Eversley GPs	15	17	6	6	8	13	10	–	16	13	18	28
Lower Farm GP	6	11	45	20	9	6	3	7	73	17	4	7
Newbury, K&A Canal	55	38	38	54	–	57	28	–	–	–	74	57
Windsor Esplanade	215	–	295	–	–	–	–	–	156	–	192	278

Counts of up to 55 were received from a further 50 sites with higher counts of 66 Horton GP Mar 20th (CL) and 67 Kennetmouth, Reading Nov 7th (MBu). **Breeding:** Confirmed at 13 locations involving 16 pairs.

BEWICK'S SWAN *Cygnus columbianus*

Uncommon passage migrant

Another poor year the only record being of 2 at Wraysbury GPs Jan 4th (BMA, BTB).

BEAN GOOSE *Anser fabalis*

Rare winter visitor

A good year with 17 flying NE over QMR on Feb 24th (CDRH) and a day later 5 Tundra's at Pingewood GP Feb 25th which remained until the following day (MO). These records were part of an influx into SE England peaking from Feb 20th-26th, the 17 at QMR being the largest flock reported throughout the region. This was, at the time, the largest flock to be recorded in Berkshire but there has subsequently been another flock of 17 (incl several juvs) in December 2004.

WHITE-FRONTED GOOSE *Anser albifrons*

Uncommon passage migrant and occasional winter visitor

There was one record of a likely wild bird at Twyford GP Dec 15th (CDRH), an adult Eurasian bird with an injured left eye and left wing presumably from a gun-shot, so may have been injured by wildfowlers. A feral bird frequented the area between Woolhampton and Theale GPs from March until the end of the year (MO). The second year with just a single wild record.

GREYLAG GOOSE *Anser anser*

Common introduced and increasing resident

Monthly maxima at the main sites were:

	Jan	Feb	Mar	Apr	May	Jun	Jul	Aug	Sep	Oct	Nov	Dec
Cockmarsh	–	–	18	7	11	50	–	–	–	–	–	–
Padworth Lane GP	57	–	6	17	–	–	–	205	–	–	–	–
Pingewood GPs	25	12	21	4	–	–	–	82	4	–	–	–
Summerleaze GP	–	30	49	3	–	–	–	60	–	–	–	–
Theale/Moatlands GPs	70	100	113	3	9	–	6	27	243	38	–	–
Woolhampton GPs	–	–	2	2	–	–	–	52	10	–	–	–

Most counts for Theale GPs came from Bottom Lane Floods. However the high count of 243 (a county record) was for Hosehill Lake on Sep 16th (BU). Elsewhere, counts of up to 24 were received from a further 45 sites with higher counts of 40 Brimpton GP Jan 22nd (JPM); c100 Cookham, Switchback Road Aug 16th (BDC); 45 Arborfield, Hall Fm Sep 10th (DJB) with c50 there Nov 7th and 34 Nov 25th (DJB); 116 Wargrave, Borough Marsh Oct 5th (ABT); c70 R. Thames Spade Oak Reach Nov 5th (LM); c50 Shinfield, Carters Hill Nov 7th (DJB) and 38 Bisham Nov 26th (DJB). **Breeding:** Reported from only 3 sites. At Bottom Lane 4 ads with 5 y were located on May 18th (JA) whilst 1 pair with 5 y was also present at Frogmill, Hurley on May 18th (SJF; FMF). Finally 4 ads with 4 y were found at Aldermaston GP Jul 18th (JPM).

SNOW GOOSE *Anser caerulescens*

Occasional escapee and regular visitor to one site where it has bred

All records relate to feral birds. Monthly maxima at the main site were:

	Jan	Feb	Mar	Apr	May	Jun	Jul	Aug	Sep	Oct	Nov	Dec
Eversley GPs	13	13	11	11	–	–	–	–	–	9	10	9

Elsewhere: 4 Denford Mill Jul 30th (RGS); 1 Dorney Wetlands Aug 23rd (JOB) and 1 Frogmill, Hurley Sep 18th (SJF, FMF).

CANADA GOOSE *Branta canadensis*

Common and widespread introduced resident

Monthly maxima at the main sites were:

	Jan	Feb	Mar	Apr	May	Jun	Jul	Aug	Sep	Oct	Nov	Dec
Aldermaston GP	4	4	27	28	10	42	23	41	122	42	34	–
Dinton Pastures	206	90	46	–	–	150	–	–	–	–	17	–
Eversley GPs	60	68	101	57	55	86	106	–	32	182	80	176
Dorney Wetlands	40	5	26	–	–	16	–	220	–	–	–	–
Lower Farm GP	244	151	54	43	88	66	99	200	130	64	192	220
Lower Farm Trout Lake	108	–	–	–	–	–	–	–	–	–	–	30
Padworth Lane GP	102	–	8	4	–	–	–	25	22	–	–	–
Thatcham GPs	82	215	70	36	66	105	120	203	186	158	176	160
Windsor Esplanade	196	–	–	–	–	–	–	–	409	–	381	59
Windsor Great Park	2	2	221	–	–	–	–	–	–	–	–	–

Counts of up to 80 were received from a further 38 sites with higher counts of 150 West Meadows Jan 12th (IW, JL); 101 Enborne, K&A Canal Jan 31st (JPM); 100 Pingewood GPs Feb 6th (BDC); 87 Theale GP Jul 6th (SAG); c400 Cookham, Switchback Road Aug 16th (BDC); 514 Twyford Aug 21st (MFW); 500 Woolhampton GP (Rowney's) Aug 31st (GEW); c100 Borough Marsh Oct 5th (ABT); 140 Maidenhead, R. Thames Nov 5th (DF); 143 Maidenhead, Towpath fields Dec 17th (DF) and 140 Odney Island Dec 20th (DF). **Breeding:** Reported from many sites, a crèche of 50 at Dinton Pastures CP on Jun 1st (CN) was the largest count reported.

BARNACLE GOOSE *Branta leucopsis*

Rare vagrant and localised feral visitor/resident

All records relate to feral birds. Monthly maxima at the main site were:

	Jan	Feb	Mar	Apr	May	Jun	Jul	Aug	Sep	Oct	Nov	Dec
Eversley GPs	200	200	173	15	29	100	22	30	30	90	100	222

Occasional records were received from sites away from the Eversley stronghold: 1 R.Thames Pangbourne Jan 5th (MJS); 1 Black Swan Lake Jan 7th ((MFW) and throughout first half of year; 8 Hosehill Lake May 24th (RCr); 1 Borough Marsh Jun 3rd (ABT); 1 Twyford GP Aug 2nd (AR); 1 Summerleaze GP Aug 16th and Sep 26th (CDRH); 1 Cookham, Switchback Road Aug 16th (BDC); 1 Cookham Rise Aug 19th (CDRH) and 1 Bray GP Aug 29th (CDRH). **Breeding:** Confined to Eversley GPs where 4 pairs bred, rearing 6 y (MGLR).

BRENT GOOSE *Branta bernicla*

Scarce passage migrant

There were 5 sightings involving 6 birds. **First winter:** Passage was noted at QMR where 2 flew off NE on Mar 5th (RIn) and 1circled there Mar 15th (JAS). An injured bird was present at Lower Fm GP from Apr 11th (RRK; FJC) until Apr 14th (MO). **Second winter:** One flew S over Moatlands GP on Nov 30th (JA) and 1 adult (dark-bellied) at QMR Dec 1st (CDRH).

EGYPTIAN GOOSE *Alopochen aegyptiaca*

Now locally common introduced resident / visitor

Records were received from 51 locations, 2 in W Berks, 24 in M Berks and 25 in E Berks. **W Berks:** Still a scarce species in this part of Berks with 2 seen flying over the Thames at Goring on Jan 1 (SPA) and 2 at Brimpton GPs on Jul 31st-Aug 1st (GEW) the only records. **M&E Berks:** Now a familiar bird along the Thames and to most of the larger GPs from Reading east to Slough. Most records involved 1-12 birds with higher counts being 22 at Cockmarsh on Jan 9th (CDRH), 20 Summerleaze GP Aug 2nd (BDC) with 15 there on Sep 6th (CDRH), 39 Cookham Rise area on Aug 10th (CDRH) increasing to 41 Aug 16th (BDC) and 67 Sep 9th (CDRH) a new county high count. Numbers remained high there with 52 over on Sep 24th (CDRH), 42 Sep 28th (BDC) and 50 over on Oct 6th (CDRH). Part of this flock was also encountered along the Thames at Cockmarsh where 33 were present on Sep 18th (BDC), 18 on Sep 24th (LM) and 30 there on Nov 11th (RG). Elsewhere 20 appeared at Eversley GPs (a site record) on Oct 1st (SW) then 13 there on Dec 23rd and 28th (JMC), 26 were on Borough Marsh on Oct 5th (ABT), 22 Sonning Oct 26th (ABT), 14 on the Berks side of the R.Thames at Henley on Nov 28th (NS) and 13 at Remenham on Nov 30th (DJB). **Breeding:** Was confirmed at Whiteknights Pk Lake where 1pr reared 3y (PG; MBu), 1pr reared 4y at Mill Pond Bracknell (RDi; MFW), a pair with 9y at Theale Main GP on Apr 13th (DHu) had lost all but 2 by May 1st (RRK), 2 prs with broods of 4y & 2y in Windsor Park on May 25th (CDRH) and 1pr with 6j were found in Windsor Pk on Jul 19th (MMc). Only 10 years ago 10-15 were regarded as high counts.

SHELDUCK   *Tadorna tadorna*

Uncommon passage migrant and summer visitor

Monthly maxima at the main sites were:

	Jan	Feb	Mar	Apr	May	Jun	Jul	Aug	Sep	Oct	Nov	Dec
Aldermaston GP	2	–	4	2	2	12	–	–	–	–	–	–
Crookham Common	–	–	6	4	–	–	–	–	–	–	–	–
Greenham Common	–	3	10	2	6	–	–	–	–	–	–	–
Hungerford, Home Farm	–	1	1	–	8	8	7	–	–	–	–	–
Lower Farm GP	2	6	5	7	4	4	7	–	–	–	1	4
Padworth Lane GP	2	4	3	4	1	15	9	–	–	–	–	–
Pingewood GPs	5	4	11	8	7	2	–	–	–	–	–	–
Queen Mother Reservoir	1	5	2	9	10	5	8	7	–	1	6	1
Theale/Moatlands GPs	–	2	2	3	11	–	–	–	–	1	–	5
Woolhampton GPs	6	2	14	12	8	–	–	–	–	–	–	–

Counts of up to 4 were received from a further 33 sites with higher counts of 7 Dorney Wetlands and Slough STW May 23rd (CDRH), and 6 Bray GP Nov 29th (WAS). An unusual report concerned 2 on flooded fields at East Ilsley on Mar 24th (ABT) increasing to 6 on Apr 5th (JOB). **Breeding:** Confirmed at Aldermaston GP, 1pr with 10y on Jun 2nd (JPM); Hungerford, Home Fm, 1pr with 6y May 28th (RGS) and Padworth Lane GP, 1pr 8y Jun 10th (RCr). Elsewhere, 7 (including 6y) Lower Fm GP Jul 6th (IW;JL) may have been the result of breeding there and a female with 7 fledged juvs at QMR on Jul 22nd (CDRH) may have been of local origin.

MANDARIN DUCK   *Aix galericulata*

Localised and increasing introduced resident

Monthly maxima at the main sites were:

	Jan	Feb	Mar	Apr	May	Jun	Jul	Aug	Sep	Oct	Nov	Dec
Eversley GPs	14	8	7	6	12	4	–	2	4	3	5	1
Whiteknights Park	20	4	–	1	3	–	–	–	–	–	–	–
Windsor Great Park	–	–	6	9	4	–	–	–	50	64	–	–

The high count of 64 at Windsor Pk occurred on Oct 2nd (CDRH). Elsewhere, counts of up to 9 were received from a further 53 sites with higher counts of 18 between Maidenhead and Cookham, R. Thames May 8th (LM); 21 R. Thames near Boulters Lock Jul 3rd (LM) and 10 Wraysbury GPs Nov 23rd (CDRH). The only reports west of Aldermaston involved 4 records from Lower Fm GP with 1pr Jan 19th (JW; IW; JL) and Jan 26th (JC), a drake associating with a Canada Goose on Mar 22nd (DJB) and a drake on Sep 12th (RH). **Breeding:** Confirmed at Quarry Woods where 2 nest boxes contained 8 and 9 eggs on May 1st (BDC), 1f with 7y on the Colnbrook at Wraysbury May 5th (AFd), 1f with 5y on the Thames at Mapledurham May 28th (KJ), 1f with young at Maiden Erlegh Lake May 28th (AM), 1f with 9y R Thames Bray May 31st (RAns; JAns), 1f 6y on the Emm Brook at Lavell's Lake Jun 5th (RDa), 1f 5y Thames Meadows Jun 6th (MJS), 2f 2y Aldermaston GP Jun 21st (JPM), 6y Boulters Lock Jul 3rd (LM), with a second brood of 4y also on R. Thames Maidenhead in Jul (DF). At Eversley GPs 6 boxes held clutches of from 12 to 24 eggs and it is thought that 8f were involved. Up to 96 eggs were laid producing 70 young (KBB).

WIGEON *Anas penelope*

Locally common winter visitor and rare summer visitor

Monthly maxima at the main sites were:

	Jan	Feb	Mar	Apr	May	Jun	Jul	Aug	Sep	Oct	Nov	Dec
Bray GP	34	–	–	–	–	–	–	–	4	2	–	–
Burghfield GPs	–	–	80	1	–	–	–	–	56	50	20	–
Dinton Pastures / Lavell's Lake	40	3	30	1	–	–	–	–	57	225	250	40
Eversley GPs	576	167	67	4	–	–	–	2	30	107	197	351
Lower Farm / Racecourse GPs	112	142	64	20	–	–	–	–	12	22	19	85
Pingewood GPs	237	199	157	37	–	–	–	2	87	105	300	100
Theale/Moatlands GPs	206	147	185	40	–	–	–	2	27	104	8	85
Wraysbury GPs	–	–	–	–	–	–	–	–	57	244	454	–

The high count of 576 at Eversley GPs occurred on Jan 7th (MGLR). Counts of up to 27 were received from a further 17 sites with 54 at West Meadows Jan 12th (IW, JL); c100 Reading, Rosekiln Lane Feb 8th (ABT), 60 Feb 9th (TGB), 100 Feb 10th (MJT), and 150 Feb 15th (JMC); 121 Ruscombe floods Mar 11th (CDRH), 120 there Mar 17th (DJB); 40 Twyford GPs Dec 7th (TGB); c60 Summerleaze GP Dec 24th (CDRH) with 40 there Dec 27th (BDC). 1 female at Horton GPs on Jun 27th still present on Jul 24th (CDRH) suggests possible summering. Latest spring departure was 1m at Pingewood GPs on Apr 28th (RCr; ABT). Earliest arrivals were 2 at Eversley GPs (MGLR), 1m at Pingewood (JOB) and 2 at Moatlands GP (BU), all on Aug 26th.

Wigeon by Helen Chadburn

GADWALL *Anas strepera*

Common winter visitor now breeding in several locations

Monthly maxima at the main sites were:

	Jan	Feb	Mar	Apr	May	Jun	Jul	Aug	Sep	Oct	Nov	Dec
Bray GPs	35	31	4	1	–	–	–	–	–	–	7	1
Burghfield GPs	–	85	10	5	–	–	–	–	139	–	90	–
Dinton Pastures	90	57	2	3	–	–	1	–	122	20	31	42
Eversley GPs	166	113	24	17	12	3	3	9	31	68	96	297
Lower Farm GP	19	18	50	18	16	16	11	20	39	9	25	42
Pingewood GPs	1	6	6	6	2	10	1	20	–	1	25	1
Theale/Moatlands GPs	29	13	15	6	6	5	9	40	117	164	25	38

Counts of up to 18 were received from a further 39 sites with higher counts of c50 Reading, Rosekiln Lane Feb 8th (ABT) and Feb 9th (TGB) and 38 Orlitts Lake North Oct 29th (BDC). **Breeding:** Confirmed at Lower Fm GP, 1f 7y Jun 15th-Jul 19th (IW; JL); Field Fm 1f 8y Jul 5th & 20th (RCr); Slough SF, 1f 11y Jul 8th (CDRH) and Moatlands GP, 1f 4y Jul 26th (MFW) to Jul 29th (RCr).

TEAL   *Anas crecca*

Common winter visitor and rare summer visitor

Monthly maxima at the main sites were:

	Jan	Feb	Mar	Apr	May	Jun	Jul	Aug	Sep	Oct	Nov	Dec
Aldermaston GP	–	29	4	–	–	–	–	–	–	9	–	–
Bray GPs	60	20	5	10	–	–	–	4	–	52	27	6
Burghfield GPs	73	–	20	1	–	–	–	–	4	2	–	–
Dinton Pastures	55	50	31	13	–	–	–	–	40	1	4	–
Eversley GPs	42	50	16	20	3	1	2	10	34	46	60	58
Dorney Wetlands	40	30	14	10	–	–	–	3	6	7	–	–
Lavell's Lake	50	40	55	7	–	2	1	26	50	73	24	27
Lower Farm GP	70	72	20	17	1	–	1	13	59	49	141	100
Pingewood GPs	38	65	34	15	2	3	3	16	33	33	45	62
Ruscombe floods	–	64	23	16	–	–	–	–	–	–	–	–
Slough SF	5	50	–	–	–	–	–	1	8	9	5	–
Theale/Moatlands GPs	150	100	100	30	–	–	1	15	8	34	10	91
Woolhampton GPs	80	2	5	5	–	–	–	2	–	–	–	–

Counts of up to 13 were received from a further 21 sites with higher counts of 55 Widbrook Com Jan 9th (CDRH); 210 Wraysbury GPs Jan 12th (CDRH); 50+ Kintbury, K&A Canal Jan 24th (DJB); 30 Pingewood GP Feb 6th (BDC); c200 Fobney Marshes Feb 8th (ABT); 120 Reading, Rosekiln Lane Feb 15th (JMC). No evidence of breeding was submitted but 3m (2 injured) remained at Burnthouse Lane throughout the summer period (RCr *et al*); a single male remained at Eversley GP as late as Jun 2nd (NRG) and a pair, possibly early returning birds, were at Lavell's Lake on Jun 17th (RR) to Jun 20th (MBu) then 1m to Jul 4th (MFW).

MALLARD   *Anas platyrhynchos*

Common and widespread resident and winter visitor

Monthly maxima at the main sites were:

	Jan	Feb	Mar	Apr	May	Jun	Jul	Aug	Sep	Oct	Nov	Dec
Eversley GPs	39	31	14	26	20	38	33	59	34	30	52	69
Lower Farm GP	21	21	12	13	11	22	21	74	91	79	57	52
Muddy Lane GP	220	nc	100	161	128	203	140	155	236	200	245	142

The high count of 245 at Muddy Lane GP, Thatcham occurred on Nov 11th (GJS). Elsewhere no counts exceeded 100 birds.

PINTAIL   *Anas acuta*
Scarce winter visitor

First winter: An exceptional year with the highlight being unprecedented numbers which spent much of February on the flooded meadows around Fobney and Rosekiln Lane, Reading. A flock of 58 was located there on Feb 2nd (BTB) which increased to 80 on Feb 9th (BDC), 96 Feb 11th (CDRH), 105 Feb 16th (DJB) and 97 Feb 17th (PBT). There were no further records (due to freezing weather) until Feb 26th when 6 were present (RCr) then increased significantly to 150 on Feb 28th (MBu) before declining to 6 on Mar 1st (JOB), the last record. At Pingewood GPs birds were present from Jan 4th (MGM) to Mar 6th (PBT) with high counts of 38 Feb 15th (JOB) and 34 Feb 19th (MGM). These records easily exceeded the previous high count for Berks, a flock of 28 over Horton GPs on Dec 31st 1974. Elsewhere there were 3 at Cookham Rise and nearby Widbrook Com from Jan 6th-8th (CDRH); 2 Remenham Jan 8th (CDRH); 4 Summerleaze GP Jan 11th (CDRH); 2m Lower Fm GP Jan 13th (PH), 1pr there Jan 20th (RAH), 5 Feb 12th (GJS) and 2 Feb 13th (GJS; RAH); 3 Woolhampton GP Jan 27th (CDRH); 1 Bray GP Jan 31st (DJB); 1pr Eversley GPs also on Jan 31st (SFa; NS); 1 Dinton Pastures Feb 2nd (TGB) and 2 on flooded fields at East Ilsley Feb 25th (CDRH). **Second winter:** A return to more usual numbers with 1f/imm Theale GP Sep 22nd (MGM); 1 Bray GP Sep 26th (BDC), 1f QMR Oct 31st (DJB; CL) and 2 (1f 1imm male) Wraysbury GPs Nov 9th (CDRH).

GARGANEY   *Anas querquedula*
Scarce passage migrant and rare summer visitor

A poor year with 8 records involving 11 birds. **Spring:** 2 Dinton Pastures Apr 8th until at least Apr 15th (MO); 2 Eversley GP Apr 13th (AF *et al*) and 2 QMR Apr 14th (JAS). **Autumn:** A probable juv at Pingewood GP on Jul 2nd (MGM), 1 j Hosehill Lake Aug 11th (ABT), 1 Moatlands GP Aug 27th (BU), 1 eclipse m Twyford GP Sep 6th (BTB; MFW) and 1 circled Wraysbury GPs with c 20 Shoveler on Sep 21st (CDRH).

SHOVELER   *Anas clypeata*
Locally common winter visitor and rare summer visitor

Monthly maxima at the main sites were:

	Jan	Feb	Mar	Apr	May	Jun	Jul	Aug	Sep	Oct	Nov	Dec
Aldermaston GP	4	37	25	2	–	–	–	–	–	–	–	1
Bray GPs	15	32	5	–	–	–	–	1	–	13	41	–
Burghfield GPs	–	70	6	2	–	–	–	2	2	6	6	–
Eversley GPs	16	32	50	16	–	–	–	2	7	9	29	28
Dorney Wetlands	5	30	4	2	–	–	–	5	17	50	30	–
Lavell's Lake	7	6	7	4	–	–	–	2	9	4	9	21
Lower Farm GP	47	71	62	12	2	–	1	16	50	72	98	60
Pingewood GPs	6	115	46	42	–	–	1	–	–	–	–	4
Slough SF	4	24	–	–	–	–	–	3	–	2	9	–
Thatcham GPs	43	5	–	2	–	–	–	–	–	–	–	–
Theale GPs	2	37	25	1	–	–	–	13	104	92	38	69
Twyford GPs	36	10	14	–	–	–	–	–	–	–	90	50

The high counts of 115 at Pingewood GPs occurred on Feb 1st (MGM) and the 104 at Theale GPs occurred at Hosehill Lake on Sep 21st (RCr). Elsewhere counts of up to 18 were received from a further 15 sites with higher counts of c50 Fobney Marshes/Rosekiln

Lane on Feb 8th (ABT) and 60 there on Feb 9th (TGB); 20 circling Wraysbury GPs Sep 21st (CDRH) and 23 Whiteknights Park Nov 18th (PG). A pair remained at Lower Fm GP until May 21st (MJT, GJS) and there were 4 drakes at Horton GP on May 31st (CDRH). The earliest return date was Jul 31st with single females at Lower Fm GP (JCh) and Pingewood GPs (MGM).

RED-CRESTED POCHARD *Netta rufina*

Scarce winter visitor but presumed feral birds occur annually in small numbers

All records are believed to relate to escaped or feral birds. At Burghfield GPs a male was reported on Feb 2nd (PBT) then single males were reported on Mar 22nd (JLe), Mar 23rd (BTB), 2 males on Mar 28th (GBr), 1f Apr 3rd, 1m Apr 5th (JLe) and 1m Apr 9th (PMC). The next report was 1m on May 19th (JLe) then 1m on Jun 20th (JA) and 26th (CDRH). In Sep there was 1m on Sep 2nd and 1f Sep 23rd (KBW), 3 (2m 1f) Oct 18th (JOB) then 1pr on Nov 1st (JA), 7th (MFW) and 13th (RJB; LM). At Pingewood GPs single males were seen on Feb 27th-28th (MGM) Mar 1st (PBT) then 2m on Mar 8th (MFW). There were no further records until July when a male moulting into eclipse was seen on Jul 1st-2nd (MGM), Jul 5th (AFd; RJB) and Jul 6th (TGB). The next crop of records there came in November with 2m from Nov 11th to Dec 4th (MGM) then 3m on Dec 5th-7th (MJT; DKP; RJB) and 1m on Dec 8th (MGM) and Dec 17th (PBT). Movement of the same birds between these two sites is probable which points to 1m having been present in the area from Feb to Dec. Elsewhere there was 1f at Datchet Moor GP on Nov 10th (CDRH).

POCHARD *Aythya ferina*

Common winter visitor and passage migrant, scarce summer visitor

Monthly maxima at the main sites were:

	Jan	Feb	Mar	Apr	May	Jun	Jul	Aug	Sep	Oct	Nov	Dec
Aldermaston GP	–	20	24	–	–	–	–	–	–	52	31	13
Bray GPs	124	162	36	–	–	–	–	–	90	40	165	150
Burghfield GPs	181	–	2	2	–	–	–	–	–	–	–	–
Dinton Pastures / Lavell's Lake	120	150	40	6	–	1	–	1	1	19	42	30
Eversley GPs	83	76	24	2	1	3	7	4	6	39	54	95
Old Slade GP	3	–	–	–	–	–	2	29	65	4	–	16
Pingewood GPs	156	122	47	8	1	5	12	13	27	4	–	30
Thatcham area GPs	142	100	55	–	1	2	–	2	7	5	23	34
Theale/Moatlands GPs	264	65	79	1	1	1	1	9	–	95	150	229
Twyford GPs	72	54	7	–	–	–	–	–	1	–	120	40
Woolhampton GPs	26	31	30	1	2	–	–	–	–	–	–	–
Wraysbury GPs	155	100	30	–	–	–	35	–	75	73	38	73

Counts of up to 29 were received from a further 18 sites with higher counts of 40 Horton GP Jan 30th (JOB) and 62 Brimpton GP Reedbeds Oct 27th (JPM). Other summer records included 5 (2m) at Marsh Benham on May 4th (DJB), 1f there on May 10th (DJB) and 1m on May 13th (MES; JPM). Nine (8m 1f) were at Horton GPs on Jun 14th (CDRH) and 1m Dorney Wetlands Jun 30th (BDC).

TUFTED DUCK *Aythya fuligula*

Common throughout the year

Monthly maxima at the main sites were:

	Jan	Feb	Mar	Apr	May	Jun	Jul	Aug	Sep	Oct	Nov	Dec
Bray GPs	23	95	37	–	–	–	2	–	–	–	89	–
Burghfield GPs	–	–	60	100	–	–	–	–	280	–	150	–
Dinton Pastures	174	174	105	80	1	–	–	–	–	16	50	–
Eversley GPs[1]	237	187	109	110	45	12	92	60	60	75	137	128
Dorney Wetlands	50	12	20	1	20	1	110	145	–	–	–	–
Lavell's Lake	25	25	18	70	3	13	1	18	20	43	43	29
Lower Farm GP	25	37	50	26	30	28	22	36	20	12	17	19
Lower Farm Trout Lake	26	50	–	–	–	–	–	–	–	–	10	4
Pingewood GPs	50	28	42	40	20	–	4	–	36	21	50	25
Summerleaze GP	42	56	22	70	–	–	–	–	–	–	–	–
Thatcham Lakes	73	53	26	22	6	2	5	14	7	6	22	45
Thatcham Marsh	3	47	23	19	6	1	2	–	–	4	2	26
Theale/Moatlands GPs	250	122	176	80	60	–	40	–	–	247	49	107
Twyford GPs	146	121	132	–	–	10	–	–	–	–	150	60
Windsor Esplanade	120	–	–	–	–	–	–	–	–	–	31	59
Woolhampton GPs	86	62	99	79	28	–	7	11	20	–	–	–
Wraysbury/Horton GPs[2]	391	2303	526	–	–	–	–	–	368	635	420	729

1 Record count for Eversley GPs occurring on Jan 6 (KBB)
2 Figures are constructed from WeBS counts at 9 of the Wraysbury area lakes

Counts of up to 43 were received from a further 37 sites with a higher count of 52 at Orlitts Lake South Jan 18th (DR). A partial albino drake at Wraysbury GPs on Sept 27th had normal body plumage but completely white wings (CDRH). **Breeding:** Confirmed at Aldermaston GP, 1f 6y (JPM); Donnington Valley GC,1f 5y (SAG); Dorney Wetlands, 6 broods (BDC); Eversley GPs, 17 nests located on Tern Island in June, 4 broods reared (MGLR); Field Fm GP, 32y from 4 broods (RCr); Lavell's Lake, 5 broods (LM); Lower Fm, 3-5 broods (MO); Moatlands GP, 2 broods, (RCr); Newbury Trout Lake, 5y (SAG); Searles Lane GP, 1f 3y, (KBW); Thatcham Reedbeds, 2 broods (LM) and Woolhampton GP, 1f 6y (JPM).

SCAUP *Aythya marila*

Scarce passage migrant and winter visitor

There were 10 records involving probably only 7 birds, a fairly average year. **First winter:** The f/w fem from 2002 remained at Horton GP until at least Jan 18th (LM); 1 ad m QMR from Jan 3rd until Feb 8th (JAS), with an ad fem there Feb 22nd (JAS); 1m Wraysbury GPs Jan 17th and 24th presumably the QMR bird (CDRH) with 1f there on Jan 21st, Feb 7th and 11th presumably the Horton bird (CDRH) and 1 Theale Main GP Feb 21st (RAd). **Second winter:** 1 f/w QMR Oct 7th (CDRH; RIn), 1f Theale GP Oct 30th (CL) and 1 f/w fem Bray GP Nov 12th to Nov 26th (CDRH), which subsequently appeared at Dorney Wetlands Dec 12th (CDRH) and Dec 21st (WG).

EIDER *Somateria mollissima*

Rare vagrant

A female found by K Butts at Lea Farm Pit north of Lavell's Lake Apr 21st remained until the following day (MO). This is the 12th record for Berks and the first since the wintering imm male at Theale Main GP in 1996-97.

COMMON SCOTER   *Melanitta nigra*

Scarce passage migrant / winter visitor

An above average year with 8 records involving 12 birds, from 4 sites. **First winter:** 1m Moatlands GP Feb 15th (MFW *et al*); 1m on the Jubilee River between the A355 and railway on Feb 19th (BDC; AJM) and Feb 20th (LM; LJF). **Spring:** At QMR there were 2 (1m 1 f) on Apr 6th (JAS; CDRH; RIn), 1m on Apr 30th (CDRH, JAS), 3 inc 1m there May 2nd-3rd (JAS; CDRH), 1m May 5th (JAS) and 2m there on Jun 23rd (CDRH) to Jun 24th (JAS). **Autumn / Second winter:** 1f/imm was seen on Theale Main GP on Dec 17th (CDRH) and Dec 19th (NRG).

GOLDENEYE   *Bucephala clangula*

Locally common winter visitor

Monthly maxima at the main sites were:

	Jan	Feb	Mar	Apr	May	Jun	Jul	Aug	Sep	Oct	Nov	Dec
Burghfield GPs	4	13	3	–	–	–	–	–	–	3	7	23
Dinton Pastures	43	27	4	–	–	–	–	–	–	–	10	12
Eversley GPs	6	7	6	4	–	–	–	–	–	3	4	8
Pingewood GPs	4	3	1	–	–	–	–	–	–	7	6	6
Theale/Moatlands GPs	35	35	43	3	–	–	–	–	–	8	15	15
Twyford GPs	38	–	10	–	–	–	–	–	–	–	2	1
Wraysbury/Horton GPs	42	37	10	8	–	–	–	–	–	6	19	40

The first winter was exceptional with counts exceeding 30 being received from 4 locations. The counts of 43 at Dinton Pastures on Jan 11th (FJC) and 38 at Twyford GPs on Jan 25th (BTB) both exceed these sites previous highest counts by some margin. Counts of up to 4 were received from a further 7 sites including 3 in West Berks, Muddy Lane GP 1f on Jan 9th-10th (GJS, DJB), Lower Fm GP 2f Feb 4th (RAL) and Racecourse GP 1imm Nov 23rd (IW, JL). Earliest arrivals were a fem/imm at Silverwings Lake (Wraysbury GPs) Oct 7th (CDRH) and a fem/imm at Pingewood GPs on Oct 10th (MGM). Latest departure was Apr 23rd at Eversley GPs (MGLR).

SMEW   *Mergus albellus*

Uncommon winter visitor but regular at preferred sites

Monthly maxima at the main sites were:

	Jan	Feb	Mar	Apr	May	Jun	Jul	Aug	Sep	Oct	Nov	Dec
Bray GPs	–	4	3	–	–	–	–	–	–	–	–	–
Theale/Moatlands GPs	3	2	2	–	–	–	–	–	–	–	–	–
Twyford GPs	12	4	–	–	–	–	–	–	–	–	–	1
Wraysbury/Horton GPs *	15	11	2	–	–	–	–	–	–	–	8	11

* Figures are constructed from WeBS counts at 8 of the Wraysbury area lakes

Singles were recorded at a further 6 sites with higher counts of 4 Dinton Pastures Jan 11th (BTB; MDD); 6 QMR Jan 11th and Jan 12th (JAS) and 4 rh Lower Fm Trout Lake with an additional 1rh at Lower Fm GP Jan 19th (FJC). Earliest arrival date was Nov 15th at Village Lake (Wraysbury) (CDRH) and latest departure was Mar 21st at Bray GP (LM).

RED-BREASTED MERGANSER   *Mergus serrator*

Scarce winter visitor and passage migrant

An above average year with 6 records, involving 10 birds. **First winter:** 1m and 4rh QMR were seen to arrive and depart on Jan 11th and 1rh there on Jan 12th (JAS) was followed by a report of 1rh at Theale Main GP on Jan 24th (TABCG), 1rh Lower Fm GP Feb 22nd (SAG) and 1rh Moatlands GP on Mar 6th (PBT). **Second winter:** 1rh Wraysburys GP Nov 29th to Dec 19th (CDRH *et al*).

GOOSANDER   *Mergus merganser*

Uncommon winter visitor but regular at preferred sites

Monthly maxima at the main sites were:

	Jan	Feb	Mar	Apr	May	Jun	Jul	Aug	Sep	Oct	Nov	Dec
Eversley GPs	45	24	20	–	–	–	–	–	–	–	3	35
Theale/Moatlands GPs	6	3	1	–	–	–	–	–	–	–	1	4
Wraysbury/Horton GPs *	28	25	2	–	–	–	–	–	–	–	3	20

* Figures are constructed from WeBS counts at 6 of the Wraysbury area lakes

First winter: Elsewhere there were 5 Muddy Lane GP Jan 5th (GJS) with 10 there Jan 11th (JL, IW); 8 rh Woolhampton GP Jan 8th (CDRH) with 9 there Jan 11th (JPM); 1m over Widbrook Com Jan 9th (CDRH); 2 m Sandhurst GP Jan 10th (RJG); 1m1f QMR Jan 18th (JAS), 1m R. Thames, Thames Valley Park Jan 19th (ABT); 1rh Lower Fm GP Jan 19th (JW), and 1rh there on Mar 7th (MJT;DCr), 1on the R. Blackwater at Swallowfield Mar 24th (CRW) and an unusually late record of 1rh at QMR May 3rd (JAS). **Second winter:** First reports involved 1rh at Heron Lakes Wraysbury on Nov 2nd (CDRH). Other records not represented in the table were 2rh at Racecourse GP on Nov 9th (SAG), 3rh Heathlake Crowthorne on Nov 28th (IT) to Dec 6th (JOB) and 1rh QMR Dec 2nd (DJB). Latest departure date (excluding the QMR record above) was Mar 30th Eversley GP (BMA).

Goosanders by Andrew Brooks

RUDDY DUCK   *Oxyura jamaicensis*

Uncommon but increasing resident and winter visitor

Monthly maxima at the main sites were:

	Jan	Feb	Mar	Apr	May	Jun	Jul	Aug	Sep	Oct	Nov	Dec
Lower Farm GP	10	8	13	13	4	3	6	14	14	18	16	13
Wraysbury/Horton GPs	5	29	5	–	–	–	–	–	4	8	8	6
Smallmead GP	1	1	1	–	2	–	–	–	–	–	–	–
Moatlands GPs	–	5	–	–	–	–	–	–	4	1	–	4
Queen Mother Reservoir.	1	–	–	–	–	–	–	–	2	3	2	1

The Lower Fm Count of 18 on Oct 17th (DJB) is a site record. Elsewhere, the only count to exceed 2 was 12 at Windsor Great Park Apr 3rd and 4 on Sep 25th (CDRH). Sightings of 1 or 2 came throughout the year from Pingewood GPs; Dinton Pastures; Dorney Wetlands; Hosehill Lake; Thatcham Marsh; Twyford GP and Woolhampton GP. As in 2002 there was successful breeding at Lower Fm, where 1f reared 1 chick (IW; JL; JLS).

RED-LEGGED PARTRIDGE   *Alectoris rufa*

Common resident in suitable habitat with numbers inflated in the autumn by released birds bred for shooting

Records were received from 70 locations, 38 in W Berks, 14 in M Berks and 18 in E Berks. The monthly maxima at the main sites are shown in the table:

	Jan	Feb	Mar	Apr	May	Jun	Jul	Aug	Sep	Oct	Nov	Dec
Aldworth/Compton	nc	2	11	nc	14	3	nc	77*	750*	500*	56	nc
Cookham	19	1	1	nc	2	nc	nc	nc	nc	24	2	42
Englefield	nc	nc	5	2	nc	4	1	11	5	nc	4	4
Streatley	nc	nc	7	4	4	nc	nc	nc	nc	60*	25	nc

*Indicate birds released for shooting
nc = no count made

As the table shows, counts were erratic and in 2003 large numbers were turned out for shooting. The high counts on the Compton Downs were made on Sep 21st (JOB) and Oct 5th (MFW). Elsewhere birds were turned out en masse in the Combe area where DJB witnessed hundreds being shot on Sep 27th and BMA estimated many hundreds concentrated around feeders on Oct 11th. At most other locations records involved 1-15 birds with many sites reporting single figure counts on 1 date only. Higher counts came from Frogmill near Hurley where 23 were present on Nov 4th (SJF; FMF) and at Little Templeton near Kintbury with 17 on Dec 23rd (DR). The count of 42 at Cookham on Dec 25th (BDC) is the highest count there for many years although the possibility that these birds had been released cannot be ruled out. **Breeding:** Was confirmed at 4 sites; at Lower Fm GP, 1 pair with 6 yng (5 being reared) was located on Jul 13th (RAH) with another pr with 1yng on Jul 19th (RRK). Nearby at the Trout Lake a pr with 4yng were located on Aug 16th (RRK), an ad with 4 juvs were present on Walbury Hill on Aug 17th (SAG) and 1pr with 5yng were at Englefield on Aug 24th (RCr). A nest at Brimpton was predated, probably by a Badger (GEW).

GREY PARTRIDGE   *Perdix perdix*

Localised and declining resident

Records were received from 39 locations, 24 (18 from the downs) in W Berks, 9 in M Berks and 6 in E Berks. The monthly maxima at the main sites were:

	Jan	Feb	Mar	Apr	May	Jun	Jul	Aug	Sep	Oct	Nov	Dec
Aldworth/Compton	nc	13	4	nc	nc	nc	nc	12	1	nc	12	nc
Bury/Cow Down	10	8	7	nc	2	nc	3	nc	18	3	Nc	7
Englefield	nc	2	3	nc	4	4	7	4	8	12	6	6

The count of 18 at Bury Down occurred on Sep 30th (BMA) and involved 2 coveys of 10 and 8 birds. Elsewhere only 2 localities had counts in excess of 10 birds, 12 at Woodlands Park, Maidenhead on Jan 6th (DJB) and 11 at Lower Barn Brightwalton on Jan 12th (GDS). Most other sites recorded less than 5 individuals. **Breeding:** Only confirmed at Woolley Down where a pair reared 3+ yng (GDS). Away from the downs, the Grey Partridge is in serious decline, with fewer and fewer areas holding sustainable populations. In Mid and East Berks away from Englefield and Woodlands Park, the highest reported counts involved just 7 birds at Pingewood GPs in Nov and Tidmarsh in Dec. Further east no site could produce more than 3 birds with nearly all locations recording the species on just 1-2 occasions. A bird seen at Moor Green Lakes on Jun 16th (C Rose) was the first at this site since 1994.

QUAIL   *Coturnix coturnix*
An uncommon summer visitor most regular on the downs

A poor year with singing males only located late in the season at 2 possibly 4 downland locations. On Jul 1st up to 6 singing males were located at 2 sites on the Berks Downs (CDRH). More exact reports came from the Wellbottom/Crog hill area with 4 singing on Jul 9th (GDS), 1 on Jul 18th (JLe) 2 on Jul 20th (IW; JL) and Jul 27th (BTB). Three singing on the Compton Downs on Jul 14th (MJT), may refer to the sites on Jul 1st. Elsewhere 1 was seen at Englefield on Aug 12th (RCr) and 1 was flushed just south of Woolstone Down on Aug 16th (GDS).

PHEASANT   *Phasianus colchicus*
Widespread and locally abundant resident

Highest counts all involved released birds with 150+ at Englefield on Aug 17th (RCr), several hundreds at Combe on Oct 11th (BMA) and 48 by Long Lane Cookham on Oct 25th (BDC). A melanistic male was found at Marsh Benham on Oct 5th (SAG), but in the Combe area the majority of the released birds were melanistic (which could make the landscape appear to be populated with Black Grouse!).

RED-THROATED DIVER   *Gavia stellata*
Rare winter visitor

One in winter plumage was located at QMR on Feb 10th and seen intermittently until Feb 22nd (JAS *et al*). What was presumed to be the same bird was also seen at Wraysbury GPs on several dates from Feb 14th (RIn) to Feb 26th (RCr) and finally at Horton GP on Feb 27th (PIn).

GREAT NORTHERN DIVER   *Gavia immer*
Rare winter visitor / passage migrant

The recent increase in spring records continued in 2003 with 1 in w/p Theale Main GP May 2nd (RHS *et al*) and 1ad in w/p QMR May 17th (JAS). Two May records in the same year is unprecedented.

LITTLE GREBE *Tachybaptus ruficollis*

Common resident and apparent passage migrant

Monthly maxima at the main sites were:

	Jan	Feb	Mar	Apr	May	Jun	Jul	Aug	Sep	Oct	Nov	Dec
Eversley GPs	1	4	3	3	4	4	6	16	19	16	6	5
Dorney Wetlands	8	6	4	2	2	3	10	17	12	8	10	–
Lower Farm GP	2	3	12	12	15	15	15	15	10	5	1	–
Marsh Benham	4	–	6	–	–	–	–	–	–	4	–	1
Old Slade GP	1	–	–	–	–	–	5	2	4	12	14	5
Padworth Lane GP	6	6	5	1	–	–	–	10	16	–	–	1
Pingewood GPs	–	–	1	–	–	–	1	3	7	1	1	–
Rapley Lake	–	–	5	6	6	3	–	–	–	–	–	–
Thatcham Marsh	1	–	5	2	2	2	2	–	4	5	2	1
Theale/Moatlands GPs	5	16	12	7	4	9	22	28	3	–	–	–
Woolhampton GPs	6	–	1	–	1	–	–	–	–	–	–	–
Wraysbury GPs	–	1	2	–	–	–	–	–	6	7	8	2

The high count of 28 (inc 7 juvs) at Theale GPs occurred at Field Fm GP on Aug 1st (RCr). Elsewhere counts of up to 3 were received from a further 43 sites with higher counts of 7 near Benham Lock Jan 3rd (DR); 6 (3prs) Avington Jun 14th (DR) with 7 there Sep 13th ; 8 Burghfield GP Oct 1st (KBW); 6 Shinfield, Lane End Fm Reservoir Oct 15th (MDB) and 7 Lower Fm Trout Lake Dec 14th (JL). **Breeding:** Confirmed at Aldermaston GP; Lower Fm GP (2 broods); Dorney Wetlands (3 broods); Eversley GPs; Field Fm GP (2 broods); Hungerford Portdown; R.Kennet, Kintbury; Moatlands GP; Simons Wood and Thatcham Marsh.

GREAT CRESTED GREBE *Podiceps cristatus*

Common resident and winter visitor

Monthly maxima at sites with frequent counts were:

	Jan	Feb	Mar	Apr	May	Jun	Jul	Aug	Sep	Oct	Nov	Dec
Eversley GPs	23	14	8	12	8	8	6	6	9	22	29	20
Old Slade GP	2	–	–	–	–	–	2	1	5	21	–	–
Theale/Moatlands GPs	4	11	10	10	10	–	32	43	26	27	–	–
Woolhampton GPs	13	9	10	14	19	–	–	20	20	–	–	–

Counts of up to 14 were received from a further 37 sites with higher counts of 16 QMR Mar 12th (BDC) with c40 there Sep 19th (DJB); 48 Horton GP May 6th (JOB) and 21 Woolhampton GP (Rowney's) Aug 8th (GEW) with 17 there Sep 12th. **Breeding:** Confirmed at Boulters Lock; Brimpton GPs; Colebrook Lakes at Eversley GPs; Dorney Wetlands (4 broods); R Thames at Frogmill; Hosehill Lake; Burghfield GPs (2 broods); Lower Fm GP; Midgham GP; Newbury Trout Lake; Summerleaze GP (2 broods); Thatcham Lakes (4 broods); Whiteknights and Woolhampton GP (2+ broods).

RED-NECKED GREBE *Podiceps grisegena*

Scarce winter visitor and passage migrant

First winter: The bird which first arrived at Woolhampton GP in November 2002 had moulted into full summer plumage by the time it finally left on May 6th (FJC). **Second winter:** There were three sightings, all from QMR with 1, a probable f/w, on Oct 6th

(CDRH), 1 Nov 17th (CL) and 1 on Dec 11th (CDRH), probably all the same mobile individual that was also seen at KGVI Res in Surrey.

BLACK-NECKED GREBE *Podiceps nigricollis*
Uncommon winter visitor and passage migrant

Only three records were received, all from the second winter period. One in w/p Theale Main GP Sep 13th (MFW *et al*), 1 w/p Wigmore Lane trout fishery on Oct 23rd (RCr) and a long staying bird seen by MO at Moor Green Lakes (Eversley GPs) from Sep 22nd (IT) to Nov 18th (BMA).

FULMAR *Fulmarus glacialis*
Very rare vagrant

One Newbury Jul 9th found freshly dead on Old Bath Rd (PBy). This is the 4th record for Berkshire and the first since one flew over the R Thames at Cliveden on Sep 4th 1989. Records show no discernable pattern having been in March, May, July and September.

STORM PETREL *Hydrobates pelagicus*
Rare storm-blown vagrant

One QMR Dec 2nd found by CDRH at 10.20 hrs, being chased by Black-headed Gulls and later by a Peregrine which subsequently caught and consumed it at 13.45hrs. A sadly short stay for a very rare visitor!
This is the 8th record for Berkshire.

Storm Petrel by Martin Hallam

CORMORANT *Phalacrocorax carbo*
Common winter visitor and now summer visitor

Monthly maxima at the main sites were:

	Jan	Feb	Mar	Apr	May	Jun	Jul	Aug	Sep	Oct	Nov	Dec
Aldermaston GP	15	24	31	39	30	32	6	8	2	6	2	2
Burghfield GPs	–	–	10	1	–	–	–	–	–	–	30	–
Dinton Pastures / Lavell's Lake	22	20	20	8	3	6	11	18	22	28	33	18
Eversley GPs	51	65	25	4	4	6	12	3	9	15	37	80
Lower Farm GP / Thatcham Marsh	15	3	4	1	4	4	22	22	12	31	18	60
Pingewood GPs	–	–	–	–	–	–	1	3	24	–	18	–
Queen Mother Reservoir	7	–	91	–	–	–	–	–	–	1480	1500	–
Twyford GPs	15	6	6	5	–	–	–	–	–	–	30	15

Low water levels led to high numbers visiting QMR in Oct/Nov with maximum counts of 1480 on Oct 31st (DJB) and an estimated 1500 on Nov 2nd (ABT) both exceeding the previous county maximum count. Counts of up to 12 were received from a further 34 sites. The only counts to exceed 12 were 150 at Wraysbury GPs Aug 30th (CL) and 20 at Summerleaze GP on Dec 27th (BDC). **Breeding:** The only colony continues to prosper with 23 active nests on Mar 28th and many young fledged during the period of Mar-Jul

(JPM). Colour ringed birds were located at Dinton Pastures (a bird of Danish origin, ring number H18 seen in both winters: MFW) and Lower Fm GP (ring lettered RP seen on Dec 9th: MSt). Finally 1 flying over Brightwalton on May 6th (SWi) was unusual.

BITTERN   *Botaurus stellaris*
Scarce but increasing winter visitor

Fewer records this year with probably 10 birds involved. **First winter:** The individual found at Hosehill in Dec 2002 remained to Mar 5th (BU), briefly joined by a 2nd bird on Jan 31st (DHK). The long staying bird at Lavell's Lake was seen on Jan 25th (BTB), with 2 birds present there from Jan 27th (BTB) to at least Mar 21st (PMC). Elsewhere singles were located at Horton GP on Jan 11th (MFW) and Jan 31st (CL), Eversley GPs from Jan 13th to Feb 23rd (N Silver *et al*), Brimpton GPs on Jan 18th and Mar 29th (GEW) and Kintbury on Feb 19th (CL). **Spring/summer:** The Lavell's Lake individual remained throughout the summer, although elusive (MO) and may be the first confirmed record of summering in Berkshire since about 1780 (Lamb 1880). Unfortunately it was found dead on Sep 16th (RR) and was bearing a French ring. **Second winter:** One was located at Lavell's Lake on Nov 3rd (FJC) and remained into 2004 (MO) and 1 showed at Horton GP on Dec 24th (CL).

LITTLE EGRET   *Egretta garzetta*
Uncommon visitor principally in winter

Jan/Mar: Regularly reported from Theale GPs where 1 was present at Bottom Lane Floods on Jan 1st (MFW), increasing to 2 on Feb 11th (DHu), 3 Feb 23rd (DHu) and 4 on Mar 14th (RCr). Further sightings at Theale involved 1 at Main pit on Jan 11th (BMA), Feb 6th (CDRH) and Feb 26th (MGM). These birds also visited the nearby Pingewood GPs with 1 on Jan 6th (MO) and Jan 8th (MGM) and Burghfield Mill GP on Jan 30th (KJ) and Feb 5th (MGM). Elsewhere records were also received from the South Reading/Burghfield GPs area with singles at Southcote on Feb 2nd (MBu), Burghfield GP Feb 7th (PBT), 2 there on Feb 14th (JOB), Fobney on Feb 9th (MGM) and 1 regular at Rosekiln Lane in March (MBu; A Lawson). **Apr/Jun:** One was still present at Bottom Lane until Apr 4th (RCr; DHu) and 1 was located at or near the Burghfield GPs Heronry on Apr 8th (CRW), 9th (RR) and 18th (JA). Four flew over Dinton Pastures on Apr 12 heading NE (TGB; JOB) with 1 at Lavell's Lake on Apr 13th-14th (CN; SJo; D Callum *et al*) and Apr 25th (BTB; KCr). In May, there was 1 at QMR on May 13th and 2 at Dorney Wetlands on May 28th (CDRH). **Jul/Sep:** Four were briefly at Woolhampton GPs on Jul 15th (JPM) with 1 the same day at Lower Fm GP (SFu) which had increased to 3 j on Jul 30th (CDRH). These birds remained at this site or the nearby trout lake until the last record of 1 on Nov 16th (MJD). Elsewhere, 1 showed at Hosehill Lake on Jul 18th (DHu), 1 at Dorney Wetlands on Aug 5th (BDC; DF), 1j Windsor Pk Aug 13th-14th (CDRH), 1j Pingewood GP Aug 14th (CDRH) to Aug 21st (MGM), 1 Woolhampton GP Aug 15th (RRK), 2 Padworth Lane GP Aug 16th (RHS) and 1 there Aug 23rd (MFW), 1 Greenham Com Aug 23rd (J Swallow), 2 there Aug 24th (SAG) and 1 Wraysbury GPs on Sep 21st (CDRH). **Oct /Dec:** One juv Lavell's Lake Oct 1st (MFW; PBT) was followed by singles at Dorney Wetlands on Nov 16th (S Pavlou), Hosehill Lake Nov 17th (BU), Theale Main GP Nov 18th (CDRH) and Dec 21st (RJB). Finally 1 at Eversley GPs on Dec 12th (KCr) had increased to a max of 3 by Dec 29th (MGLR).

Great White Egret
by Martin Hallam

GREAT WHITE EGRET   *Egretta alba*

Very rare vagrant

One Theale GP Feb 25th flew low over the water from western end gained height over M4 and then lost to view drifting high NE at 10:57 (RAd). First county record. Record accepted by BBRC (although does not appear to tie in with any other records in the UK at this time: Recorder).

GREY HERON   *Ardea cinerea*

Locally common resident and winter visitor in small numbers

Monthly maxima at the main sites were:

	Jan	Feb	Mar	Apr	May	Jun	Jul	Aug	Sep	Oct	Nov	Dec
Burghfield GPs	6	6	8	9	15	–	–	–	–	–	4	–
Eversley GPs	4	4	3	3	2	3	7	7	7	7	4	6
Hungerford, Home Farm	–	–	–	–	–	30	25	8	–	–	–	12
Lavell's Lake	2	3	3	3	3	3	4	4	15	4	2	1
Queen Mother Reservoir	–	–	6	–	–	–	–	–	–	27	–	–

Counts of up to 9 were received from a further 67 sites. The only counts to exceed 9 were 10 Donnington Lake Apr 27th (SAG) and 18 Lea Fm Pit Sep 14th (SJo). Breeding counts were made at all known heronries as part of the BTO annual survey and in addition, as this was a special survey year (75th anniversary), extra effort was made to locate new or lost heronries. Counts of occupied nests (per CR) were as follows:- Englefield 4 (CR); Aldermaston GP 5 (JPM): Searles Lane (Burghfield GPs) 19 (JA); Twyford 20 (Stephanie and Ian Brown); Donnington Park 6 (SAG); Heath Lake 2 (BMA); Theale Main 6 (CR); Wraysbury 3 (CR); Bray Lock 6 (CR). See "The Growth of Herons in Berkshire 1992-2003" by Chris Robinson.

SPOONBILL   *Platalea leucorodia*

Rare passage migrant

A good year with two separate sightings. Two flew over Finchampstead May 7th heading south (PBT) and an imm at QMR Nov 2nd (ABT) remained until Nov 25th (JOB). These were the 13th and 14th records for the county and means there have now been four sightings in as many years.

RED KITE *Milvus milvus*

Formerly a rare vagrant, now frequently recorded following its successful reintroduction

Regularly encountered throughout north and central Berks, less so in the south with very few records in the SE of the county from Moor Green Lakes (2 records) to Wraysbury GPs where none were reported (although 1 was at QMR: May 30th). The monthly maxima from the main areas where this species is encountered is shown in the table.

	Jan	Feb	Mar	Apr	May	Jun	Jul	Aug	Sep	Oct	Nov	Dec
Aldworth, Streatley & Compton area	1	3	4	2	2	0	1	6	5	4	4	4
Bury Down, West Ilsley area	9	5	0	0	0	0	3	2	1	7	2	2
Caversham	0	1	4	4	5	1	3	5	4	4	5	2
Cold Harbour, White Waltham AF area	0	0	0	1	1	1	1	2	1	4	2	0
Cookham and Pinkneys Green	1	2	2	2	0	1	2	1	1	2	2	1
Farnborough, Woolley, Brightwalton	3	18	15	10	2	0	0	6	9	20	42	19
Hurley to Remenham	5	2	6	2	2	4	3	4	3	5	2	3
Lambourn Downs	0	2	1	0	1	1	0	5	0	0	0	4
Tilehurst and Purley	1	1	2	3	1	2	1	0	1	2	1	0
Twyford, Hurst and Dinton Pastures	1	1	2	1	4	3	4	3	3	2	2	2
Walbury and Combe Hills	0	1	0	1	0	1	1	1	1	0	2	0

The highest counts all came from West Berks with exceptional numbers reported from the Woolley Down roost, the high of 42 being reported on Nov 16th (GDS). Nearby 20 were noted at Brightwalton on Oct 8th (SWi) and 17 at Nine Acre Wood on Nov 2nd (GDS). A count of 27 on the Berkshire Downs on Jan 25th (CDRH) probably refers to this area. Away from the west, high counts involved 4-5 at Remenham on Jan 8th (CDRH), 6 at Frogmill Hurley on Mar 11th (SGF; FMF) and 5 at Caversham on several dates in May, Aug and Nov (TGB). At Hurst Tip, a regular site for the species, an individual with orange and blue wing tags present on May 24th (MFW) and Jun 24th (FJC) had originated from the Yorkshire reintroduction scheme (MFW). **Breeding:** This may have taken place in one area of West Berks where a group of 6 (a possible family party) were reported on Aug 17th (GDS). Display was observed at Frogmill on Mar 11th (SJF; FMF) and juveniles were noted at Thurle Down, 3 on Aug 5th (CDRH) and 1 drifted over Shottesbrooke on Aug 30th (DJB).

MARSH HARRIER *Circus aeruginosus*

Scarce passage migrant

The recent increase of Marsh Harriers in Britain has also changed its status in Berkshire. From a less than annual visitor up to the mid nineties it has now become annual since 1997, albeit still in small numbers. Three records were received in 2003; **Spring:** A first year circled Wraysbury GPs on May 6th (CDRH). **Autumn:** Passage occurred during August with 2 downland records of single females at Woolley Down on Aug 10th (GDS) and Knighton Bushes on Aug 16th (GDS).

HEN HARRIER *Circus cyaneus*

Scarce passage migrant and winter visitor

A better than average year with 7 records, all from the Downs, although not necessarily of different birds. **First winter:** A ringtail located at Bury Down on Jan 11th (JOB) proved popular and was regularly reported to Jan 21st (GJSu) and again on Feb 8th (RMu). Other ringtails were reported from Eling, on Feb 1st (CDRH), Sheepdrove on Mar 18th (BDC) and Apr 10th (JPB), South Fawley on Mar 20th and West Ilsley on Apr 10th (SWi). **Second winter:** An adult female at West Ilsley on Nov 11th (NJD) was the only record. However a male was reported just over the county boundary at Churn Oxon on Dec 14th (SR).

MONTAGU'S HARRIER *Circus pygargus*

Rare passage migrant and summer visitor

Summered again on the Downs with at least 1 pair successfully breeding in Oxon. In Berkshire, birds were reported from May 4th when 2 males and 2 females were present (ABT) to Jul 20th, a single male (IW; JL). This is the 8th consecutive year that Montagu's Harriers have been reported in this area.

GOSHAWK *Accipiter gentilis*

Rare visitor

2002   The observer of the Jan 19th record for Wigmore Lane was (ABT)

2003   The problem of separating this species from large female Sparrowhawks means that the records committee continues to err on the side of caution when considering records of Goshawk and will not accept any report without a written description. An extremely useful guide to the identification of Goshawk by Keith Vinicombe appears in the March 2005 edition of Birdwatch magazine. Although there were 5 reports in 2003 none were accompanied by descriptions for consideration by the Records Committee.

SPARROWHAWK *Accipiter nisus*

Common and widespread resident

Records were received from throughout the county, usually of 1-3 birds. Higher counts consisted of 5 at Horton GPs on Jan 14th (JOB), 4 at Wishmoor Bottom on Aug 12th (BMA) and 4 at Larkshill Bracknell on Sep 9th (MFW). **Breeding:** In spring display was noted at Tilehurst (GJSu), Quarry Woods (BDC) and Dinton Pastures (FJC). Birds carrying prey at this time were seen at Wishmoor and Windsor Great Park (DJB). Breeding was confirmed at Broadhouse Plantation Farnborough (1pr rearing 2 young: (GDS); Cemetery Junction Reading, 2-3 juvs heard on Aug 3rd (PG) and Warren Row, 1 pair with 2 juvs on Aug 7th (DJB). Juveniles were also reported from Kintbury Cressbeds (RGS), Inkpen (LS), Lavell's Lake (FJC), Wishmoor (MDD) and Wraysbury GPs (PJC) all indicating local breeding. Food items involved the usual small bird prey and additionally there were 3 reported instances of adult males taking Collared Doves, a species of comparable size. A female repeatedly swooped down and mobbed an adult female Peregrine which was feeding on a pigeon at White Waltham Airfield on Feb 18th (DJB).

BUZZARD   *Buteo buteo*

Common resident and increasing passage migrant

Records were received from throughout the county, the monthly maxima from the main areas is shown in the table:

	Jan	Feb	Mar	Apr	May	Jun	Jul	Aug	Sep	Oct	Nov	Dec
Bury Down/West Ilsley	6	1	3	nc	1	4	2	nc	1	7	2	2
Combe/Walbury Hill	8	8	6	5	1	2	2	11	6	7	2	4
Compton to Streatley	5	nc	9	nc	3	2	4	3	5	4	5	4
Dinton Pastures/LCA	nc	nc	2	3	6	3	1	7	9	2	1	1
Hurley to Remenham	1	nc	1	3	nc	nc	1	2	3	3	5	1
Inkpen and Kintbury	3	nc	2	2	1	2	1	4	6	2	1	2
Lambourn Downs	6	12	7	3	4	5	1	4	2	nc	1	4
Pingewood/Theale GPs	2	2	1	3	2	1	3	3	2	1	1	2
Ruscombe/Twyford	1	nc	nc	1	2	3	3	2	1	4	nc	1
Shurlock Row area	1	3	6	5	nc	4	nc	nc	6	3	1	nc
Windsor Great Park	3	7	2	2	3	3	nc	nc	5	nc	nc	nc
Woolley area	nc	2	6	7	7	12	12	21	nc	nc	nc	nc

Counts remained highest in W Berks, exceeding 10 at Sheepdrove, 12 on Feb 25th: (BDC) and Combe Bottom, 11 on Aug 30th (IW; JL). Numbers continued to increase in M and E Berks with maximum counts of 9 at Lavell's Lake on Sep 12th (FJC) and 7 at Windsor Great Park on Feb 21st (DTu). **Breeding:** Courtship display was noted at Great Shefford (GDS), Woolley (GDS), Lambourn (BDC) and Winterbourne (MJT) in the west and at Cookham Rise (BDC) and Rapley Lake (DJB) in the east. Nest building was observed at Compton on Mar 24th (ABT) and breeding confirmed in the Woolley Down area where 6 pairs reared a minimum of 9 young (GDS) which accounts for the figure of 21 in the above table. Breeding was also confirmed at Crookham Com with 1pr with 3 nestlings on Jun 30th (JPM), 1ad and 1juv was located at Inkpen on Aug 10th-14th (LS), there were 2 fledged young on the county boundary at Crog Hill on Aug 16th (GDS) with a further 2 young nearby just south of Woolstone Down the same day (GDS). An adult with 2 juvs appeared at Pingewood GPs on Aug 31st (RCr) and 1pr with 1juv showed at Shurlock Row on Oct 6th (RAl).

OSPREY   *Pandion haliaetus*

Scarce but increasing passage migrant

Numbers were down on recent years but still above average with records received from 11 locations but probably involving no more than 8 individuals. **Spring:** First reported on Apr 12th when 1 flew N over Woolhampton GPs (IW; JL) and 1 flew N over Dinton Pastures CP (L G R Evans per BLSE). There followed 2 reports on Apr 18th which may have involved the same bird, 1 flying NW over Pingewood GPs (JA; RPo) and over Thatcham Marsh (Birdtrack). One was located resting on the ground at Greenham Com on May 8th (RF) and finally 1 was located at Marsh Benham on Jun 17th (IW; JPM; DL). **Autumn:** One took up temporary residence in the Kennet Valley, being seen regularly in the Brimpton area from Jul 17th to Aug 20th (GEW). It was probably this bird that wandered to Lower Fm GP on Jul 17th (SAG) and West Meadows on Jul 18th (DL; JPM; IW). Further sightings involved 1 over Tilehurst on Aug 26th (JA) and 1 seen distantly from QMR flying over Home Park Windsor and Wraysbury on Sep 21st (CDRH).

KESTREL   *Falco tinnunculus*

A common and widespread resident

A familiar sight throughout Berks, Kestrels tend to be under recorded with most reports involving 1-4 birds. The only count to exceed 4 involved 5 over Walbury Hill on Aug 17th (SAG). **Breeding:** Evidence of breeding (display) was noted at Summerleaze GP on Mar 23rd (BDC) and at Winter Hill on Apr 5th (BDC). Breeding was confirmed at Moor Green Lakes where 1pr reared 2 young (MGLR); Dorney Wetlands, 1ad with 2 juvs on Jun 28th (BMA); Kintbury, 1pr & 2 juvs on Jul 3rd (RRK) and Lower Fm GP, 1ad & 2juvs on Jul 12th (IW; JL).

RED FOOTED FALCON   *Falco vespertinus*

Rare vagrant

A first summer male, found at Pingewood GPs on Jul 4th (RCr *et al*), entertained many visiting admirers until Jul 9th (MO). Accepted by the BBRC, it is the 7th record for Berkshire and the first to be seen in July. Of the previous 6 records 5 occurred between June 4th-12th in 1973, 1989, 1992, 1999 and 2000 whilst the other was found on Sep 27th 1973.

MERLIN   *Falco columbarius*

Uncommon winter visitor and passage migrant which has increased in recent years

A good year for this diminutive falcon, birds were reported from a surprising 16 locations, 9 in W Berks, 4 in M Berks and 3 in E Berks and probably involved between 20 and 23 birds. The monthly distribution was:

	Jan	Feb	Mar	Apr	May	Jun	Jul	Aug	Sep	Oct	Nov	Dec
Number of sites	4	8	4	0	0	0	0	0	0	0	4	2
Number of birds	4	9	4	0	0	0	0	0	0	0	4	2

First winter: A F/imm was located at Englefield on Jan 4th (RCr) and was followed by a male (a returning 2002 bird?) at Cold Harbour from Jan 8th (DJB), seen regularly by MO to Mar 12th (DJB). Jan 12th produced 2 records; an imm male at East Ilsley (CDRH) and a female at Warren Down Lambourn (MJS). February and March continued the high standard set by Jan with 1 flying over Lavell's Lake on Feb 3rd (RR), 2 males at Cold Harbour on Feb 11th (DJB), 1f Sheepdrove Lambourn on Feb 14th (JPB; JLe), 1f Catmore (JOB), 1 Compton Downs (JOB) and 1 Woolley Down (GDS) all on Feb 18th, 1f West Ilsley on Feb 21st (JOB) and 1 male Bury Down on Feb 22nd (JOB). A male (possibly the Bury Down bird) was located at West Ilsley on Mar 2nd (JOB), an imm male was again at East Ilsley on Mar 11th (CDRH), a male caught a Skylark at Ashampstead Com on Mar 15th (CDRH) and a male was reported from the Compton Downs on Mar 24th (DDC). **Autumn/second winter:** A notable influx took place in November. A female at Cold Harbour on Nov 5th and 11th (DJB) was followed by an imm male at Field Fm GP on Nov 8th (JA), 1m at Pingewood GPs on Nov 11th (MGM) and 1m at Pinkneys Green on Nov 12th (BDC). Further records involved 1 flying over Cockmarsh into Bucks Dec 14th (MM; RAn) and finally a male had returned to Cold Harbour on Dec 24th and remained into 2004 (DJB).

HOBBY   *Falco subbuteo*

Uncommon summer visitor and passage migrant which has increased in recent years

Hobbies were reported from 87 locations throughout the county, the monthly distribution is shown in the table:

	Mar	Apr	May	Jun	Jul	Aug	Sep	Oct
Number of sites	0	18	34	27	21	30	31	1
Minimum number of birds	0	28	58	37	31	51	50	2

Spring: There were no sightings until the fairly usual date of Apr 13th when singles were noted at Cookham Rise (BDC) and Thatcham Marsh (JPM). There followed a steady (though fairly uneventful) passage through Apr – May. Counts only exceeded 3 birds at 4 sites with 5 at Summerleaze GP on Apr 29th (CDRH), 4 by the Thames at Bray on May 2nd (RAns; JAns),11 together at Wraysbury GPs on May 6th (CDRH), 4 feeding on Mayflies by the Thames at Cliveden on May 8th (LM) and 6+ at Horton GPs on May 26th (CDRH). At Wraysbury GPs an individual was observed chasing Bats (without success) at dusk on Apr 28th (DJB). **Summer:** Recorded from 39 locations in Jun – Jul, thus indicating a fairly healthy summering population. Numbers were highest at Horton GPs where 5 were present on June 9th (CDRH), Pingewood GPs where 4 were present on Jun 23rd (RCr) and up to 6 on Jul 7th (RDr). **Breeding:** Confirmed at 3 sites in E Berks with pairs rearing 2 young at 2 sites (PJC) and 1pr rearing 1 young at the other (BDC). Unfortunately a further pair was disturbed by forestry operations in Swinley Forest and so failed to breed (PJC). **Autumn:** Passage began in Aug, continuing through Sep. High counts of 4 birds were at Lavell's Lake on Sep 4th (FJC), Ockwells Park Maidenhead on Sep 9th (DNTR) and Wraysbury GPs where 2ads were feeding 2 juvs (local breeders) on Sep 15th (CDRH) and Sep 19th (DJB). At Pingewood GPs, up to 3 juvs were present with adults on several dates in Sep (MO) and may also indicate local breeding. Passage continued to the end of Sep with 1 at Windsor Park on Sep 30th (CDRH), the only Oct record involved 2 over Brimpton GPs on Oct 7th (GEW).

PEREGRINE FALCON   *Falco peregrinus*

Uncommon visitor throughout the year

Another good year with records received from 36 locations, 16 in W Berks and 10 in both M and E Berks. The monthly status is shown in the table:

	Jan	Feb	Mar	Apr	May	Jun	Jul	Aug	Sep	Oct	Nov	Dec
Number of sites	8	7	3	2	6	3	5	3	6	9	12	8
Number of birds*	8	8	3	2	8	5	6	3	8	10	14	10

* These figures do not account for the possibility of individual birds visiting various different locations

As the table shows, unlike 2002 records were spread more evenly throughout the year with reports for May-July more than doubling. Most records still involved 1 bird but records of 2 or more were of an adult male and female at Lavell's Lake on Feb 21st (CL), 3 (an adult pr plus 1 over) at Theale Main GP on Sep 25th (RCr) with the pair remaining to the years end (MO), 1ad and 1 imm female on the Compton Downs on Nov 15th (DJB) and an adult male and female at Bury Down on Dec 30th (IW; JL). Several areas attracted Peregrines on a regular basis. At Dinton Pastures/Lavell's Lake birds were regular during the summer, exploiting the large numbers of birds that are attracted to the CP and nearby landfill site at Hurst. At least 3 individuals (ad m & f & 1 imm/m) were identified during this period

(FJC) and possibly as many as 5 individuals may have visited the site during the year. In the Theale/Pingewood GPs area, birds were reported in every month except for June and may have involved 4-6 birds including the pair taking up winter residence on the Theale Main GP pylon. Other long staying individuals could be found at QMR where a juv female took up residence from Oct 2nd to at least Dec 25th (CDRH) and a Juv female was located at Lower Fm GP on Oct 4th (BMA) then seen intermittently until Dec 28th (SAG). Prey items included a Mallard at East Ilsley on Jan 8th (GDS), 1 was observed mantling a pigeon in the middle of a busy road in Reading on Nov 12th (MJS), a Golden Plover was taken at Thatcham on Dec 9th (CDRH) and to the despair of many the Storm Petrel eventually fell to the Juv f at QMR on Dec 2nd (MO). A lucky escape involved a Wood Pigeon that was forced to land on the water at QMR to escape its pursuer (CDRH). An over-confident juv briefly attacked a Grey Heron in Windsor Great Park on Sep 15th (CDRH).

WATER RAIL   *Rallus aquaticus*

Uncommon winter visitor and a rare summer resident

Records were received from 31 locations, 11 in W Berks, 12 in M Berks and 8 in E Berks. The monthly maxima at the main sites is shown in Table 1, the monthly status is shown in Table 2.

Table 1

	Jan	Feb	Mar	Apr	May	Jun	Jul	Aug	Sep	Oct	Nov	Dec
Dinton Pastures	3	1	1	0	0	0	0	0	0	1	1	1
Hosehill Lake	4	3	3	0	0	0	0	0	0	3	3	1
Kintbury Cressbeds	6	3	7	1	1	1	nc	3	2	2	1	2
Lavell's Lake	3	2	5	0	0	0	0	0	3	4	3	2
Moatlands GPs	nc	3	2	0	0	0	0	0	0	1	1	2
Thatcham Marsh	3	3	7	3	3	3	3	4	3	2	2	2

Table 2

	Jan	Feb	Mar	Apr	May	Jun	Jul	Aug	Sep	Oct	Nov	Dec
Number of sites	15	17	15	4	2	2	1	3	3	10	9	12
Minimum no of birds	34	36	37	6	4	4	3	8	8	17	14	19

First winter: The high counts at Kintbury Cressbeds were made on several days in both Jan and Mar (RGS) and are low estimates of the site's wintering population. The count of 7 at Thatcham Marsh occurred on Mar 22nd (DJB) whilst the 5 at Lavell's Lake on Mar 19th (ADB) is a high count for this site. At Bottom Lane Floods, good numbers were present throughout the period with a maximum of 6 on Feb 26th (RCr). However bank repair work carried out by the Environment Agency to the K&A canal starved the site of water causing this valuable wetland to dry out thus making it unsuitable for Water Rails in the second winter. One was seen in the jaws of a cat at Kintbury on Apr 29th (LS).
Summer: Summering took place at Kintbury Cressbeds and Thatcham Marsh, but the only evidence of breeding came from the former site where a juv was heard on Aug 13th (RGS). At Thatcham Marsh up to 3 territories had been located (IW; JL) but evidence of breeding was not forthcoming. **Second winter:** Returning birds were first located in Aug with 1 at Slough SF on Aug 29th (BDC). Birds had repopulated Lavell's Lake in Sep but it was not until Oct that the main winter influx began with 4 at Lavell's Lake on Oct 1st (MFW) and Oct 14th (FJC) being the highest counts for the period.

MOORHEN *Gallinula chloropus*

Common and widespread resident, found almost anywhere where there is open water

The monthly maxima at the main sites are shown in the table.

	Jan	Feb	Mar	Apr	May	Jun	Jul	Aug	Sep	Oct	Nov	Dec
Lavell's Lake	5	4	5	4	3	8	nc	7	7	6	6	5
Lower Fm GP	11	22	17	16	10	12	11	17	11	12	13	13
Muddy Lane GP	10	6	2	3	4	1	2	4	10	12	19	23
Moor Green Lakes	4	5	12	12	6	6	7	nc	11	23	17	25

Other high counts involved 16 at Dorney Wetlands on Mar 26th (Birdtrack), 13 Windsor Esplanade on Oct 23rd (DFu) and 12 there on Dec 19th (DFu). An interesting record involved 1 in a Farnborough garden on Mar 25th (GDS), nowhere near any water.

COOT *Fulica atra*

A common resident and winter visitor

A disappointing year for records with very few if any counts coming from the more important waters such as Theale, Wraysbury and Dinton Pastures CP. The monthly maxima at the main sites that were covered is shown in the table:

	Jan	Feb	Mar	Apr	May	Jun	Jul	Aug	Sep	Oct	Nov	Dec
Aldermaston GPs	2	9	14	14	7	8	7	15	1	1	2	1
Lower Farm GP	98	101	104	80	63	71	50	72	73	53	31	50
Moatlands GPs	220	84	18	nc	nc	nc	nc	nc	nc	113	109	122
Moor Green Lakes	229	106	37	18	37	57	110	nc	128	227	193	236
Muddy Lane GP	48	24	22	9	7	13	23	22	51	63	64	60
Pingewood GPs	28	23	12	nc	nc	65	nc	nc	136	142	nc	91

Away from these sites the only count to exceed 100 was 115 at Woolhampton GPs on Jan 3rd (JPM). **Breeding:** Records were received from many sites with 8 occupied nests at Rapley Lake on Apr 4th (DJB) being the highest count.

CRANE *Grus grus*

Very rare vagrant

A flock of 9 was watched distantly from Hedgerley Bucks, flying over from the SW at 1015-1030hrs on Mar 2nd (CDRH; RIn; CDR Jones; D Willis). Following an examination of maps and discussion between CDRH, RIn (the LNHS recorder for Middlesex) and CDRJ, it was agreed that this group were certainly seen in Berks airspace when first spotted flying in from the SW and then again when they continued E above the northern outskirts of Slough. This was part of a national influx which was detailed in the May 2003 edition of Birdwatch magazine (Birdwatch 131:50-51). Not recorded in Berks until 1987 when 2 singles seen in Jan. The only other record is of 3 birds in 2002. County total now 5 records involving 14 birds.

OYSTERCATCHER *Haematopus ostralegus*

Uncommon but regular passage migrant and occasional winter visitor

Monthly maxima at the main sites were:

	Jan	Feb	Mar	Apr	May	Jun	Jul	Aug	Sep	Oct	Nov	Dec
Queen Mother Reservoir	–	–	1	–	2	–	3	–	–	–	1	–
Theale/Moatlands GPs	–	–	–	1	1	1	2	–	–	–	–	1

Singles were recorded at a further 10 sites as follows: **Spring:** Lower Fm GP Mar 23rd (MJD; RRK), Mar 24th (DDC) and Apr 28th (GJS; RAL); Summerleaze GP Apr 4th (BAJC); Burghfield GPs Apr 5th (JLe) and Apr 12th (TGB); Pingewood GPs on Apr 11th (JPM) and Apr 21st (JEM); Eversley GPs Apr 13th (PBa), Apr 18th (B Harland), Apr 21st (IT) and Apr 27th (N Silver); over Twyford GPs Apr 28th (AR); Lea Fm GP May 2nd (MFW) and Dorney W on May 14th (SP). **Autumn:** Pingewood GPs Jul 13th (RJB); over Westbrook, Boxford Jul 30th (MSt) and over Tilehurst Aug 25th (MGM). A juv present at QMR from Nov 21st to Nov 28th was observed feeding on exposed Zebra Mussels before moving to open grass to feed on earthworms (CDRH).

AVOCET *Recurvirostra avosetta*

Rare passage migrant

A good year for this species in Berks with 4 records involving 12 birds. **First winter/spring:** Singles at QMR Feb 25th (JAS), Dorney W Mar 4th (MDD) and Woolhampton GP Mar 9th (TGB *et al*). Unusually for this species the Woolhampton bird was present all day, allowing many local birders to enjoy the spectacle. **Autumn/second winter:** A flock of nine were at QMR Nov 29th (CDRH) which repeatedly landed on open water in the centre of the Res from 12.10 hrs to 13.30 hrs although often harried by gulls, the largest count since 14 were seen at Theale GPs on Mar 27th 1983. [Note: Nov 29th also produced flocks of 6 at Staines Res, Surrey, 8 at Testwood Lakes, Hants and 20 at Hanningfield Res in Essex.]

STONE CURLEW *Burhinus oedicnemus*

Scarce and localised summer visitor

First recorded from the Downs Mar 29th (JOB). Evidence of breeding included 1 ad and 2 juv Jun 13th (CL), and 2 ads and 2 juvs Jun 15th (LM) and 2ads with 1juv on Jul 14th (MJT). Post breeding gatherings included 12 Sep 14th (JOB, MFW) and 17 Sep 21st (JOB). The RSPB survey recorded six breeding pairs in Berkshire which fledged six young. In addition a juvenile colour-ringed as a chick in Wiltshire was seen in the autumn roost.

LITTLE RINGED PLOVER   *Charadrius dubius*

Uncommon summer visitor and passage migrant

Monthly maxima at the main sites were:

	Jan	Feb	Mar	Apr	May	Jun	Jul	Aug	Sep	Oct	Nov	Dec
Crookham Common	–	–	5	6	2	–	–	–	–	–	–	–
Eversley GPs	–	–	–	3	3	6	5	–	–	–	–	–
Greenham Common	–	–	3	8	9	–	–	–	1	–	–	–
Dorney Wetlands	–	–	6	8	8	5	2	1	–	–	–	–
Lavell's Lake	–	–	1	3	2	2	–	–	–	–	–	–
Lea Fm Pit	–	–	–	2	7	2	–	–	–	–	–	–
Lower Fm GP	–	–	3	6	8	7	3	2	–	–	–	–
Padworth Lane GP	–	–	4	4	–	1	5	–	–	–	–	–
Pingewood GPs	–	–	3	6	4	3	1	–	–	–	–	–
Theale/Moatlands GPs	–	–	2	5	2	2	1	–	–	–	–	–
Twyford GPs	–	–	2	3	2	–	2	–	–	–	–	–
Woolhampton GPs	–	–	3	4	4	–	3	–	–	–	–	–
Total at 10 other sites	–	–	7	4	2	4	14	–	–	–	–	–

Counts from the 10 other sites included a high of 11 at Slough SF on Jul 9th (CDRH).
Breeding: This was confirmed at Eversley GPs where 1pr reared 3 young (NRG),
Pingewood GPs, 1juv on Jun 23rd (RCr), Lower Fm GP, 2 juvs on Jun 29th (IW; JL),
Padworth Lane GP, 1pr with 3 chicks on Jul 5th (RCr), Dorney Wetlands, 1 ad with 2
chicks on Jul 11th (BDC) and Woolhampton GPs where an anxious pair was located on Jul
19th (GEW) and 1pr with 2 young on Jul 22nd (JPM). Juvs were also reported at Bray GP,
Moatlands GP and Hosehill Lake and although breeding may have occurred at the latter
2 sites the possibility of these birds being migrants cannot be ruled out. Displaying birds
were noted at Greenham Com, Lea Fm GP and Wasing Woods. Away from the river valleys
1 was located on flooded fields near East Ilsley on Mar 24th (ABT). Extreme dates for
arrival were singles on the very early date of Mar 3rd at Eversley GPs (KBB) and Mar 7th
at Dorney Wetlands (BDC). The latest departure involved 1juv at Greenham Com on Sep
25th (GEW) the latest departure date since 1996.

RINGED PLOVER   *Charadrius hiaticula*

Uncommon passage migrant and summer visitor

Monthly maxima at the main sites were:

	Jan	Feb	Mar	Apr	May	Jun	Jul	Aug	Sep	Oct	Nov	Dec
Greenham Common	–	1	3	6	8	2	–	–	–	–	–	–
Dorney Wetlands	–	1	4	6	18	1	–	–	–	–	–	–
Lower Fm GP	–	–	2	4	3	6	4	2	–	–	–	–
Pingewood GP	–	–	–	7	1	–	1	–	–	–	–	–
QMR	–	1	–	1	3	1	–	1	9	–	1	–
Total at 11 other sites	–	–	8	6	8	4	9	2	1	–	–	–

Counts of up to two were received from the further 11 sites. The only counts to exceed
two were three Slough SF May 23rd and 6 ads there on Jul 8th, (CDRH). The high count
of 18 at Dorney Wetlands was made May 16th during heavy rain (JOB) and is the highest
Berks count since 40-50 were seen at this site on May 27th 1998. **Breeding:** Confirmed at
Greenham Com, 1pr with 3 yng May 30th (RRK) and 1pr with 2 chicks May 31st (BDC),
Lower Fm GP where 1juv was located on Jun 21st, Jun 29th and Jul 6th (IW; JL), 2 juvs Jul

23rd (CDRH) to Jul 27th (MO) and 1 juv was located at Padworth Lane GP on Jul 19th (KEM). However this bird and the late July records from Lower Fm GP probably refer to migrants. The high count of 9 (all juvs) at QMR occurred on Sep 16th-17th and was part of a period of passage at this site that extended from Sep 4th (2 juvs) to Sep 22nd (3 birds) (CDRH). Extreme dates for arrival and departure were Feb 22nd at Greenham Com (JL) and QMR (JAS) and Nov 3rd at QMR (CDRH), the first November record since 1991. The last date was exceptionally late with the second latest bird being recorded from QMR on Sep 22nd (CDRH).

GOLDEN PLOVER *Pluvialis apricaria*
Common but local winter visitor and passage migrant

Monthly maxima at the main sites were:

	Jan	Feb	Mar	Apr	May	Jun	Jul	Aug	Sep	Oct	Nov	Dec
Bury Down	400	284	60	60	–	–	–	–	–	120	70	75
Greenham Common	70	26	250	150	–	–	–	–	–	250	300	80
Dorney Wetlands	200	200	416	8	–	–	–	–	–	6	–	–
Lower Fm GP	40	16	26	31	–	–	–	2	2	200	550	120
Slough SF / Eton Wick	100	360	270	–	–	–	–	–	5	4	450	700
White Waltham Aerodrome	–	1	–	–	–	–	–	–	–	32	–	250

Counts of up to 80 were received from a further 28 sites. **First winter:** Counts exceeding 80 involved 250 Cookham, Long Lane Jan 19th (BDC); 200 Catmore Fm Feb 21st (JOB); 120 flying S over West Meadows Marsh Benham Feb 23rd (IW, JL); 100 Farnborough Down Feb 25th (BDC); 90 Winterbourne Mar 5th (MJT); 200 Crookham Com Mar 28th (JPM) with 85 there Apr 5th (BTr); c110 West Ilsley, Cow Down Apr 11th (GDS) and a staggering c2500 flying W over Hungerford Apr 26th (RGS) the latest first winter date and the highest ever April count – see note below. **Second winter:** Counts exceeding 80 involved c180 Brightwalton Nov 2nd (GDS); 400 Newbury Racecourse Nov 3rd (SAG); c100 over Farnborough Down Nov 16th (GDS); 450-500 West Ilsley Nov 28th (DJB); c200 Shaw, Turnpike Road Dec 9th (GJS); 300+ between Langley & Old Slade Dec 30th (CCH) and 200 Thatcham, Lower Henwick Fm Dec 31st (RSJ). Extreme dates for departure and arrival were Apr 26th at Hungerford (RGS) and Aug 10th at Lower Fm GP (JCh, RRK). **Note:** The latest spring record was all the more remarkable as it consisted of an estimated 2,500 birds! The next to last date was Apr 24th when there were just 5 at Greenham Com (CDRH). The count of 2,500 was made as they passed, calling, quite low over the centre of Hungerford moving west. This appears to be the first time such strong late passage has been observed in Berkshire although it is not unknown in some years in adjacent counties, e.g. over 5000 at Aldfield Com, Oxon on Apr 3rd 1983 (Birds of Oxfordshire: *JW Brucker et al*) and 1500 at Damebury Hants on Apr 2nd 1978 with 1265 there on Apr 11th 1982 (Birds of Hampshire: *Clark and Eyre* who presumed this late passage involves birds which have wintered further south) (Recorder).

GREY PLOVER *Pluvialis squatarola*
Uncommon but regular passage migrant

One in w/p Pingewood GP Apr 6th (MFW) and another there Apr 27th (BTB) were the only records.

LAPWING *Vanellus vanellus*

Common breeder, and abundant migrant and winter visitor

Monthly maxima at the main sites were:

	Jan	Feb	Mar	Apr	May	Jun	Jul	Aug	Sep	Oct	Nov	Dec
Eversley GP	250	150	20	15	16	44	15	105	238	200	400	500
Lavell's Lake/Hurst Tip	1500	500	–	–	–	1	3	27	–	29	1000	300
Lower Fm GP	222	200	50	20	30	150	300	210	60	230	262	500
Slough SF	500	500	–	–	–	20	–	100	86	127	500	–

Counts were received from a further 109 sites. **First winter:** Counts in excess of 400 involved 5000+ at Smallmead Fm on Jan 2nd with 2500 still there on Jan 21st (RCr), 1600 Green Pk Reading Jan 3rd (RCr) and 1000 there Jan 19th (RJB), 1000+ near Grazeley at Amners Fm Feb 7th (RCr) with 700 there Feb 14th (RJB) and 800 at Catmore Fm on Feb 21st (JOB). **Summer:** Display was observed at Bury Down, Dorney W, Farnborough Down, Greenham Com, Hawthorn Hill, Midgham GP, Home Fm Snelsmore, Upper Bucklebury, Widbrook Com and Windsor Great Park. **Breeding:** Was confirmed at Brimpton, nest with 4 eggs Apr 5th (GEW); Ruscombe, 3 nests Apr 24th , 1 brood of 4 Apr 27th decreasing to 3y May 3rd (DJB); Swallowfield Pk, 1 sitting and 1pr with 2y May 8th (DJB); Thurle Down, 4+ broods May 10th (DJB); Hungerford Newtown, juvs present May 31st (LS); Pingewood GPs, 1juv Jun 1st (RCr); Woolhampton GPs, 2juvs Jun 20th (GEW); Lower Fm GP, 2juvs Jun 21st (IW; JL); Eversley GPs, 8prs attempted to breed, rearing 5y (MGLR); Field Fm GP, 1ad with 1chick Jul 13th (RCr). **Second winter:** The largest post breeding flock encountered was 300 at Lower Fm GP on Jul 10th (GJS). Later counts exceeding 400 involved c500 at White Waltham AF on Nov 5th (BDC; DF), c660 Remenham Nov 6th (DJB) and 1000+ at Amners Fm Grazeley on Dec 24th with 600 on Dec 28th (RJB).

Lapwing by Helen Chadburn

KNOT   *Calidris canutus*

Scarce passage migrant and winter visitor

A good year for this species with 4 records all involving single birds. **Spring:** one in s/p Lower Fm GP May 16th (MJT; JC) to May 18th (MO). **Autumn:** There was a run of records at the near empty QMR with 1 f/w on Oct 17th to Oct 19th (CDRH; JOB *et al*) a different f/w there Oct 22nd- 23rd (JOB *et al*) and 1f/w with 3 Dunlin on Nov 17th (CDRH; LGRE). Although there have been years when more birds have been recorded, 2003 is the first year to produce 4 records.

SANDERLING   *Calidris alba*

Scarce passage migrant

There were 11 records of 12 individuals reported from 2 sites. **Spring:** one w/p QMR Apr 11th - 12th (CDRH) and possibly the same Apr 15th (JAS), ad fresh s/p May 1st (CDRH, JAS) and May 2nd (JAS) and singles in full s/p May 15th, May 20th (JAS), Jun 3rd (JAS; CDRH) and Jun 6th (JAS). At Pingewood GPs 1 in s/p was present on Apr 27th (FJC) and 1 there May 19th (BTB). **Autumn:** At QMR, there was 1 on Aug 24th (BTB, CL), 1juv Sep 4th, 2 juvs Sep 9th (CDRH) and Sep 11th (CDRH, CL).

LITTLE STINT   *Calidris minuta*

Scarce passage migrant, principally in autumn

Just two records,1 spring and 1 autumn, both at Lower Fm GP with singles on May 15th (MJD, RRK) and Sep 13th (IW, JL, RRK).

TEMMINCK'S STINT   *Calidris temminckii*

Scarce passage migrant, predominantly in spring

Two at Lower Fm GP on Apr 18th - 19th (MJD, RRK *et al*) is the first April record for this species in Berks and is only pre-dated by an exceptional record of 1 at Ham SF on Mar 18th 1948.

PECTORAL SANDPIPER   *Calidris melanotos*

Rare vagrant

Two records, possibly relating to the same bird involved a juv at Eversley GP from Nov 1st to Nov 7th (C Gent *et al*) and then 1 juv at Slough SF and briefly Dorney Wetlands on Nov 12th (CDRH *et al*) and Nov 13th (JOB). The lack of records elsewhere in Britain at this time (only 1 reported in Scotland per Birding World) does strengthen the case that these records involved the same bird. This bird represents the 13th record for Berks - and the latest ever - and is the 6th record for Slough SF with the last record also a juv at Slough SF from Oct 5th to 13th 1996.

DUNLIN *Calidris alpina*

Common passage migrant and winter visitor

Records were received from 12 locations throughout the county. Monthly maxima at the main sites were:

	Jan	Feb	Mar	Apr	May	Jun	Jul	Aug	Sep	Oct	Nov	Dec
Eversley GP	–	–	–	2	4	1	1	1	–	–	1	–
Dorney Wetlands	–	–	2	5	4	1	–	–	–	–	–	1
Lower Fm GP	–	–	–	1	3	1	4	2	–	2	1	–
Queen Mother Reservoir	–	1	1	9	10	1	1	2	1	1	4	–
Slough SF	–	–	–	–	4	–	2	1	1	1	2	–
No at other sites	2	–	5	7	5	1	2	3	–	–	–	–

First winter/Spring: Records began in Jan with 1 at Pingewood GPs on Jan 8th (MGM) and 1 near Summerleaze GP on Jan 14th (CDRH). Away from the main sites, the only count to exceed 2 was 4 on flooded meadows at Charvil on Mar 15th (CDRH). The high counts at QMR occurred on Apr 28th and May 12th (CDRH). Late single migrants were reported from Lower Fm GP (IW; JL) and QMR (JAS), both on Jun 7th. **Autumn/Second winter:** Early return passage was observed at Horton GP where 1 was seen "flying with Tufted Ducks" on Jun 27th (CDRH) and at Dorney Wetlands, 1 in s/p on Jun 29th (JOB). Apart from these early records, passage was slow with no counts exceeding 4 birds. However due to low water levels at several sites, small numbers remained into the winter with the last report being 1 at Dorney Wetlands on Dec 12th (JEM).

RUFF *Philomachus pugnax*

Uncommon passage migrant and winter visitor

There were 9 records of 10 individuals reported from 8 sites. **Spring:** Singles Pingewood GPs, Mar 13th (MO) and Mar 28th (MGM); 1 Charvil on Mar 15th (CDRH); 2 on a flooded field at East Ilsley Mar 22nd-24th (ABT *et al*) and 1 male Lower Fm GP Apr 18th (MO). **Autumn:** A juv commuting between Dorney W and Slough SF from Aug 11th (SP) to Aug 19th (RR; JOB) was followed by a juv reeve at Windsor Great Park on Aug 13th -17th (CDRH), 1juv Lower Fm GP Aug 25th (IW; JL) and Aug 28th (MO) and 1juv male at Greenham Com on Aug 29th (CDRH), possibly the Lower Fm bird?

JACK SNIPE *Lymnocryptes minimus*

Uncommon localised winter visitor and passage migrant

Reported from 10 sites during the first winter period and 6 sites during the second winter period. A wide spread of records but in lower numbers than in 2002 when the peak count was 9 at Horton GP. **First winter:** Three Eversley GPs Jan 6th (KBB; R Haynes), 2 Horton GP Jan 11th (MFW) with 1 there Jan 14th (JOB) and Jan 31st (CL); singles Pingewood GP Feb 2nd (ABT), Dorney W Feb 23rd (SP), Greenham Com Feb 25th (AJT, IW, JL), Lavell's Lake Feb 27th (RBal), Eversley GPs Mar 1st (KBB), Mar 16th (RAH) and Apr 2nd (CRo) to Apr 6th (MO), Apr 14th (MGM) and Apr 24th (TC; PBT; MFW) the latest departure date, Fobney Marshes Mar 6th (RAd), Hackney Bottom Mar 26th and 30th (CDRH), Woolhampton GP Mar 29th (MFW) and Apr 2nd (GEW, RHS) and Lower Fm GP Apr 6th (JC). **Second winter:** Began with singles at Windsor Great Park Sep 30th (CDRH), Lower Fm GP Oct 12th (MJD), Lavell's Lake Nov 5th (ADB) 2 there on Nov 6th (S Hughes) then 1 to Nov 20th (MFW). There were 4+ at Dorney W on Nov 17th and

1 on Dec 3rd (CDRH), 1 Brimpton GP Dec 7th (CDRH) and finally 1 at Horton GP Dec 24th (CL).

SNIPE   *Gallinago gallinago*
Common winter visitor, scarce in summer

Monthly maxima at the main sites were:

	Jan	Feb	Mar	Apr	May	Jun	Jul	Aug	Sep	Oct	Nov	Dec
Aldermaston GP	–	1	18	4	–	–	–	–	–	1	–	–
Eversley GPs	46	4	7	7	–	–	–	1	4	3	4	3
Lavell's Lake	35	24	25	2	–	–	–	1	5	6	9	2
Lower Fm GP	5	4	8	9	2	–	1	9	10	5	6	1
Pingewood GPs	25	29	10	11	–	–	–	2	–	–	–	8
Slough SF	67	10	4	2	–	–	–	1	6	7	12	–
Theale GPs	3	5	22	18	1	–	–	1	1	1	–	1

Counts of up to 15 were received from a further 41 sites. The only count to exceed 15 was 17 at West Meadows Marsh Benham Jan 12th (IW, JL). The high count of 67 at Slough SF was made on Jan 17th (CDRH) and the 46 at Eversley GPs on Jan 25th (MGLR). The high numbers that occurred in Dec 2002 at Lavell's Lake continued into 2003 thus making the 2002/3 winter the best ever for this site. The only May records were at Hosehill Lake May 1st (BU), Lower Fm GP May 3rd (JLS) with 2 there May 4th (IW, JL) and 1 May 10th (AG). Extreme dates for departure and arrival were at Lower Fm GP, May 10th (AG) and Jul 27th (IW, JL), perhaps indicating local summering.

WOODCOCK   *Scolopax rusticola*
Localised resident in small numbers; recorded more widely in winter

Records were received from 12 locations during the winter months with 4 in W Berks, 3 in M Berks and 5 in E Berks. The BTO survey of this species during the summer showed Woodcocks to be present at an encouraging 25 locations, 16 in W Berks, 3 in M Berks and 6 in E Berks. **First winter:** Singles were located at 7 sites, the only higher count involved birds leaving their roost at Lavell's Lake where after 1 was located on Jan 11th (BTB; FJC), reports of 1-2 were regular to Feb 24th (FJC) peaking at 3 on Feb 15th (DDC). **Spring/ summer:** Survey work produced the following results (r=roding). *W Berks:* Single birds were reported from Greenham Com (MO), Inkpen (LS), K&A Canal Kintbury (JLS), Kintbury (JLS), Bradley Court (JLS), Sandleford (IW; JL), Stockcross (SAG) and Sole Com (RF). Higher counts were received from Hampstead Marshal, 2r Apr 23rd (JPM); Marsh Benham, 2r Apr 23rd (RF;LS); Hermitage, 10 contacts on May 1st, 13 on May 16th, and 7 on May 28th (JLe); High Copse Frilsham, 12 contacts involving 5-6 birds on May 4th, increasing to 22 contacts on Jun 12th (RCr); Bucklebury Com, 5 on May 8th (JA) and 1pr plus 1 Jul 4th (GJS); Snelsmore Com, 6 contacts on Jun 6th (MSt) and c4r Jun 13th -14th (JLS;LS); Crookham Com, 3 together Jun 15th (RAH) and Bucklebury, 5 contacts Jun 28th (RCr). *M Berks:* Single birds were reported from Moor Copse on Apr 27th (JLe), Padworth Com May 20th (DHu) and Decoy Heath Jun 25th (RF). *E Berks:* As would be expected most records came from the Swinley and Windsor Forests. In Swinley Forest roding birds were noted at 16 locations during May-Jun (DJB). Another high count in this area involved 12 contacts at Caesars Camp on May 24th (WAN). In Windsor Forest, 3-4 were roding at South Forest on Apr 21st (DJB) and 3 were roding at Cranbourne Chase on Jun 3rd (BAJC) and 2-3r plus 1pr on Jun 28th (DJB). Elsewhere 2 were roding in Windsor Pk on May 23rd (BAJC; DJW), 5r Swinley Brickpits Jun 6th (DJB) and 1 was located at Gorrick Wood on Jul 24th (BMc; RMc). There were no reports from the Ashley Hill area this year, a site that usually holds a significant population. The survey, based on the number of roding males, points to a county population in the range 50-70 (Recorder). **Breeding:** This was confirmed at Snelsmore Com where 2 recently fledged juvs were located on Jul 9th (IW; JL; JPM). **Second winter:** Two intriguing reports of 1 flying over Tilehurst gardens on Sep 15th (JA) and Oct 3rd (JLe). Two birds flew over the A322 Bagshot Rd at Rapley Fm on Oct 23rd and 1 on Oct 24th (DKP). Singles were noted at Pinkneys Green on Nov 12th (BDC) and Hermitage on Dec 7th (CDRH).

BLACK-TAILED GODWIT   *Limosa limosa*

Scarce passage migrant

A record year for numbers with 12 records of 38+ individuals reported from 6 sites. **Spring:** 3 Lower Fm GP May 3rd (RRK; SAG) and 2 flying SW over Dorney W May 4th (CDRH, LGRE). **Autumn:** A party of 14 at Eversley GPs on Jul 1st (CRG) is the largest count since 15 at Slough SF on Aug 18th 1958. There followed a run of Records at Lower Fm GP, with 10 Jul 6th including one with coloured rings on both legs (IW, JL) with 1 there Jul 11th (RF), two Jul 18th (JCh), a late record Nov 13th (PAdn) to Nov 14th (SAG) and presumably the same bird Nov 22nd (IW, JL) and Nov 23rd (RAH). Elsewhere singles were reported from Padworth Lane GP Jul 19th (KEM); Woolhampton GP Jul 30th (JPM); Dorney W Sep 2nd (BDC) and finally two juvs Slough SF Sep 10th (CDRH). A Godwit species seen flying high SW over Caversham on Jun 29th was thought more likely to be Black-tailed than Bar-tailed (TBa).

BAR-TAILED GODWIT   *Limosa lapponica*

Scarce passage migrant

Two records, both from QMR: one May 12th on size and plumage considered to be a female, circled twice then flew off NE (CDRH) and an adult in w/p May 14th that flew off SW (JAS).

WHIMBREL   *Numenius phaeopus*

Uncommon passage migrant

There were 21 records involving 57 individuals reported from 8 sites with peak passage Apr 11th to 28th and Jul 9th to 19th. **Spring:** Four Pingewood GP Apr 11th (FJC *et al*) with 2 there Apr 21st (MGM *et al*); 1 flying NE over Moatlands GP Apr 16th (JOB; FJC); 1 over Dorney W Apr 18th (JOB), 2 there Apr 27th (SP) and 1 left to the north May 19th (JOB); 3 QMR Apr 23rd (JAS) with 12 flying N over there Apr 28th (CDRH), 2 flying N May 1st (CDRH) and 1 flying NW May 14th (CDRH); 3 Eversley GPs May 2nd (JJW) and 1 there May 9th (JBS); 1 Brimpton GP May 19th (GEW) and 1 heard calling there at 11pm May 20th (GEW). **Autumn:** one Eversley GP Jun 30th (TC); 1 calling over QMR Jul 9th with 5 SE over there in groups of 2, 1 and 2 Jul 17th (CDRH); 4 flying S/SW over Brimpton Jul 17th (AHo) and 8 flying S over there Jul 19th (GEW); 1 Lower Fm GP Jul 11th (RF); 1 heard calling over Warfield Aug 14th (FJC); 1 Pingewood GP Aug 26th (MGM). A flock of 9 Whimbrel/Curlew flew SE over QMR at dusk Aug 18th (CDRH).

CURLEW *Numenius arquata*

Uncommon passage migrant and now summer visitor in small numbers

There were 3 records during the first winter period: one Sonning Jan 13th (CDRH); 1 over Upper Bucklebury Feb 1st (RF) and 1 heard at night over Sandhurst Feb 27th (RJG). **Spring:** 2 Dorney W Mar 2nd (SP), 1 flying N over Twyford GP Mar 20th (ADB), 1 flying N over QMR Mar 29th with 3 there Apr 27th (JAS), 1 Pingewood GP Apr 7th (MGM), 1 Lower Fm GP May 26th (JC). **Summer:** The first birds returned to the Downs during March with 1 heard W of Fawley Mar 20th (PBT) 2 Lambourn Downs Mar 23rd (JOB) and 3 Bury Down Mar 31st (SWi), and were present into July. The highest count was 12+ displaying at Crog Hill on the Berks/Oxon border Jun 15th (IW, JL). Elsewhere 3 were on the Compton Downs May 14th (ABT) and 1 there May 30th (CL). **Autumn:** juv Lower Fm GP Jun 22nd with 1 there Jul 11th (JC) and 2 flying over E Aug 21st (SAG), 1 flying S over Thatcham Jun 26th (RR), 1 Pingewood GP Jul 10th with 1 there Sep 18th (MGM), 1 QMR Jul 13th (JAS) with 3 there Aug 24th (BTB, CL). There were no records during the second winter period.

SPOTTED REDSHANK *Tringa erythropus*

Scarce passage migrant

There was an early spring record of one in winter plumage at Lavell's Lake Mar 15th (BTB *et al*). In autumn, one circled over Moatlands GP Aug 13th calling then dropped down low over the old wader pit before departing low E (MGM) and a juv was at Windsor Great Park Aug 13th and Aug 19th (CDRH).

REDSHANK *Tringa totanus*

Locally common passage migrant and summer visitor in small numbers

Monthly maxima at the main sites were:

	Jan	Feb	Mar	Apr	May	Jun	Jul	Aug	Sep	Oct	Nov	Dec
Eversley GPs	–	1	2	5	4	4	1	1	1	–	–	–
Greenham Common	–	–	2	2	4	–	–	–	–	–	–	–
Dorney Wetlands	–	1	3	4	4	4	1	1	1	–	–	–
Lavell's Lake	–	–	2	3	1	1	1	–	–	–	–	–
Lea Fm Pit	–	–	–	2	5	–	–	–	–	–	–	–
Lower Fm GP	–	1	4	8	7	7	1	–	1	–	–	–
Moatlands GPs	–	–	4	4	4	3	1	1	–	–	–	–
Padworth Lane GP	–	–	1	–	1	3	1	–	–	–	–	–
Pingewood GPs	–	–	6	8	4	1	3	1	–	–	–	–
Ruscombe floods	–	–	3	2	2	–	–	–	–	–	–	–
Thatcham Lakes	–	–	3	2	–	1	–	–	–	–	–	–
Theale GPs	–	3	9	10	1	1	–	–	–	–	–	–
Twyford GPs	–	–	2	6	–	–	–	–	–	–	–	–
Woolhampton GPs	–	1	4	2	–	1	2	1	–	–	–	–
Total at 10 other sites	7	–	13	3	2	1	7	1	3	–	–	–

Counts of up to 2 were received from the 10 other sites with higher counts of 3 Widbrook Com Jan 10th and Jan 11th (CDRH); 7 Charvil Meadows Mar 15th (CDRH) and 7 Hungerford, Home Fm Jul 6th (IW, JL). Although birds were present at several sites during the spring and summer the only confirmed breeding record was from Dorney W where there were 2 juv Jun 29th (JOB) and Jun 30th (BDC). Three juvs at Pingewood GP Jul 13th

(RCr) were likely to have been migrants. First reported from Widbrook Com, 1 on Jan 9th (CDRH), last report 1 Lower Fm GP on Oct 27th (SAG).

GREENSHANK *Tringa nebularia*
Uncommon passage migrant

Monthly maxima at the main sites were:

	Jan	Feb	Mar	Apr	May	Jun	Jul	Aug	Sep	Oct	Nov	Dec
Dorney Wetlands	–	–	–	1	–	–	–	5	–	–	–	–
Lower Fm GP	–	–	–	–	–	–	1	4	2	–	–	–
Queen Mother Reservoir	–	–	–	–	–	–	1	6	8	–	–	–
Total at 11 other sites	–	–	–	6	5	–	2	8	2	–	–	–

In what was an above average year, records were received from 14 locations, with the heaviest passage occurring in the autumn. **Spring:** Passage began on Apr 14th with singles at Smallmead Fm GP (CDRH) and Pingewood GPs (RAd; BTB). At the latter site 2 were located on Apr 19th (JOB) to Apr 21st (MO), 1 remaining to Apr 23rd (RCr) then 2 on May 2nd (PBT; CDRH). Elsewhere there were 2 at Burghfield GPs on Apr 15th, 1 Hosehill Lake Apr 15th (RCr; BU) and May 1st (BU), 1 Dorney Wetlands Apr 17th (JOB) and finally 2 at Greenham Com on May 29-30th (CDRH). **Autumn:** Passage was more widespread with records being received from 11 locations, beginning with 1 at Hosehill Lake on Jul 13th (RJB). This was followed by singles at QMR on Jul 14th (JAS), Lower Fm GP Jul 17th (SAG) and Eversley GPs on Jul 22nd (MGLR). However, the main passage occurred from mid August with most records from 3 sites: *Lower Fm GP*; 1 on Aug 8th (DJB; JC), Aug 13th (RRK; MFW), 3 Aug 17th (IW; JL) increasing to 4 Aug 25th (IW; JL; SAG) then 1-2 to Sep 17th (MO). *Dorney W*; 1 on Aug 11th (JOB), Aug 15th-17th (JOB; CRe) increasing to 5 Aug 18th (JOB), 3 (2 flying over from Slough SF) Aug 19th (PBT) then 1-2 to Aug 31st (MO). *QMR*; 2j Aug 17th increasing to 4j Aug 20th (CDRH), 6 on Aug 24th (BTB), Aug 29th and Sep 2nd (CDRH) and 8 on Sep 6th (ABT), numbers then declined to 1 on Sep 19th (DJB) the latest record. Elsewhere 1 was present intermittently at Bray GP from Aug 8th to 18th (MMc) and Aug 29th (JOB), 1 Woolhampton GPs Aug 10th (GEW), 3 Greenham Com on Aug 18th, 1 Aug 29th (CDRH) and 1 Sep 2nd (GEW), 1 Moatlands GP Aug 24th (BU) and 1j Windsor Park Sep 5th (CDRH).

GREEN SANDPIPER *Tringa ochropus*
Locally common passage migrant and winter visitor

Monthly maxima at the main sites were:

	Jan	Feb	Mar	Apr	May	Jun	Jul	Aug	Sep	Oct	Nov	Dec
Eversley GPs	4	3	3	1	–	1	1	1	5	1	5	1
Dorney Wetlands	2	1	2	9	–	–	1	3	2	4	–	1
Lavell's Lake	–	–	–	1	–	3	3	2	1	–	–	–
Lower Fm GP	2	2	2	1	–	3	5	4	2	2	–	2
Padworth Lane GP	1	–	3	1	–	–	3	1	2	2	–	–
Slough SF	3	–	2	–	–	1	–	12	6	7	11	9
Theale GPs	4	5	5	4	–	–	–	–	–	–	1	–
Woolhampton GPs	2	–	3	1	–	6	6	1	2	–	–	–
Total at 26 other sites	6	5	9	5	–	3	8	14	9	11	5	5

Of records from the 26 other sites counts exceeding 2 come from Smallmead Fm GP with 3 on Feb 24th (MGM), 3 Bray GP Mar 24th (CDRH), 5 Home Fm Hungerford Jul 27th (IW; JL) and 6j at Windsor Great Park on Aug 14th and 4 there Sep 5th (CDRH). 6 were found at Jubilee River (Dorney Wetlands to Blackpots) Oct 24th (BDC). The latest departure date was Apr 26th at Lavell's Lake and Lea Fm Pit (TOA; TGB; MFW), first returning, 1 Horton GPs Jun 11th (CDRH). The high count of 9 at Dorney Wetlands occurred on Apr 18th and involved a party of 9 flying over into Bucks (SP) and is the highest spring count since 10 at Slough SF on Apr 22nd 1989. The high counts of 11 on Nov 12th and 9 on Dec 3rd (both CDRH) at Slough SF are the highest winter counts in Berks since at least 1974.

WOOD SANDPIPER *Tringa glareola*
Scarce passage migrant

Three records. **Spring:** Dorney W May 4th (JOB *et al*). **Autumn:** 1 Dorney W Aug 18th to Aug 20th (BDC *et al*); juv Slough SF Aug 27th (MMc) and probably the same bird at Dorney W Aug 29th (JOB).

COMMON SANDPIPER *Actitis hypoleucos*
Common passage migrant, rare in summer and uncommon in winter

Monthly maxima at the main sites were:

	Jan	Feb	Mar	Apr	May	Jun	Jul	Aug	Sep	Oct	Nov	Dec
Bray GP	–	–	–	–	–	–	–	3	3	–	–	–
Eversley GPs	–	–	1	2	3	–	9	–	1	–	–	–
Dorney Wetlands	–	–	1	2	3	–	5	4	1	–	–	–
Lower Fm GP	1	–	1	2	1	–	4	3	3	–	–	–
Pingewood GPs	–	–	–	2	3	–	2	5	1	–	–	–
Queen Mother Reservoir	–	–	–	4	3	2	19	11	4	–	–	–
Slough SF	–	–	–	–	–	–	5	6	–	–	–	–
Theale GPs	–	1	2	5	2	–	2	5	1	–	–	–
Woolhampton GPs	1	1	–	1	4	–	–	2	–	–	–	–

Counts of up to 2 were received from a further 24 sites. As in previous years Padworth Lane GP hosted a wintering bird from Jan 5th (KEM) into Mar (MO), more unusually another wintered at Woolhampton GP from Jan 6th (JPM) to Feb 2nd (RF) with further records at Lower Fm GP, 1 on Jan 18th (JOB) and Bottom Lane Theale, 1 Feb 27th (MR). There were no reports of wintering in the second winter, the latest being 1 at Racecourse GP on Nov 12th (SAG). The high count of 19 at QMR was made Jul 18th (CDRH).

TURNSTONE *Arenaria interpres*
Scarce passage migrant

There were 12 records of 22-26 individuals reported from 6 sites which exceeds the previous best year of 24 birds in 1993. Unusually for this species there was a winter record of one at Widbrook Com Jan 10th and Jan 11th (CDRH) only the third mid-winter record, the previous being singles at QMR in Jan-Feb 1987 and Feb 1989 which also visited Horton GP. **Spring:** 3 s/p Dorney W Apr 18th (JOB *et al*), 1 Hosehill Lake Apr 30th (KEM, MJS) 1 Moatlands GP May 1st (MGM) with 2 on May 3rd (BU), 3 flew low over Theale Main GP May 2nd (RCr); 1 Lavell's Lake May 20th (MO), and 1 flying over Greenham Com May 31st (ABT). **Autumn:** All records came from QMR: 2 flying SE Jul 17th (CDRH), ad and juv Aug 11th (CDRH), 5 juvs Sep 4th (seen earlier over Arthur Jacob NR before flying

NW towards QMR), 3 flying over Sep 11th (HRN) and 1 Nov 21st (CDRH) the first Nov record since 1 at Ham SF in 1949.

GREY PHALAROPE   *Phalaropus fulicarius*
Rare storm-blown vagrant

One f/w was located at QMR Nov 15th (CL *et al*) and remained to Nov 20th (CDRH). First record since 1999 when one was at Theale GP on Sep 29th and Sep 30th. The 24th record for Berks.

POMARINE SKUA   *Stercorarius pomarinus*
Very Rare vagrant

A remarkable flock of 13 birds circled over QMR for a few minutes on the evening of Apr 25th before departing to the North (CDRH). Inland occurrences in spring are extremely rare and this is the first such record for Berkshire, the first multiple occurrence, and indeed only the 4th county record of Pomarine Skua. See "A Spring Flock of Pomarine Skuas in Berkshire" by Chris Heard for further details.

ARCTIC SKUA   *Stercorarius parasiticus*
Rare vagrant, principally in autumn

A pale morph juv was found at QMR on the morning of Oct 18th (MMc) and remained until 20th (CL), constituting the 13th county record. This bird completed a remarkable year for *Stercorarius* Skuas in Berkshire with all three species being seen, two of which by many observers.

LONG-TAILED SKUA   *Stercorarius longicaudus*
Very rare vagrant

A dark phase juv was found at QMR on Aug 17th (CDRH *et al*) but to the disappointment of many departed early in the afternoon. This is only the second Berkshire record of Long-tailed Skua the other, also a juvenile, was seen over Wraysbury GPs on Aug 30th 1978.

Long-tailed Skua
by Martin Hallam

70

MEDITERRANEAN GULL *Larus melanocephalus*

Scarce passage migrant and winter visitor

There was a good spread of records of this attractive gull in 2003, covering the full range of ages and plumages, but since some birds were clearly seen on multiple occasions and at a variety of sites, it is difficult to be certain as to the number involved, an estimate being between 18-24 birds. There were records for all months except March, May and July with peaks in January, April and June. **Jan/Mar:** The year began with 2 records on Jan 3rd, an ad w at Dorney Wetlands (SP) and 1ad w and 1 f/w at QMR (RIn). What was possibly the same ad appeared at Remenham on Jan 8th (CDRH), Dorney Wetlands on Jan 14th (CDRH) and Jan 19th (SP; RAll) and QMR on Jan 21st (CDRH) where a f/w and s/w were present on Jan 31st (CL). In Mid Berks a f/w was located on floods at Theale on Feb 6th (CDRH) and a s/w was present at Hurst Tip on Feb 25th (MFW). **Apr/Jun:** After no reports in March, a small influx occurred in April with a s/s at Wraysbury GPs on Apr 4th moving to QMR on Apr 5th , where a s/p ad was located on Apr 10th and a f/s on Apr 16th (all CDRH). Elsewhere there was an ad at Dinton Pastures CP on Apr 11th (NRG). A second influx occurred in June with 2 records from QMR involving a f/s with a missing right foot on Jun 17th, a f/s with both feet on Jun 28th and nearby at Poyle GP a s/s on Jun 30th (CDRH). This influx coincided with record numbers of 150 at Dungeness Kent on Jun 25th. **Jul/Sep:** Reported only from QMR where a s/w (not the June bird) was seen on Aug 11th, 13th, 18th and 20th, and 1 juv moulting into f/w on Sep 14th, 15th, 19th and 20th (CDRH). **Oct/Dec:** At QMR records involved an ad w on Oct 2nd (CDRH), a f/w on Oct 25th (PBT), 1ad w Nov 18th -19th (CDRH) and 1ad w on Dec 24th (CDRH). Elsewhere an ad w appeared at Wraysbury GPs on Nov 22nd (CDRH) (the QMR bird?) and a f/w was located at Lavell's Lake on Dec 5th (PBT).

LITTLE GULL *Larus minutus*

Scarce passage and winter visitor

There were two first winter records of this delicate gull, a f/w at QMR on Jan 4th (JAS) and an ad w/p at Temple on Jan 11th (CDRH). **Spring:** There was a good spring passage of at least 89 birds, beginning with a f/w present around Moatlands GPs from Apr 3rd (BTB) until 10th (RCr), joined by an ad from 7th (MJT; MGM; KEM). In the east of the county, the first spring birds were an ad and a s/s together at Wraysbury GPs on Apr 8th (CDRH). This was followed by 2 ads at QMR on Apr 12th (JAS) and a period of heavy passage at this site with 46 in groups of 23 ads/imms, 5 ads and 18 ads/imms on Apr 16th (JAS) and by several groups totalling 24 birds on Apr 17th (JAS; CDRH). The last two groups of 4 and 8 at QMR seem to have passed through Dinton Pastures CP earlier on the same morning (17th DR), if so indicating that a group of Little Gulls can cover the 30km between the 2 sites in as little as 40 minutes. Two further ads were seen later on the 17th at Dinton Pastures CP (FJC), rising to 4 on Apr 18th (D Callum; CN). Two further ads were seen at QMR on Apr 20th (JAS) with 1 ad on Apr 21st (CDRH), mirrored at Moatlands GP with 1 ad on Apr 20th (BU) and 3 ads on Apr 21st (CDRH), followed by a f/w on May 1st (TGB *et al*) which circulated between there, Theale Main GP and Hosehill Lake until May 16th (ABT) and was joined by an ad on 2nd (PBT). Back at QMR, a f/s flew east on May 12th (CDRH) and nearby at Horton GP a f/s was present on the late dates of Jun 9th -13th (CDRH). **Autumn:** Passage began early with a single bird at Lower Fm GP on Jul 15th (SFu) and 4 there on 20th (PJO). The month of August was unusually quiet with just an ad w/p at QMR on Aug 12th (CDRH) and a group of 3 birds there on Aug 29th (CL). September was no better, producing two records of single juvs at QMR (CDRH) and Moatlands GPs (BU) on the 5th. There was a stronger showing in October, with 5 (4 w/p ads and 1 f/w) at QMR on Oct 2nd (CDRH), followed by a s/w on Oct 6th , 1ad and a s/w Oct 7-8th, joined by a f/w on Oct 9-10th (all CDRH). The ad w/p and f/w were still present on Oct 11th (JO) and 2 ads were reported on Oct 14th (PBT). As in spring one (a f/w) remained for an extended period in the Moatlands area from Oct 19th (PBT) until unfortunately found dead on Nov 2nd (MFW). Finally a f/w at Lower Fm on Oct 24th (JC) bought the autumn total to at least 22 birds.

BLACK-HEADED GULL   *Larus ridibundus*

Abundant winter visitor and passage migrant, which now breeds

First winter: Black-headed Gull remains the most abundant wintering gull in Berkshire but is now an all-year-round resident, and breeding numbers and sites have continued to increase. High counts in the first winter period include 400 at Caversham on Jan 13th (JL), an estimated 2000 at Dinton Pastures CP on Jan 17th (FJC), 600 over Woodley on Jan 19th (NA) and 215 at Moor Green Lakes on Feb 23rd (IHB). In West Berks, 148 birds were in a flooded field at Beenham on Jan 22nd (JPM) and 400 at Lower Fm GP on Feb 16th (JL) and Mar 12th (GJS). There were few counts from East Berks, but 200 were noted at QMR on Mar 12th (BDC). **Summer:** The largest breeding concentration was the 46 pairs counted at Theale Main GP on May 1st (PDT) and together with 28 pairs at Hosehill LNR May 26th (RCr), the local gull population now significantly outnumbers the Common Terns. Colonisation continued with the first breeding at Moor Green Lakes, with 8 pairs rearing 21 young (IHB). **Late Summer / Second Winter:** 500 were noted on ploughed land at Shottesbrooke on Aug 30th, increasing to c1000 on Oct 5th (DJB), but the really high counts of the autumn resulted from some diligent counting at Theale Main pit, with 10,000+ on Oct 21st and Nov 12th (RCr), and counts at similar levels until the year's end with 5,200 on Dec 19th (RCr). Other high autumn counts were of 2000 at Dinton Pastures Oct 23rd (RR), 1,300 at Searle's Farm Lane GPs Dec 5th (RCr), and 350 at Lower Fm GP on Dec 29th (JL). Dyed birds from the tracking programme at Hedgerley tip (Bucks) were observed at Lower Fm on Nov 15th (SAG) and at Dinton Pastures CP on Nov 16th and Dec 12th (ADB).

COMMON GULL   *Larus canus*

Common winter visitor and passage migrant

January saw a very large concentration of Common Gulls on flooded fields at Remenham, with 1,600 estimated on 9th (DJB). Subsequent large counts were 350 at Frogmill on Feb 12th (SJF, FMF) and 300 at Easthampstead on the same date (MGM). Downland records included 100 on Compton Downs on Feb 21st (DJB) ad 147 on Thurle Down on Mar 16th (MFW). The latest spring record was a single at Lower Fm GP on Apr 21st (JL). A s/p adult was present at QMR on May 28th (CDRH) and 3 including 1 ad at this site on Jun 17th (CDRH) suggests either attempted summering or more likely early returning birds. A gap of nearly 1 month then ensued before the next record, an ad at Lower Fm GP on Jul 13th (JC), followed by small numbers through August and September, including an ad with a distinctly pale iris at Eversley GPs on Sep 17th-18th (MFW). Up to 35 were at Eversley GPs in December (BMA) and 50 at Moatlands on Dec 19th (RCr) but the only three-figure count from the second winter period was of 100 at Streatley on Dec 30th (ABT).

LESSER BLACK-BACKED GULL   *Larus fuscus*

Common passage migrant and winter visitor

Lesser Black-backed Gull is the most numerous of the large gull species in winter gull roosts in Berkshire, although numbers of this species are highest in early autumn as the large British breeding population moves south, with peak counts in September reaching 3 or 4 times the maximum winter count. Scattered records of individuals or small groups occur across the county in all months and like Herring Gull groups of non-breeding birds remain throughout the summer. **First winter:** Daytime counts in the hundreds were made at several sites, including 250 at Green Park, Reading on Jan 3rd (TBa), 150 at Sheepdrove Fm, Lambourn Downs on Feb 15th (JPB) and 600 at Lower Fm GP on Jan 25th (S Graham) and 1000 there on Feb 16th (JL). The winter roost at QMR is certainly sizeable, but unfortunately there are no counts available from this site. Numbers dwindle in spring, but a large late spring flock of 320 imm birds was at Amners Fm, Grazeley on May 22nd (RCr), with smaller numbers of imm birds in the same area through June and July. The only other sizeable summer count was of 250 birds at Lavell's Lake on Jun 21st (FJC). **Autumn / Second Winter:** The first juvs noted were 3 at Lavell's Lake on Aug 15th (RR); although not thought to be of immediately local origin, the first breeding records for Buckinghamshire occurred at High Wycombe in 2003, perhaps indicating that this species is soon likely to be a future addition to the breeding birds of Berkshire. By mid August numbers at Englefield had reached 700 (RCr) but the truly large numbers occurred in a series of counts from the September roost at Theale Main Pit, peaking at an estimated 22,000 birds on 23rd (RCr). Counts from the same site had fallen to 5,000 by Oct 23rd and 4,000 on Nov 15th and 3,000 were on nearby Moatlands GP on Dec 19th (all RCr). At Market Lane, Langley a count of 134 birds was made on Oct 9th, including a few darker birds presumed to be of the Scandinavian race *intermedius* (RDr). Lower Fm GP counts also built up through September, but only reached 100 on Oct 18th (BMA) and 400 by the end of November (SAG), and peaked at 1200, Dec 6th (ABT), mostly arriving around dusk and presumably roosting there. Pre-roost gatherings also occurred at Burghfield GPs where 1500+ were present on Nov 13th (RJB) and 2200+ on Dec 5th (RCr)

HERRING GULL   *Larus argentatus*

Common passage migrant and winter visitor

In addition to being a widespread and numerous winter visitor at rubbish tips and inland waters, the trend for non-breeding and immature Herring gulls to spend the summer inland continues. **First winter:** Counts of up to 100 were made at several sites, but the maximum count was an impressive estimated 1000 birds on Jan 17th at Hurst tip near Dinton Pastures CP (FJC), the majority of which were ads; this was in a period where there were high daytime counts of several gull species in the area. Two aberrant birds were seen, a leucistic ad with pale flight feathers at Lower Fm GP on Jan 24th (DJB) and either the same or another at Smallmead GP on Jan 25th (MFW). Late winter and spring counts remained at fairly low levels although counts at Jubilee River regularly reached 30 – 60 birds (MO) and 90+ were recorded at Burnthouse Lane GP (part of Pingewood GPs) on Apr 23rd (RCr); this group of mostly imm birds remained through May. **Summer:** Birds were present at Wood Lane Weir, Dorney Wetlands with 28 (inc 4 ads) on Jun 11th (CDRH) and from Lavell's Lake, with 50 birds on Jun 21st (FJC). A juv bird was noted from Lower Fm GP on Jul 30th (JC). Summering ads in urban locations along the Thames have given rise to suspicions of inland breeding, as has been recently confirmed in adjacent counties, but there was no definitive evidence in 2003 to prove this species as having bred in Berkshire. **Autumn:** Counts were mostly low, apart from 262 at Langley Park on Oct 9th (RDr) and 50 at Hurst on Oct 12th (GBa). Many of the wintering birds in Berkshire are of the Scandinavian argentatus race (with ads separable on their larger size, darker mantle shade and more heavily streaked heads) and the first returning birds of this form were 1 ad and 4 subads at QMR on Aug 11th (CDRH). From November onwards a number of birds were seen that had been caught, colour-ringed and marked with orange dye at Hedgerley pit (Bucks) as part of a Central Science Laboratory project to monitor daytime gull movements. See article "Wintering Gulls in the Thames Valley" by Paul Cropper.

YELLOW-LEGGED GULL *Larus michahellis*
Uncommon but increasing autumn passage migrant and winter visitor

Yellow-legged gulls were recorded in small numbers at reservoirs and GPs across the county, and this race (at the time of printing recognised as a full species) was reported in all months except May. Most records were of ads, for which the leg-colour is a diagnostic feature, but also in autumn and early winter the ad plumage can be very striking in its contrast between clean white head and neck and dense grey upper parts, by which they stand out from flocks of dull and streaked Herring Gulls. First winter and older sub-ad birds were apparently scarce, but this could be because these plumages are somewhat harder to distinguish from the commoner large gulls. **First winter/Spring:** Numbers as usual during this period were low, maximum counts being 6 QMR on Jan 21st (CDRH) and 6 at Burghfield GP on Feb 13th (MGM). Numbers dwindled into the spring, the last birds being 2 at Dinton Pastures on Apr 21st (FJC). **Autumn/Second winter:** There was only a short period before 3 imms (a f/s a s/s and a 3/s) were located at QMR on Jun 9th (CDRH). The only counts in double figures were in the post-breeding dispersal period, with the highest being 61 (54ads and 7 imms) at QMR on Jul 24th, increasing to an impressive 70 birds, of which 66 were ads, on Aug 11th (CDRH). The first juv was reported from the same site on Jul 17th (CDRH), and the probability of this being a domestic-bred bird must be considered, since small numbers are now breeding at several locations along the south coast. In the second winter period small numbers of up to 4 birds of all ages were recorded from several sites, most frequently from the QMR/Wraysbury area (CDRH).

CASPIAN GULL *Larus (argentatus) cachinnans*
Rare (under-recorded?) autumn/winter visitor

First winter: At QMR a small adult (presumably female) that was first seen on Dec 25th 2002 was again present on Jan 3rd (RIn) and the same or another at Wraysbury on Feb 14th (RIn). A co-operative f/w bird was in the flooded meadows at Rose Kiln Lane, Reading from Feb 7th – 10th (PBT *et al*), providing the chance for a number of birders to familiarise themselves with the distinctively clean f/w plumage of *cachinnans*. A f/s bird (a presumed male) was at Smallmead GP on Apr 14th (CDRH). Further east, at QMR a f/w was present on Mar 5th and 31st and a f/s probably a female was present there before flying to Colnbrook on Apr 4th with what was presumed to be the same bird in the gull roost there on Apr 17th (all CDRH). **Autumn / Second Winter:** QMR presented a variety of individuals in different plumages, with a s/w bird seen and photographed (MMc) on Oct 28th, and probably earlier on 24th, a juv moulting to f/w plumage on Nov 24th and Dec 1st (CDRH), and an ad at the same site on Dec 2nd-3rd (PBT *et al*, photographed

JOB) and a further f/w was present on Dec 31st (CDRH). Further west, a f/w bird was seen at Pingewood GPs on Nov 25th (MGM), a lame ad, presumed to be male (per CDRH) based on size, was at Twyford GP on Dec 5th (CDRH) and a large presumed male at the nearby Lea Fm landfill site on Dec 15th (PBT). While some individuals of this form may look very distinctive, a number of lookalikes can arise in related species and so it is important to use the full suite of identification features (CDRH).

ICELAND GULL   *Larus glaucoides*

Rare winter visitor

The presumed returning ad bird was seen several times in the roost at QMR, first on Jan 26th (CDRH) then again in early February, through to early March, being last seen on the 8th (DKP). During the day this bird could frequently be seen several miles to the north at Hedgerley tip in Buckinghamshire. At the close of the year what is presumed to be the same bird was seen for its 6th successive winter in the QMR roost on Dec 31st (CDRH).

GLAUCOUS GULL   *Larus hyperboreus*

Rare annual winter visitor

A s/w bird was seen at QMR on Feb 20th (CL) and a 2nd summer was there on Apr 11th (CDRH); presumed to be the same bird (neither actually roosted there). Note that two Glaucous X Herring hybrids were also noted at this site during April (see HYBRIDS). Both the white-winged gulls put in just a single appearance in 2003.

GREAT BLACK-BACKED GULL   *Larus marinus*

Uncommon passage migrant and winter visitor

As with most of the other common gull species, birds are now present in Berkshire almost throughout the year, and Great Black-backed Gull was recorded in all months of 2003 except June. In the first winter period there were flocks in Jan of up to 80 at Green Park (TGB), close to the main Reading tip, and 70 at Dinton Pastures close to Hurst Tip (FJC). The last spring records were of a s/s bird at Pingewood GPs on May 9-10 (PBT) and an ad at Dorney Wetlands on the latter date (DJB). There was a flyover midsummer record at the unusual location of Inkpen on Jul 19th (LS) and a lingering f/s bird was at Pingewood GPs on Jul 30th (PBT). There were only single records in August and September but records were more widespread in October and November, predominantly ads. The highest counts in the second winter period were 87 adults at QMR on Nov 22nd and 153 birds (150 ads, 3 imms) at the same site on Dec 29th (both CDRH).

KITTIWAKE   *Rissa tridactyla*

Scarce spring migrant and winter visitor

There was a typical scattering of records of Kittiwake in 2003, beginning with an ad at Lower Fm GP on Jan 26th (JC). Spring records comprised a tight-knit flock of 10 ads at QMR on Apr 3rd (CDRH) and a f/s bird shortly afterwards at the same site on Apr 6th (CL). In the second winter period Lower Fm GP contributed a second record with an ad on Dec 14th (JC), and there were 1-2 further ads at QMR on Dec 24th (CL, CDRH).

SANDWICH TERN *Sterna sandvicensis*

Uncommon passage migrant

In 2003 there was a good spread of Sandwich Tern records totalling at least 60 birds; in fact there were occurrences in seven months during the year, with June the only blank month between March and October. Despite the number of records, this species is typically a very short stayer in Berkshire and consequently is hard to catch up with. **Spring:** The first records were at QMR in the last week of March, with a single briefly on the morning of Mar 24th and then 4 together for half an hour on Mar 31st (JAS). QMR's run of records continued from mid April, with a succession of small groups through on several dates, totalling 29 birds with a maximum day count of 13 birds on 17th (JAS). The only other spring records were 2 staying for only 10 minutes at Moatlands GP on April 22nd (CDRH), 1 at QMR early on May 4th (JAS), 1 through Thatcham Marsh LNR on May 11th (IW, JL) and 1 at QMR on May 29th which flew off NE (CDRH). **Autumn:** Passage began early with a single bird, presumably a failed breeder, departing to the south from Lower Fm GP on the evening of Jul 10th (CDRH). Four south over Tilehurst on Aug 11th constituted an excellent garden record (JA), with these birds possibly included in the group of 6 present at Moatlands GP on the morning of 13th (MGM). September records comprised a group of 6 at QMR on 14th (CDRH) and a single on the same date at Field Fm GP (BU). A mixed-age group of 1 f/w, 1 w/p ad and 1 s/w was at QMR on Oct 2nd (CDRH) and the final record of the year was a single at Wraysbury GPs on Oct 11th (CL).

COMMON TERN *Sterna hirundo*

Common passage migrant and regular summer visitor in small numbers

Arrival / Breeding: 2003 saw two early Common Tern records, with a single bird at Dinton Pastures CP on Mar 26th-27th (PBT) and another at Eversley GPs on the same dates (BMA). By April 1st the first small group of 4 had arrived at Dinton Pastures (BirdTrack), and 2 were at Muddy Lane GPs on the same date (GJS), followed by scattered records in

Common Tern
by Andrew Brooks

Mid and West Berks and along the Thames, but the main arrivals did not take place until mid-month. The largest flocks were recorded from Moatlands GP with 30 on Apr 14th (CDRH) and 120 on Apr 30th (BU), with counts close to the 100 mark throughout the month of May. The size of the local population on Moatlands GP was c.30 pairs raising at least 35 young (BU) and on Hosehill Lake, c.15 pairs (RCr). A new tern raft at Lower Fm GP attracted 3 pairs, raising at least 2 young (SAG), and at Colebrook Lake, Eversley GPs 19 pairs, undeterred by the Black-headed Gulls which colonised their breeding island, raised 30 young (IHB), the first of which hatched on Jun 4th. Other sites where breeding was noted were Aldermaston, Bray, Padworth Lane, Summerleaze and Woolhampton GPs, Lavell's Lake and the first pair at QMR for several years raised 3 young (JAS). In total at least 70 pairs nested in Berkshire in 2003. **Autumn:** Many of the locally bred juvs were in evidence through the late summer, with departure dates for family groups in mid August noted at Lower Fm and Woolhampton. The peak autumn count was 50 at QMR on Aug 20th (CDRH). The last records were a f/w at QMR on Oct 4th-6th (CDRH) and another at Searle's Fm Lane GPs on Oct 8th (JA).

Monthly maxima at the main sites were:

	Jan	Feb	Mar	Apr	May	Jun	Jul	Aug	Sep	Oct	Nov	Dec
Bray GP	–	–	–	–	–	–	12	5	–	–	–	–
Dinton Pastures	–	–	1	23	28	2	10	11	–	–	–	–
Eversley GP	–	–	1	20	16	27	4	1	–	–	–	–
Dorney Wetlands	–	–	–	6	32	2	3	12	–	–	–	–
Lower Farm GP	–	–	–	4	8	8	25	3	2	–	–	–
Pingewood GP	–	–	–	30	–	–	4	2	–	–	–	–
Theale GP	–	–	–	120	122	80	70	30	–	–	–	–
Woolhampton GP	–	–	–	–	–	4	18	6	–	–	–	–

ARCTIC TERN   *Sterna paradisaea*
Uncommon passage migrant in small numbers

Spring: The first record of the year was of 2 at Moatlands on the early date of Apr 6th (MFW), with 3 there on Apr 9th (MO) and a further 3 on Apr 14th (RAd). There was then a sequence of records at Dinton Pastures and Lavell's Lake, with 1 on 15th, 2 on 16th, 1 on 17th and 2 on 19th (MO), most probably all different birds. QMR recorded a disappointing total of only 2 birds, together on Apr 21st (JAS). The highest spring count was a mere 4 birds at Moatlands on Apr 30th (RCr), with possibly the same birds at Field Fm the following day, which together with a single at Dinton Pastures (MFW) concluded a fairly light spring passage. **Autumn:** In contrast to spring, all the autumn records were at QMR. There were single juvs on Aug 17th (CDRH), Aug 25th (BTB), Sep 3rd, 2 juvs Sep 4th (CDRH), 5 on Sep 11th (CL), 2 juvs identified with 3 "Comics" before departing on Sep 21st (CDRH), 2juvs with 2 Common Terns that departed mid morning and an additional juv lingering late morning on Sep 28th and finally 2juvs on Sep 30th (CDRH).

LITTLE TERN   *Sternula albifrons*
Scarce passage migrant

There was a typical single spring record at Dinton Pastures on Apr 15th (FJC/CDRH *et al*) a bird which stayed for half a day and was enjoyed by many observers.

BLACK TERN *Chlidonias niger*
Uncommon passage migrant

Spring: Passage began on Apr 15th, with two birds at QMR (JAS) and one present there on the following day (CDRH). Apr 17th saw a spread of records across west and central Berkshire, indicating a wider inland movement; 2 birds were at Lower Fm GP (JPM), 4 were together at Woolhampton GP (ICB), a single was at Theale Main Pit (ICB) and 4 more were at Eversley GPs (DJB, B&RMc). These were followed by a bird at Moatlands on Apr 30th to May 1st (MO), joined by a second bird on May 1st (AFd, RR), and presumably one of these two was at nearby Pingewood GPs on May 2nd (BTB). Finally one s/p flew east from QMR on May 30th (CDRH). **Autumn:** Passage also began early, with a single moulting ad at QMR on Jul 16th (CDRH), and another ad at Dinton Pastures CP on Jul 20th (MO). There were 3 moulting adults and 1juv at QMR on Aug 11th (CDRH). The next records were in early September, with 3 ad and 3 juv together at QMR on Sep 4th (CDRH, CL), 1 ad on Sep 8th, and 2ad and 3 juv on Sep 15th (CDRH). A single bird was reported from Theale Main Pit on Sep 8th (BU) with a juv moving between there and Moatlands Sep 13th – 17th (MO).

FERAL PIGEON *Columba livia*
Abundant urban resident

As usual, few records were submitted, despite the species obvious presence in most town centres. The only count to exceed 4 was a flock of 30 on a barn roof at Field Barn Fm, Beenham Jan 2nd (BMc; RMc). **Breeding:** Reported from Maidenhead, where there was a pair with a chick aged 1-2 weeks on Jan 14th (BB).

STOCK DOVE *Columba oenas*
Common resident and winter visitor

Records were received from 84 sites. The number of big flocks reported was well below the 2002 figures though flock sizes were similar. Counts of over 50 came from 7 sites, the largest flock being 305 adjacent to Drift Road at Braywoodside on Oct 1st (CDRH) increasing to c550 on Oct 6th (DJB). Other notable counts were 50-100 in stubble at Finchampstead on Jan 7th (BMc; RMc), c100 Broadcommon Hurst Mar 10 (DJB), 89 Englefield Mar 11th (TM), 60 Aldworth May 4th (TGB), 65 near Eversley GPs Nov 15th (BMA) and 60 Sheepdrove Lambourn on Dec 31st (ABT). **Breeding:** Probably occurred throughout the county (numerous birds present during the breeding season). Reports of pairs or singing /displaying birds came from Ambarrow Court, Mar 19th (KBW), Aldermaston GP on Apr 16th (JPM), Swinley Park - 5 calling + 1pr May 4th (DJB) and Caesar's Camp May 19th (WAN). Occupied nests were reported from Eversley GPs Apr 5th (MJT), Hell Corner Fm Inkpen Apr 21st (LS), Hamstead Park Jun 26th (JPM), Benham Stud Aug 20 (JPM) and Hamstead Marshall Aug 27th (JPM). A juv was present with 2 adults at Dorney Wetlands on Jun 30th (BDC).

WOODPIGEON *Columba palumbus*
Abundant resident and winter visitor

Due to its familiarity throughout the county, Wood Pigeons are usually overlooked, thus comparatively few records were received. As usual the highest counts (500 or more) were reported during the 2 winter periods. **First winter:** Highest counts were from the Downs with 500 at Bury Down on Jan 18th (JOB), c500 in Oilseed Rape at Farnborough Down on Feb 4th increasing to c750 on Feb 18th (GDS) and 2000 at Sheepdrove Lambourn on Feb 25th (BDC). **Second winter:** Up to 800 were located feeding in stubble at Cold Harbour on Oct 3rd (DJB), 2-3000 were being constantly harassed by an imm Peregrine on the Compton Downs on Nov 1st (DJB), 530 flew south over Twyford GPs in 10 minutes on Nov 9th (TGB) and c800 had returned to Farnborough Down by Dec 6th (GDS). **Breeding:** An unusual report involved a pair nesting in a Carrion Crow's nest on Aug 15th shortly after the original inhabitants had vacated the site (GEW).

COLLARED DOVE   *Streptopelia decaocto*
Widespread and common resident

Counts of up to 10 were received from 20 sites with higher counts of 52 on wires near farm buildings at Wawcott, W Berks, Sep 12th (JPM); 100+ Carters Hill, Shinfield Sep 23rd (DJB); 20 Manor Fm Oct 10th (GEW); 172 Pinkneys Green Nov 12th (BDC); 172 Cookham garden Dec 16th (BDC) and 25 Strand Water, Cookham Dec 27th (BDC). The species was reported from a Twyford garden in all 12 months with a maximum of 21 in August and a minimum of 8 in Apr/May/Jun (SPA). There was no evidence of breeding other than the presence of numerous birds during the breeding season.

TURTLE DOVE   *Streptopelia turtur*
Widely, but now only thinly, distributed summer visitor

The first reports of the year were of single birds at Woolhampton GPs (JPM), Bottom Lane GP (RCr) and Ruscombe (CDRH; DJB) all on Apr 29th and the latest records were 1 at Bucklebury Com on Sep 21(RF) and 1 at Brimpton GPs on Sep 24th (GEW). Birds were reported from a total of 28 sites, 8 in W Berks, 15 in M Berks and 5 in E Berks. Birds were present through the breeding period at 6 sites (Aldermaston GPs, Brimptom, Greenham Com, Hosehill Lake, Ruscombe, Thatcham), and pairs were reported from Binfield on May 28th (DJB) and Aldermaston GPs on Jul 18th (JPM). A juvenile was seen at Brimpton on Aug 14th (GEW). The only count to exceed 3 was 13 at Brimpton GPs on Aug 20 with 10 seen there on Aug 25th and 4 there on Sep 5th (GEW).

ROSE-RINGED PARAKEET   *Psittacula krameri*
Common but localised resident in East of County. Uncommon elsewhere

This species is well established in its core area along the Thames from Wraysbury to Cookham, and there are signs of a gradual increase in numbers since the 1990s (e.g. this year's peak count of 227 at the Bray roost site on Aug 20th (MMc) was a record for Berkshire) but counts fluctuate so much that the trend is obscured. There are signs of an increase in the Warfield/Winkfield area, which produced 7 records e.g. 2 at Warfield Hall on Jun 26th (GG) and 1-3 on several dates at Winkfield Row from Sep 29th to Nov 5th (DJB). The table below lists the peak counts per month from the main sites. Counts of up to 8 were received from 26 areas away from the main sites. There was no firm evidence of breeding other then the presence of birds during the spring/summer, some reports of pairs coming to feeders and a group of 4 juveniles on May 1st at Frogmill, Hurley that may have been raised on an island in the Thames (SJF/FMF).

Monthly peak counts

Site	Jan	Feb	Mar	Apr	May	Jun	Jul	Aug	Sep	Oct	Nov	Dec
Bray area	4	15	20	7	1	0	10	227	0	0	16	2
Cookham area	10	5	2	4	1	4	0	24	4	0	5	0
Dorney Wetlands	10	0	21	3	0	2	1	5	2	0	15	0
Datchet/Horton area	5	7	6	5	1	0	0	0	3	60	7	0
Maidenhead area	4	9	8	8	4	6	10	20	16	1	30	11
Wraysbury	4	12	5	2	0	0	0	54	51	30	130	2
Birds at other sites	10	9	16	9	19	19	0	14	11	9	20	13
Number of other sites	4	4	7	5	4	5	0	5	5	5	5	5

CUCKOO   *Cuculus canorus*

Common summer visitor

Records came from 62 distinct areas all over the county. Almost all reports were of singles, but there were reports of 4 (3 singing + 1 female) at Thatcham Marsh on Jun 14th and 3 there on May 3rd (IW/JL), also 3 birds at Wishmoor on May 7th (DJB). After the first report on Apr 12th of 1 calling at Inkpen (LS), there were singles at Maidens Green on 13th and at Moatlands GP on 14th (JPM), followed by 19 records from 15th to 18th. The approximate numbers (making allowance for duplicate reports) reported in the county for the 5 weeks from 1st Apr were 0, 3, 7, 19 and 20. The table below shows the number of birds (sum of maxima at each site) reported over the summer. The latest record was from QMR on Aug 19th (CL) but a report of an adult at Moatlands GP on Jul 26th is noteworthy (MFW).

	April	May	June	July	August
Number of birds	35	63	19	2	1
Number of sites	35	48	15	2	1

Definite evidence of breeding was, as usual, scarce, but the presence of so many singing males suggests that it happened all over the county. A male and female were seen at Thatcham Lakes on May 10th (BMA). A juvenile being fed by 2 wrens at Swinley Park on Jun 14th (DJB) and another juv was reported from Moatlands GP on Jul 30th (PBT) having apparently left the nest very recently.

BARN OWL   *Tyto alba*

Uncommon and localised resident but nest box schemes are likely to increase number of records.

An excellent year with records received from 48 sites, 28 in W Berks, 11 in M Berks and 9 in E Berks. The monthly recorded distribution is shown in the table; numbers of chicks are in brackets.

		Jan	Feb	Mar	Apr	May	Jun	Jul	Aug	Sep	Oct	Nov	Dec
W Berks	No of Sites	2	12	7	5	4	6	8	7	1	0	2	4
	Min no of Birds	2	14	8	5	4	6	15(5)	8	1	0	2	4
M Berks	No of Sites	1	2	3	1	1	3	4	1	1	2	2	2
	Min no of Birds	2	4	4	1	1	7(2)	5	1	2	2	3	2
E Berks	No of Sites	1	1	0	2	1	0	0	1	3	3	1	1
	Min no of Birds	1	1	0	2	1	0	0	1	3	3	2	2
TOTALS													
	Sites	4	15	10	8	6	9	12	9	5	5	5	7
	Birds	5	19	12	8	6	13	20	10	6	5	7	8

Breeding: During the breeding season (May –July) records were received from 21 locations. Breeding was confirmed at 4 sites, 2 in West Berks where broods of 2 and 3 were ringed on Jul 18th (DL; JPM; IW) and 2 in Mid Berks where a pair reared at least 2 young at a well known location (MO) and a pair bred at a second location (MJS).Evidence of possible breeding was also obtained from a fifth site where an adult was seen carrying food on Jul 3rd (RRK). Unfortunately there were 3 reports of dead birds, 2 from the M4, 1 between J8/9 and 10 on Sep 1st (DJW) and 1 by the J8/9 east-bound exit on Oct 17th (DJB). An individual found dead by Environment Agency staff at Beenhams Heath on Oct 15th had wounds to its chest (cause unknown) (per DJB).

LITTLE OWL *Athene noctua*

Widespread and locally common resident

Records were received from 59 locations, 20 in W Berks, 12 in M Berks and 27 in E Berks. The monthly distribution of records is as follows:

	Jan	Feb	Mar	Apr	May	Jun	Jul	Aug	Sep	Oct	Nov	Dec
No of sites	9	15	19	15	10	11	15	10	5	7	7	5
Min no of birds	12	24	30	34	17	22	20	15	12	9	10	6

The peak in numbers in the late winter-spring corresponds to the time when this species is most vocal. Most records involved 1-2 birds, higher counts being 3 regularly calling at Woolley Down from Feb 23rd to May 25th (GDS), 3+ calling at Cockmarsh on Mar 11th (DJB) with 5 there on Apr 30th (BDC), 4 White Place Fm Cookham on Apr 4th (BDC), 3 Windsor Great Pk on Apr 21st (DJB) and 6 calling at Strand Water on Sep 7th (BDC). **Breeding:** Birds were reported from 36 sites during the breeding season (Mar-Jun) with 2 or more birds noted at 16 of these. Breeding was confirmed at 3 locations, 2 pairs bred at Aldermaston AWE (SRi), a check of nest boxes in the Strand Water area on Apr 28th found 10 occupied and 8 with eggs (BDC) and 1pair reared 2 young at Hell Corner Fm Inkpen (LS). A juv located at Brimpton on Aug 8th (GEW) would indicate local breeding.

TAWNY OWL *Strix aluco*

Widespread resident, common in suitable habitat, including urban areas

Records received from 65 sites, 19 in E Berks, 13 in M Berks and 33 in W Berks, of which 42 records are based only on calls (including young in nests). 5 birds were reported dead – 1 was found beside the A34 near Chieveley Feb 27th (SAG), 1 beside the A321 north of Wokingham Dec 4th (MFW), 1 beside the A4 west of Kiln Green Sep 30th (PBT) and, unusually, 2 within 100 yards of each other near Hurley Aug 25th (BDC).

	Jan	Feb	Mar	Apr	May	Jun	Jul	Aug	Sep	Oct	Nov	Dec
Number of sites	7	7	8	11	15	11	5	6	8	6	4	4
Number of birds	12	9	10	13	15	17	12	14	8	7	4	6

Breeding: Confirmed at 10 sites, but the presence of calling birds (sometimes pairs) at about 70% of the sites suggests widespread breeding. At Woolley Down and Farnborough Down a minimum of 3 prs raised young (GDS). Breeding was successful at Eversley GPs where 2 territories were located (MGLR). At Cookham Dean a pair used a nest box in a garden (success unknown) (MTuc), while nearby at Park Wood 2 boxes held eggs on Apr 30th (BDC). At Frogmill juvs were calling from an Island in the Thames from Jun 2nd to

Sep 8th (SJF, FMF). At Bowdown Woods, Greenham a young bird still showing extensive down sat out on a branch on Jun 8th (JLS). At Edgebarrow Heath on Jun 16 and also at Wishmoor on Jun 27th young were heard (DJB). At Maidenhead Court an adult fed 2 young between Jul 15th-23rd (DF). On Jul 22nd, 2 families of 2 and 3 young were being raised at Snelsmore Com (GDS).

LONG-EARED OWL   *Asio otus*

Resident in very small numbers and scarce winter visitor

In West Berks single birds were located at 2 sites, at one on Mar 16th and at the other on Mar 27th (CDRH).

SHORT-EARED OWL   *Asio flammeus*

Scarce winter visitor and passage migrant

2002 Sheepdrove Fm, Lambourn: 1, 17/12/02 (CDRH); is additional to the Bury Down sighting that day.

2003 An above average number of birds were recorded in the county, all but one in the Downs north and west of West Ilsley. **First winter:** On Jan 10th DJB submitted the first report of a long staying group of owls at Bury Down / Cow Down. Many records from many observers were received showing that there was a regular group of 8 birds in the area throughout late Jan, reducing progressively to 4 by the end of Feb, which remained until Mar 22nd when the last observation (of 4) was recorded (MSt). **Second winter:** A single bird, which was on the east bank of QMR at 9.30am on Nov 24th (CDRH), departed south-west at 9.40 having been mobbed by gulls and magpies. A single on Bury Down on Nov 8th (MHu) was later reported by several observers until Dec 7th (ABT) and was joined by 2 more birds by Dec 31st (NRG). An "eared owl", probably this species, at the Arthur Newberry Pk Tilehurst on Nov 26th was flushed by the observer's dog, briefly alighting on a tree before flying off (PDT).

Footnote: The continuing practice of some observers to walk through the private area of scrub on Bury/Cow Down looking for the SEO's, caused much disturbance to the birds and may cause some birds to desert the area in future winters. Birdwatchers are asked to keep strictly to the footpaths in the area.

NIGHTJAR   *Caprimulgus europaeus*

Regular summer visitor in small numbers to suitable habitat

A good year with records received from 11 locations throughout the county. **W Berks:** First reported from Snelsmore Com where 2 (1 churring) were located on May 7th (CDRH). Churring was heard from May to July with a maximum of 4 on Jun 6th (MSt) and last reported on Jul 22nd (GDS). Birds were heard at Bucklebury Com from May 27th to Jul 4th (GJS) peaking at 3 on Jun 6th (RCr). It was a poor year at Greenham Com (poor observer coverage?) with 1 on Jul 2nd (JW) the only record. **M Berks:** One was located at Padworth Com on May 20th (DHu) and nearby 3 churring males were noted at Mortimer on May 29th (RCr) and 1 was churring at Decoy Heath on Jun 25th (RF). **E Berks:** A comprehensive survey of the East Berks heaths was undertaken by DJB resulting in 46 pairs or churring males being located. The area totals were, Swinley Forest 37, Swinley Brickpits 6, Wildmoor Heath 2 and Windsor Forest 1. Birds were first reported on May 7th with 1-2 churring at Wishmoor Bottom (DJB) and 1 at Windsor (DJW).

Other counts for Windsor Forest involved 1 churring on Jun 13th (BAJC), Jun 28th (DJB) and 1 pair probably breeding (fem mobbing the observer) on Jul 9th (CDRH). Other counts of interest for Swinley Forest involved 6 churring on May 29th (BMA), 4 churring in the Hut Hill area on Jun 13th (MFSW) and 2 pairs plus 3 churring in the Caesars Camp area on Jul 14th (RDa) with the latest report 2 on Aug 8th (BMA). Elsewhere birds were regular at Gorrick Woods with a maximum of 3 churring on May 31st (BMc; RMc) Jul 11th (PJC) and Jul 24th (BMc; RMc). The total of at least 60 churring males/pairs are the best figures since at least 1974 and bodes well for the 2004 BTO survey.

SWIFT *Apus apus*

Common passage migrant and (declining?) summer visitor

The first birds were singles seen at Pingewood GPs on Apr 18th (JA) and Hosehill Lake on 19th (BU) from when numbers built up rapidly (the chart shows the largest single flock (grey), and the sum of largest flocks at all separate sites (black), week by week). The last sizeable flock was 21 seen at Newbury on Aug 27th (IW) and the latest record was 1 at Slough SF on Sep 11th (CDRH). The numbers recorded are higher than in 1996, 1997 and 2002 (the last published data) which seems to show a genuine increase in what will be largely passage birds, not just a result of there being more records, given that the reported size of flocks is larger than in those previous years. The largest flocks were at Moatlands GP, where there were 500+ on Apr 28th (RCr), 1000+ on May 2nd (JA), 500+ on May 12th (BU) and 700+ on May 16th (RCr). About 600 fed voraciously on insect swarms over oak trees at Burghfield Mill on May 22nd (RCr). The only record of breeding was of a pair with a nest in Friar Street, Reading on Jun 25th (BDC).

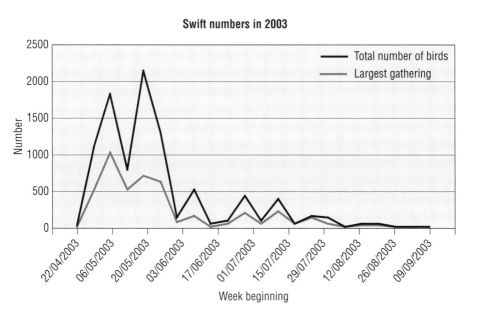

Swift numbers in 2003

KINGFISHER   *Alcedo atthis*
Common but thinly distributed resident

455 records from 98 sites were received, of which about 85% were of single birds. The table below gives a summary month by month (sum of monthly maxima at each site).

	Jan	Feb	Mar	Apr	May	Jun	Jul	Aug	Sep	Oct	Nov	Dec
Number of birds	26	21	41	24	27	22	25	29	49	35	34	20
Number of sites	21	16	28	18	22	18	21	20	34	28	24	17

2 birds (assumed to be pairs) were present at least once in the breeding period at 24 sites although 68 sites had one or more birds present at some time between Feb and Jun. Given that at well watched sites (e.g. Dinton Pastures, Woolhampton GPs, Thatcham Marsh) about one quarter of records report 2 birds, it is likely that 24 is an underestimate of the number of pairs. **Breeding:** Confirmed at Burghfield GPs, pair at nest hole 26th May (JA); Eversley GPs, pair breeding on River Blackwater May 8th (DJB); Lower Fm GPs, family party of 3 on Aug 9th (SAG) and at Marsh Meadow, 1 ad fed 1 juv, Sep 18th (BDC). Juveniles were also seen in the Woolhampton area, 1 or 2 on Jul 8th (JPM); Thatcham Marsh, 2 juvs on Aug 3rd (IW/JL) and R. Kennet, Woolhampton on Sep 9th, where an adult and immature were present (GEW).

HOOPOE   *Upupa epops*
Scarce passage migrant

A single bird seen in the Downs at Sheepdrove in 'W1 field' on 1st May by Nick Mandeville was reported by JPB.

WRYNECK   *Jynx torquilla*
Now only a scarce passage migrant

There were 3 autumn records. One was reported from Fence Wood on Sep 11th (JBu) followed by 1 at Bray GP, found at 0930hrs on Sep 14th (WAS) which became extremely elusive (probably due to disturbance from visiting birdwatchers), only being seen again at 1820hrs that evening (CDRH; BTB) and at 1650hrs on Sep 15th (CDRH). Finally 1 was located in the small plantation adjacent to the Lower Fm GP hide on Sep 27th (RAH) and remained to Sep 28th (MO).

Wryneck by
Martin Hallam

GREEN WOODPECKER   *Picus viridis*
Common resident

Reported from 117 sites across Berkshire in all months, with a peak in March/April and a trough in Nov/Dec (but no peak in Jul/Aug as there was last year). 80% of records referred to single birds, and only 30 records mentioned more than 2 birds. There were counts of 6 at Wildmoor Reserve, Crowthorne on Oct 3 (BMA), 6 at Greenham Com on Mar 21st (AJT) and on several other dates, and there were 6 at White Place Fm, Cookham on Apr 4th (BDC). Calling was reported during most months, but mostly from late Jan to mid Apr. A rare report of drumming came from Snelsmore Com on Mar 27th where there were 5 birds altogether, including 2 calling (JPM). **Breeding:** There were many reports of 2 birds, but only three identified as pairs (or m + f). There were no reports of occupied nests but juveniles were seen at 14 sites from Jun 29th to Sep 18th.

GREAT SPOTTED WOODPECKER *Dendrocopos major*
Common resident

Reports covered 128 sites all over the county in all months of the year, though about 3 times as many records refer to March to May as to Aug to Oct, presumably reflecting the birds' level of activity. Numerous reports were of birds in gardens and/or on peanut feeders. Another indication of diet comes from a sighting of one at Wishmoor on Sep 14th wedging a pine cone in a crevice to extract the seeds (BMA). Drumming was heard from early Jan until early May (with 1 report in December). Mostly records refer to 1 bird, 59 to 2 birds and 22 to more. Highest numbers (covering areas, not flocks) were 7 at Boxford Com on Jun 7th (JL), 5 at Strand Water, Cookham on Dec 27th (BDC) and 5 at Sole Com on May 29th (JLS). **Breeding:** Apparently widespread, but was confirmed at Lavell's Lake, birds going in and out of a nest hole beside the R. Lodden (SJo); Swinley Park, 7 nests with calling young on May 15th, (DJB); Wishmoor Cross, 1 occupied nest May 15th (DJB); Poppy Hills, 1 occupied nest May 18th (DJB) and Windsor Forest, 6 occupied nests May 24th-31st (DJB). Juveniles were widely reported by many observers from end of May to July.

LESSER SPOTTED WOODPECKER *Dendrocopos minor*
Uncommon resident

There were 67 records from 41 sites (10 in West Berks, 16 in Mid Berks and 15 in East Berks). All records were of single birds other than 3 near Blacknest Gate (Windsor Gt Park) on Mar 29th (PMC), a pair at Cockney Hill, Reading on May 5th (JA), 2 at Tilehurst on May 31st (JLe), and 2 at Boxford Com on Jun 7th (JL). Of those records that give the sex of the single birds, 10 were female and 12 male. Drumming was heard at Twyford on Jan 5th (MFW), Caesars Camp on Mar 19th (MFW) and Cookham Lock on Apr 17th-18th (DJB). There were 5 records of calling, 3 in Feb and 2 in Jun. Note: there were 4 records of birds 'heard' but no indication of whether this was calling or drumming. 3 records refer to feeding or foraging. 18 records describe the type of tree the bird was in – 8 in Willow, 5 in alder, 1 in birch, 1 in hawthorn and 3 in oak. The table below summarises the annual distribution of records.

	Jan	Feb	Mar	Apr	May	Jun	Jul	Aug	Sep	Oct	Nov	Dec
Number of sites	7	7	7	5	5	6	1	5	5	2	4	3
Number of birds	7	7	10	5	7	7	1	5	5	2	4	3

WOODLARK *Lullula arborea*
Summer visitor in small numbers to suitable habitat, uncommon at other times

Records covered every month except July and December. A survey by DJB and PJC of the East Berks heaths located 27 territories, all but 2 in Swinley Forest. At least 5 pairs bred in Swinley Forest with a further pair breeding at Wildmoor Heath (1 pair plus 2 juveniles on June 16) (DJB). A singing male was present at Swinley Park in March to April (DJB). Elsewhere in East Berks, 4 (2 singing) were present at Gorrick Wood on Mar 21st (KCr) and 1 singing there on Apr 15th (PJC). The other main stronghold in Berks is the Greenham Com area where there were 2 displaying, another singing and a fourth watching on Jan 24th

(JPM), a pair in the southeast corner on Mar 12th (PH) and a family party of 2 adults and 3 juveniles on May 5th (GEW). A pair bred at Aldermaston AWE (SRi) and there was a pair at Decoy Heath on Mar 14th (RF). There were a few reports from Crookham Com and Snelsmore Com (and Tadley Com in Hampshire). The table below summarizes the number of birds reported in west and Mid Berks. There were 3 records away from the usual heathland areas:- on Feb 3, 1 sang from farmland next to Pingewood GPs (MGM), 1 was at Twyford GP on Mar 24th (AR) and 1 flew south west from Cookham Rise on Nov 5th (CDRH).

	Jan	Feb	Mar	Apr	May	Jun	Jul	Aug	Sep	Oct	Nov	Dec
Greenham area commons	4	2	4	5	5	nc	nc	2	4	0	0	0
Other west and Mid Berks commons	0	0	4	3	2	0	0	0	0	0	0	0

SKYLARK *Alauda arvensis*

Common resident, passage migrant and winter visitor

There were 355 records from 65 separate areas all over the county, but with most records coming from downland, farmland or GPs. 50% of records were of 1 or 2 birds, 75% had counts of under 10 and only 20 records (6%) were of 50 birds or more. Counts of 50+ were as follows: **First winter:** At Englefield there were 60+ on Jan 4th and c110 on Mar 20th (RCr), c100 Cockpole Green on Jan 9th (DJB), 85 Bury Down on Jan 12th (TGB) and c125 at Gunter's Down Lambourn on Feb 25th (BDC). **Summer:** A high survey count of 110+ was made at Englefield on Jun 9th (RCr). **Second winter:** A flock of 50+ was present at Cold Harbour from Oct 12th into Nov (DJB). Englefield numbers built up from 70+ on Oct 15th to 240+ Nov 15th, peaking at 300+ on Dec 14th before dropping to 135+ on Dec 27th (RCr). Finally 52 were counted at Field Fm GP on Dec 31st (RCr). There were 62 records of song, 60 of these between Jan 25th and July 27th (the other 2 in Sep and Oct). A count of 35 at Greenham Com on Mar 26th contained 'many' pairs (JPM). There was no firm evidence of breeding (there was only one record of breeding behaviour of any kind other than song), but birds were present on 70 sites between Feb and Jun, and on 19 of these sites birds were present 3 times or more in the breeding season (Feb-Jun), so it is reasonable to think that breeding was widespread.

SAND MARTIN *Riparia riparia*

Locally common summer visitor and passage migrant

There were 243 records from 27 sites, but only 2 records away from lakes or GPs i.e. 1 at Brightwalton on Apr 14th (SWi) and 1 at West Ilsley on July 14th (ABT). The chart below illustrates the abundance of all three common hirundines. It shows the sum of the largest flocks in all areas week by week. The records generally support comments that it was a poor year for sand martins. **Spring:** The earliest were 3 at Lower Fm GPs on Mar 8th (DCr/JC) which were followed by small numbers on most days until the spring passage peaked during the week of Apr 26th and the following 2 weeks with 250 at Lower Fm GPs (MJT) and 100 at Twyford GPs on May 2nd (Birdtrack) and 200 at Lower Fm GPs on May 8th (MJT). **Summer:** The only report of breeding was of 3 pairs nesting in drain pipes in the river wall at Cookham (as in previous years) on Aug 22nd (BDC). **Autumn:** Flock sizes increased through the weeks beginning 16th and 23rd Aug peaking at 250+ at Pingewood GPs on Aug 26th (MGM) with only small flocks after Aug 30th other than a group of 30 on Sep 25th at Dinton Pastures (MFW) . The latest records were 3 at Lavell's Lake on Oct 2nd (FJC) and 1 over Dinton Pastures on Oct 24th (PBT).

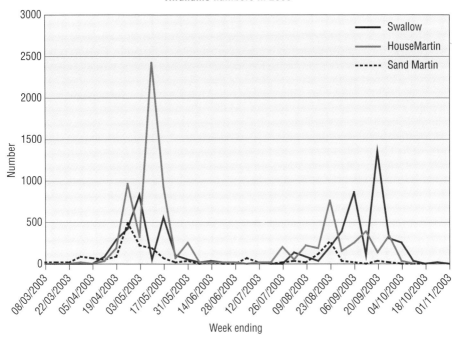

Hirundine numbers in 2003

SWALLOW *Hirundo rustica*

Abundant summer visitor and passage migrant

Records were submitted from 106 sites in 90 areas all over the county. The table included under "Sand Martin" also illustrates the abundance of Swallows. **Spring:** The first observation was of 2 birds at Woolhampton GP on Mar 30th (GRa), followed by reports of 2s and 3s on Apr 2nd, 5th, 6th and 8th and then 10 at Twyford GPs on Apr 14th (AR) which marked the beginning of the main arrival. There were c250 at Pingewood GPs on Apr 28th (MGM) and 400+ at Moatlands GPs on May 17th (BU) **Summer/Breeding:** Breeding records were sparse. A bird was carrying food at Woolhampton GPs on May 7th (JPM) and at Hungerford there were 2 nests in a bus shelter on May 31st (LS). A series of 17 records from Hell Corner Fm, Inkpen systematically record the arrival of the first bird on Apr 19th through to the departure on Sept 10 of the last of 4 juveniles raised there (LS). **Autumn:** Some big flocks built up during the return migration with c300 at Dorney Wetlands on Aug 29th (JOB), c350 (made up of a main flock followed by many groups of c30) passed over Lavell's Lake on Sep 4th (FJC) and at Hosehill Lake on Sep 15th a flock of 750-1000 flew over southwards (BU) taking 20 minutes to pass through. Flock sizes declined from then on, and the latest report of a sizeable flock was of 20 at Brightwalton on Oct 5th (SWi) followed by almost daily reports of 2 or 3 until Oct 26th when there were 2 at QMR (RIn) and finally a single straggler was at Searle's Lane GP on Nov 16th (JA) the latest date since 1 at Thatcham on Nov 24th 1994.

HOUSE MARTIN   *Delichon urbica*

Locally Common (but declining) summer visitor and common passage migrant

317 records came from 60 observers covering 84 sites in 62 areas. The table above in the "sand martin" section also illustrates house martin numbers. **Spring:** The spring movement was characterised by cycles in which a few birds arrived then a week or more passed without a record. The first sighted were 2 at Reading Mar 21st (SHa) then 3 at Lower Fm GP on Mar 27th (AJT)), 1 Eversley GPs on Apr 1st (MGLR) and 1 (with Swallows and Sand Martins) at Dinton Pastures on Apr 9th (ADB). Big numbers started to arrive from Apr 28th when there were 120 at Pingewood GPs (RCr). The largest flocks were 1150 at Theale and Moatlands GPs on May 16th (RCr), with 400 at Moatlands GP on May 17th (BU). **Summer:** There were very few records of breeding activity. Two birds were inspecting old nests at Boxford on Apr 18th (MSt), 4+ pairs nested in eaves at Stanford Dingley (BAJC) and at least 10 pairs bred at Woodlands Park, Maidenhead between May and July (DJB). Given that during June/July only 15 sites produced records and only 6 of those sites provided more than 1 record, it is possible that numbers of breeding house martins in Berkshire are declining (or are they being under-reported?). **Autumn:** The largest autumn gatherings were c200 at Lower Fm GP on Jul 30th (GJS; JL) and c500 at Dorney Wetlands on Aug 29th (JOB). Latest records were 1 flying east over Brimpton GPs on Oct 9th (JPM) and 1 at Thatcham Marsh on Oct 19th (IW JL) an earlier than usual departure.

TREE PIPIT   *Anthus trivialis*

Locally common summer visitor and uncommon passage migrant

Records were received from 18 locations throughout the county (this includes the many sites in Swinley Forest as one). **W Berks:** Birds were reported from 8 locations but only 2 produced records for more than 1 date. Single birds were reported at Crookham Com on Apr 12th (JPM); Walbury Hill on Apr 21st (CL); Mount Hill Bagnor in song on May 6th (MJT); Bucklebury Com in song on May 10th (RCr) and Woolley Down in song on May 17th (GDS). More regular sites were Snelsmore Com where 3 were reported on Apr 12th (ABT) increasing to 10 (9 singing) on Apr 26th and 8+ singing on May 10th (IW; JL) and Combe Wood with 1 singing on Apr 18th and 2 in song on May 26th (IW; JL). The last W Berks record involved 2+ at Inkpen Hill on Jul 30th (CDRH). **M Berks:** Just two records, at Hosehill Lake on Apr 13th (TABCG) and at Padworth Com on Aug 10th (JLe). **E Berks:** First reported from Swinley Forest where 1 was singing at Hut Hill on Mar 16th (JOB) the earliest ever recorded arrival in Berks. Another early bird was singing at Caesars Camp on Mar 19th (MFW) which equalled the previous earliest record of 1 at Wildmoor Heath in 1993. Migrants involved 1 at Wraysbury GPs on Apr 4th (CDRH) and 1 at QMR on May 4th (JAS). A survey of the East Berks Heaths by DJB resulted in 70 territories being located with 54 in Swinley Forest, 8 at South Ascot/Swinley Brickpits, 7 on Wildmoor Heath and 1 at Swinley Park. **Breeding:** Only confirmed from Swinley Forest where 1pr was feeding young at Round Hill on May 23rd (DJB), 1pr feeding young at Caesars Camp on May 24th (WAN) and 1juv seen at Wishmoor Bottom on Jul 1st (BMA). The latest report involved 1 over Eversley GPs on Aug 23rd (IHB).

MEADOW PIPIT *Anthus pratensis*

Abundant migrant and winter visitor, locally common summer visitor

Records were received from 81 locations, 40 in W Berks, 12 in M Berks and 29 in E Berks. The monthly site distribution of records received is shown in the table and should be looked upon as a guide to the species relative abundance as it is regularly overlooked.

	Jan	Feb	Mar	Apr	May	Jun	Jul	Aug	Sep	Oct	Nov	Dec
No of sites where reported	22	14	25	15	4	4	5	5	24	26	10	11
Minimum no of Birds	252	240	285	255	19	20	21	29	742	554	147	109

First winter: Although well distributed, flock sizes were relatively low, the highest count being 60 at Walbury Hill on Feb 23rd (FJC). **Spring:** Passage peaked during Mar-Apr and consisted of many small flocks moving north through the county, the largest being 65 at Dorney Wetlands on Apr 3rd (DJB). The first of our small breeding population also began to appear on their breeding grounds with display noted at Greenham Com on Mar 8th (JPM), 1 singing at Woolley Down on Mar 27th (GDS) and more unusually song flight at Long Lane Cookham on Mar 29th (BDC). **Summer:** Lower numbers were reported than in 2002, a total of 7 sites held birds between May-Jul. Singing was reported from the Wellbottom Down/Crog Hill area with 2 singing on May 7th (DJB), Jun 15th and 2-3s on Jul 20th (IW; JL) and there was 1 at Dorney Wetlands on May 5th (BAJC) and Jun 28th (BMA), c10 at Greenham Com (well down on previous years) on May 31st (BDC), 16 Bury Down on Jun 16th (MFW),1 Hogs Hole Combe Jun 29th (IW; JL) and 3prs at Knighton Bushes on Jul 20th (IW; JL). **Breeding:** Only confirmed at Greenham Com where 1 was feeding young on Aug 3rd (GEW; JOB). **Autumn/Second winter:** After a report of one at Dinton Pastures CP on Jul 19th (BJH) the main passage was in Sep/Oct when there were 11 reports of flocks of 50+. The largest counts involved 100+ at Hernehill Down near Farnborough on Sep 21st (ABT), Sonning Meadows on Sep 22nd (ABT) and 150 at Inkpen Hill on Sep 24th (CDRH). Numbers declined during Nov-Dec with 45 at Englefield on Nov 15th (RCr) the highest count.

ROCK PIPIT *Anthus petrosus*

Scarce passage migrant and occasional winter visitor

First winter/spring: There was 1 at QMR on Feb 26th (JAS) and 1 (the same?) there on Mar 14th (JAS). **Autumn:** One at QMR on Sep 26th (CDRH) was followed by Oct reports of 1 on 4th (ABT), 1 on 10th (CDRH) increasing to 2 on 11th (JOB), then 1 on 20th (CL), 2 on 21st (MMc) and 1 on 25th (MO). This indicates that 3-6 birds may have passed through the site during Sep-Oct. Elsewhere there was 1 at Summerleaze GP on Oct 10th (CDRH).

WATER PIPIT *Anthus spinoletta*

Scarce passage migrant and winter visitor

There were 12 records involving up to 14 birds. **First winter:** 1 was located at Midgham Quarry on Jan 1st (KEM) remaining to Jan 3rd (FJC). **Spring passage:** March is the peak month for this species in Berks and records were received from 3 locations in 2003. At Greenham Com 1 was present on Mar 4th (SWi) and 1 in s/p on Mar 26th (CDRH). At least 2 in w/p were at Woolhampton GPs on Mar 9th (CDRH) with further reports there on Mar 22nd, 1 w/p (MFW), 1 partial s/p Mar 26th (DKP), 1 s/p Mar 29th (MFW) and 2 s/p on Apr 4th (GEW; RHS). One in s/p was reported at Eversley GPs on Mar 27th-29th (CR *et al*). **Autumn:** Began with a report of 2 flying around Eversley GPs on Oct 5th (RJG) and was followed by 1 at QMR on Oct 24th (JOB) seen by MO to Oct 26th with this or another bird reappearing on Nov 6th (CL; JOB). Finally 1 in w/p was reported at Lower Fm GP on Oct 27th (RRo) and again on Nov 3rd (APJ).

YELLOW WAGTAIL   *Motacilla flava*

Common passage migrant and localised summer visitor in small numbers

Summary: There were 132 records from 32 sites all over the county, mostly near substantial bodies of water. These included two unusual records – 1 in winter and 1 of a possible hybrid – see below. As is normal, the autumn passage was much heavier than the spring passage, but numbers were significantly low this year. **Spring:** The first arrivals were 1 at QMR on Mar 25th (JAS) followed by 1 at Lavell's Lake on Mar 28th (RR). From then on there was a regular flow of 1 or 2 most days until the main movement in late Apr to early May with high counts of 7 at Woolhampton GPs on Apr 24th (CDRH) and 7 at Aldermaston on May 4th (RCr). **Summer/Breeding:** Breeding was confirmed at Aldermaston where there were 8m + 3f including 2f carrying food on Jun 9th (RCr). At Brimpton a pair was reported during June and July. At Cold Harbour where the species occurs in years when beans or peas are grown, a series of records chronicles the presence and nest-building of a pair plus 1-2 singing males, and although there is no record of breeding success, there were 5 birds there on Jul 24th (DJB). Seven reports from Lower Fm GP extend through the breeding period but with no positive indication of breeding. At QMR there was a pair on Apr 27th (ABT), 2 pairs regularly during May and an adult with a fledgling on Jul 18th (CDRH). **Autumn:** The return passage started from about Aug 14th when 4 were at Roden Down Compton (CDRH), with 11 at QMR on Aug 24th (BTB), 10 at Cockmarsh on Sep 11th (CRe) and 25 at Freeman's Marsh on Sep 18th (RF). After that a declining stream of small records lasted until Oct 24th when 1 was at Dorney Wetlands (BDC). **Second winter:** A male was present with other wagtails at Wokingham SF on Dec 17th (DJB). This is the first December record for the county the previous latest being Nov 15th 1991 at QMR. **Hybrid:** A male 'Channel Wagtail' - the hybrid resulting from Blue-headed X Yellow Wagtail (also called 'Syke's-type' because of their resemblance to the Central Asian race *M.f. beema*) - was first seen at Cold Harbour on May 7th (KEM) then by MO until May 24th (GRa). It sang and appeared to hold territory in a bean field and was presumed to be the same individual that was present at this site in May 2001.

GREY WAGTAIL   *Motacilla cinerea*

Locally common resident and winter visitor

Numbers appear to be similar to those of recent years. Records were received from 84 locations throughout the county. Nearly all were close to water bodies or SFs with the highest breeding season densities along the Thames and Kennet valleys where most breeding records originated. GPs and SFs held more birds outside the breeding season. **Breeding:** Was confirmed at 8 locations, a male was feeding a juv on the R Blackwater at Eversley GPs on Apr 27th (BMA), 1pr was feeding young at Foxhold, Crookham Com on May 4th-5th (JPM), a pair with 3 young at Wraysbury on May 9th (RDr), 1pr feeding young at Kintbury Mill on Jun 11th-14th (DR), 1pr feeding young Avington on Jun 14th (DR), a pair rearing 3 juvs during late Jun-early Jul at Frogmill, Hurley (SJF; FMF), a family party at Donnington Valley GC on Jun 29th (SAG) and 1m with 1juv at Odney Club, Cookham on Jul 12th (BDC). A pair was nest building at Hungerford Marsh on May 18th (JD) and juveniles were located at Dorney Wetlands and Slough SF during Aug (BDC; JOB) and may indicate local breeding. Pairs were located at a further 13 sites during the breeding season.

High counts involved 5 at Sandhurst SF on Jan 3rd (JMC), 14 at Wokingham SF on Jul 30th (DJB), 6 over Lavell's Lake on Sep 24th (FJC), 11 Slough SF on Oct 6th (JOB) and 8 along the Jubilee River on Oct 24th (BDC). The table below sums up the years records:

	Jan	Feb	Mar	Apr	May	Jun	Jul	Aug	Sep	Oct	Nov	Dec
Number of sites	23	17	33	23	29	18	16	10	22	24	16	13
Number of birds	32	22	55	38	46	30	39	26	42	60	23	17

PIED WAGTAIL *Motacilla yarrelli*
Common resident, passage migrant and winter visitor

Reports came from across the county throughout the year. 50% of records were of 1 or 2 birds, 90% were of 20 or fewer, there were 12 reports of more than 50 of which 6 were of over 100. Highest counts were 422 at Sandhurst SF on Jan 3rd (JMC), c100 at Thames Valley Park on Jan 12th (SH), c100 at Dorney Wetlands on Jan 21 (JOB), c100 at Wokingham SF on Dec 18th increasing to c150 by 22nd (DJB) and 519 at Sandhurst SF on Dec 24th (JMC). The table below illustrates the extent of seasonal flocking.

Month	Jan	Feb	Mar	Apr	May	Jun	Jul	Aug	Sep	Oct	Nov	Dec
Max count	422	40	21	55	7	10	10	46	60	60	50	519

Although the total number of records submitted doubled over 2002, there is no reason to suppose this accounted for the higher counts, and it seems that this species did well in 2003. There were no reports of roosts, though a gathering of 40 at Tesco's, Newbury on 1st Feb (SAG) suggests a roost nearby. Another report from Newbury on 3rd Oct of c60 flying towards Stroud Green (SAG) points to a regular roost site in that area and a pre-roost gathering of 30 was located on Windsor Station on Dec 19th (DF). Despite this being a common, familiar bird there was little hard evidence of breeding – a regular pair at Inkpen was seen collecting food on Jun 2nd (LS), otherwise the presence of pairs or family parties at several sites was inconclusive.

WHITE WAGTAIL *Motacilla (alba) alba*
Uncommon passage migrant

Spring: There were records of at least 10 birds from 8 locations. First reported at Twyford GPs where 1 was present on Mar 22nd (ADB), Mar 25th (AR) and Apr 18th (BTB). A female was at Lower Fm Trout Lake on Mar 22nd (MFW) and 23rd (RRK) and was followed by a male on fields adjacent to Pingewood GPs on Apr 1st (MGM); 1 at Moatlands GP on Apr 13th (RJB); 1m Greenham Com on Apr 15th (CDRH); 1m Dorney Wetlands on Apr 15th and Apr 24th (DNTR); 1 Lea Fm Pit on Apr 30th (BTB) and finally 1m at QMR on May 4th (JAS). **Autumn:** Before 2000 autumn White Wagtails had either been rare visitors to Berks or overlooked, the last 20th century record being 1 at Wraysbury GPs on Sep 17th 1989. However, birds have since been recorded in 2000 and 2002. This year a small influx occurred in Sep with 2 f/w birds at Summerleaze GP on Sep 25th and 5+ with 40+ Pied Wagtails at QMR the same day with a f/w still present on Sep 26th and 28th (CDRH).

WAXWING *Bombycilla garrulus*
Irregular and scarce winter visitor

First winter: A better winter than usual, but not a classic 'irruption' year. A single bird was reported from a Wokingham garden on Jan 10th (per BMc; RMc) and two f/w birds were seen at Theale motorway services at midday on Jan 27th (CDRH). A party of 6, 2ads, 4 f/w (MFW), was consistently present in trees on the roundabout next to the Running Horse PH in Bracknell from Feb 7th-27th (MO). Finally 8 were reported from a Bracknell garden on Apr 20th (D Lloyd per CMR). **Second winter:** The only record involved 1 briefly in a Burnham garden (Westlands Avenue) on Nov 23rd (RN).

WREN   *Troglodytes troglodytes*
Abundant resident and winter visitor

Reports, usually of 1 or 2, came from 50 widely distributed sites, reflecting observers' favourite sites more than the distribution of the species. It is no surprise that 75% of reports (of a species that can be skulking and difficult to find) were in Mar/Apr/May, when the birds are singing and most active. An indication of abundance comes from 2 local surveys carried out by RCr. He found 41 singing at Burghfield GPs on Mar 23rd and 27 singing around Moatlands GPs on Apr 3rd with the same number there on May 30th. **Breeding:** Was seen to be successful at Inkpen, where a family party included juveniles recently out of the nest on Jun 11th (LS), and at Brimpton on Jul 15th, where a family group of 5 included juveniles (GEW).

DUNNOCK   *Prunella modularis*
Widespread and common resident

The picture for Dunnock, being another extremely common, if rather more visible, 'garden' bird, is very much like that for Wren, though the main reporting season extended to the end of June (86% of records Mar – Jun). It was reported from all over the county in all months, almost always 1 or 2 birds, e.g. SPA reported that there were 1 or 2 and occasionally 3 birds in her Twyford garden (including 2 ad with 1 juv on Jul 18) between 16 and 24 days of every month, although in Mar – May there were usually 3 or 4 birds. Largest counts were more than 10 at Eversley GPs on Apr 23rd (BMA) and 8 at Strand Water, Cookham on Nov 7th (BDC).

ROBIN   *Erithacus rubecula*
Abundant resident

Only 15 observers took the time to report this very common, widely distributed and highly visible resident. In a garden in Twyford, 1-3 robins were present during all months, with on average 24 recorded days per month (ranging from 11 days in June to 30 days in March and May)(SPA). Highest count was 25 on Oct 24th along the Jubilee River between its confluence with the Thames near Windsor and the Berks/Bucks boundary (the west side of Dorney Wetlands) (BDC). Other high counts were 16 singing around Burghfield GPs on Mar 23rd (RCr), 12 near Swallowfield on May 28th (BMA) and 10 on Boxford Com on Jun 7th (JL). At Inkpen (Hell Corner Fm) 3-4 pairs nested (LS).

NIGHTINGALE   *Luscinia megarhynchos*
Uncommon and local passage migrant and summer visitor

Records were submitted from 17 sites/areas showing that the stronghold of this very restricted species continues to be the area of Theale GPs, with lesser populations further along the Kennet valley and isolated records from Dinton Pastures CP and at Wraysbury

GPs where 1 was singing on May 10th (DJB). A 4 year old bird was re-trapped at Brimpton GPs on Apr 22nd (JPM) and a singing bird at Kintbury cress beds on Apr 22nd was the first for several years (RGS). The highest counts were 11 singing at Moatlands GP on Apr 22nd (RAd), 11 singing at Burghfield GPs on Apr 24th (JA) and 10 (5 singing and a family group of 2ad and 3 juvs) at Burghfield GPs on Jun 20th (JA). All but 6 of the 131 records date from between April 5th (when the first was heard at Searle's Lane GP Burghfield) (JA) and Jun 8th, the period when the birds sing actively, making them fairly easy to locate. The latest record was 1 heard in sub-song at Burghfield GPs on Aug 20th (KBW) the latest since 1 at Theale GPs on Sep 8th 1991. The table below illustrates their abundance.

	Mar	Apr				May				Jun				Jul
Week beginning	30th	6th	13th	20th	27th	4th	11th	18th	25th	1st	8th	15th	2nd 29th	6th
Number of sites	1	2	10	8	8	14	6	5	6	2	1	1	0 1	1
Number of birds	1	3	17	31	14	19	10	6	11	2	1	10	0 3	1

Breeding: Was probable in 7 areas and was proved at 3 of them: 1 was collecting food at Brimpton GPs on Apr 15th (JPM), an adult fed 2nd young at Hosehill Lake on Jul 5th (RLe) and the Burghfield GP family (above).

BLACK REDSTART *Phoenicurus ochruros*

Scarce passage migrant and rare summer visitor

In Berks this species was surveyed in Reading and Slough and resulted in at least 3prs being located in Reading town centre on Apr 27th (TGB; RCr; JLe), but none were located at Slough. Birds were reported from Reading fairly regularly throughout the summer (MO) with breeding confirmed when 1f was located feeding 2 recently fledged juvs on Jun 14th (CDRH). Two males were still singing on Jun 27th (TB) and the last record from Reading involved 1f on Aug 22nd (BDC). At the other regular breeding site in Berks, the AWE Aldermaston, birds were reported during early spring (SRi) but not after although a report of 2 there on Jun 14th was received from Birdtrack. Elsewhere in the county there were 2 spring records of single migrants with an imm male at Superity Fm Compton on Mar 23rd (AJP) and 1f at Dorney Wetlands on May 3rd (WAS; JOB) and May 4th (C Barnes). Finally a fem f/w briefly appeared in BMA's Crowthorne garden on Nov 23rd (BMA).

REDSTART *Phoenicurus phoenicurus*

Localised summer visitor and uncommon passage migrant

Only 38 records were received, half were of passage birds and half from traditional breeding areas. If the East Berks heathlands survey results (submitted as a single record) are included the true number of records would be more than double this number. **Spring passage:** The first bird, a male, was at Lavell's Lake on Apr 12th (MO) and was followed by 1f at Snelsmore Com (RRK) and 1m at Hungerford Marsh on Apr 13th (GVW). A male sang at Thatcham Marsh on Apr 18th (NJMo) and 1 was at Eversley GPs on the same day (J B Sheridan). On May 15th a female was at Brimpton GPs (JPM). **Summer:** All records came from East Berks. *East Berks heathland survey:* 46 territories were located, all in Swinley Forest with 33 on Crown Estate lands and 13 on MOD lands. Nine pairs were confirmed to have bred. Nest locations include an old pine stump which has been used yearly since at least 1999 and a natural cavity in a Beech (DJB). **Autumn:** 16 birds were reported on passage which began with 1 imm at Dinton Pastures on Jul 16th (RR).

The main movement was between Aug 17th, 1f at Bottom Lane, Theale (JA), and Sep 21st, 1 f/w east of Farnborough (ABT). During this period single birds were reported from Brimpton, 1m on Aug 22nd and 1f Aug 23rd (GEW); Walbury Hill, 1 f/w Aug 22nd (DJB)); Arthur Jacob NR Horton, Aug 30th (CDRH); Dinton Pastures CP, 1 imm on Aug 31st (A Bassett per FJC); South Fawley, Sep 2nd (JD); Larden Chase near Streatley, 1m on Sep 4th (JH); Eversley GPs, 1f on Sep 7th (GR) and Lower Fm GP, 1f on Sep 7th (TGB). The only record of more than 1 bird was of 1m + 1f at Brimpton on Sep 7th (GEW). The latest were both f/imm, at Summerleaze GPs on Oct 5th (CDRH) and Wraysbury GPs on Oct 10th (CDRH).

WHINCHAT   *Saxicola rubetra*

Uncommon passage migrant

Records were received from 27 locations. The sites were well distributed across the county, with a (not surprising) bias towards the well-watched sites. Those with most birds (sum of weekly maxima during the year) were Greenham Com with 17 birds, Dorney Wetlands with 11, Lower Fm GP with 10, Slough SF with 10, Brimpton with 9, Cold Harbour with 7 and QMR with 9. Reports were confined to well defined passages in spring and autumn, as the table below shows. The autumn passage was longer and larger than that in spring (as normal). The tables present the sum of the maximum number present at each site in each week. There was no evidence of summering.

Spring

Week beginning	13/4	20/4	27/4	4/5	11/5
Number of birds	1	4	13	2	2
Number of sites	1	3	6	2	2

Autumn

Week beginning	3/8	10/8	17/8	24/8	31/8	7/9	14/9	21/9
Number of birds	1	4	17	14	21	13	7	3
Number of sites	1	1	6	7	8	6	5	2

Spring passage: The earliest bird was a male on Apr 18th at Lower Fm GP (MJD, RRK, SCC) followed on 23rd by 1 at Marsh Benham (RF). From records in which the sex was reported (many records omitted this) there were 10 males and 8 females in spring. The males came through ahead of the females (males – 18/4 to 4/5, females 30/4 to 26/5). Largest count was 5 at Dorney Wetlands on May 3rd (TGB; SP). Spring passage concluded with 1f at Greenham Com on May 26th (JC). **Autumn passage:** During the autumn, all birds were described as imm/f i.e. no males were reported possibly not reflecting the similarity of males and females at this time of year. Largest counts were 7 at Greenham Com on Aug 22nd (DJB) with at least 6 there on 31st (JLS), 4 at Cold Harbour on Aug 14th (DJB), 4 at Brimpton on Aug 18th and Sep 19th (GEW), 4 at Aldworth Downs on Aug 25th (TGB) and 4 at Lower Fm GP on Aug 31st (AJP). The latest were 1 at Marsh Meadow, Cookham on Sep 24th (LM) and 2 at Greenham Com on Sep 26th (RAH).

STONECHAT *Saxicola torquata*

Uncommon winter visitor and passage migrant; breeds locally with numbers dictated by habitat availability

Birds were reported from 45 sites. The following table summarises the distribution:

Area		Jan	Feb	Mar	Apr	May	Jun	Jul	Aug	Sep	Oct	Nov	Dec
East Berks	Min no Birds	0	3	33	44	64	45	8	5	12	12	5	2
Heaths	Number of sites	0	1	5	5	7	5	2	3	1	2	2	1
Berks Downs	Min no Birds	10	7	0	1	0	0	0	7	7	0	1	0
	Number of sites	4	5	0	1	0	0	0	1	3	0	1	0
W Berks	Min no Birds	5	5	8	7	6	2	nc	30	8	3	11	0
Commons	Number of sites	1	1	2	1	1	1	nc	1	1	2	1	0
Other sites	Min no Birds	27	15	6	1	0	1	0	2	14	16	15	11
	Number of sites	13	6	4	1	0	1	0	1	9	11	6	7
ALL SITES	Total no Birds	42	30	47	53	70	48	8	44	41	31	32	13
	Total no sites	18	13	11	8	8	7	2	6	14	15	10	8

East Berks Heaths are Swinley Forest (includes the sites of Caesars Camp, Crowthorne Wood, Wishmoor Bottom and Broadmoor RDA), Wildmoor Heath and Swinley Brickpits. There were no records from Finchampstead Ridges or Gorrick Plantation. The Berkshire Downs sites include 14 widely distributed sites mostly on the Berks/Oxon scarp (from the Compton Downs in the east to Seven Barrows in the west) and with a few on the downland scarp south of Inkpen. West Berks commons include Greenham Com, Snelsmore Com and Crookham Com. 'Other Sites', 25 of them, include all the well watched major wetland sites and a few other sites that are neither heath nor downland e.g. Tickleback Row and Englefield. **Winter/spring passage:** Quite a lot of birds were reported, as the table shows, but they were in small, scattered groups. During Jan and Feb highest counts were 5 at Greenham Com on Jan 4th (JPM) and Feb 22nd (JOB), 4 at Bury Down on Jan 12th (RCr) and 4 at Dorney Wetlands on Jan 7th and Feb 7th (JOB). In March birds started reappearing in their main breeding territory with 4 pairs at Edgebarrow on 7th and 6 pairs at Wishmoor on 16th (DJB). **Summer:** The main breeding area was on the East Berks heaths, where a survey by DJB and PJC located 28 territories, 17 in Swinley Forest with 11 pairs successfully breeding, 9 territories at Wildmoor Heath with 7 pairs breeding successfully and 2 pairs at Swinley Brickpits. At least 31 juveniles were located. The only other confirmed breeding area was Greenham Com, where numerous records of song and pairs included a report of 6 males (5 singing) + 1f on Apr 18th (JPM), followed by reports of a pair feeding young on Jun 29th (JC) and a total of 30+ birds in the area on Aug 4th including 20+ juveniles (JOB). At least 4 pairs seem to have been successful there. There is no compelling evidence to suggest that breeding took place at any other sites although a record of 2ads and 5juvs at Sheepdrove Lambourn on Aug 25th (ABT) may indicate local breeding. A juvenile located at Lavell's Lake on Jun 6th (FJC; ADB) is evidence of early dispersal from breeding grounds. **Autumn passage/winter:** As in the first winter there were numerous reports of 1s and 2s from sites (usually GPs, sewage works, etc) away from the breeding areas. Highest counts in Oct/Nov continued to come from the breeding areas, with 7 in the Wishmoor area on Oct 26th (DJB) and 11 on Greenham Com on Nov 28th (DJB). On other sites, there were 4 at Beacon Hill, Inkpen on Sep 24th (CDRH), 3 at Slough SF on Sep 29th (CDRH), 3 at Strand Water, Cookham on Nov 7th (BDC), 5 at Dorney Wetlands on Nov 12th (CDRH) with 3 there on Nov 30th (JOB) and again on Dec 12th (CDRH).

WHEATEAR *Oenanthe oenanthe*
Common passage migrant and rare summer visitor

182 records came from 54 observers at 43 sites. Where sex was noted, there were 50 males and 47 females in spring and 4 males, 5 females and 9 immature in autumn. There were no records to suggest any attempt to breed in the county. **Spring:** Passage began in early March with singles at wetland sites in East Berks. There were single males at QMR on 6th and 9th, then a female there on 11th (JAS), followed by single males at Dorney Wetlands on 12th and 13th (PMC, JOB). The chart below shows the sum of maxima at all sites through the year. Highest counts were in early May with 9 (5m + 4f) at QMR on 2nd (JAS), 11 (6m + 5f) at Crookham Com on 4th (JPM) and 7 at Greenham Com on 5th (ABT). The total minimum number of spring and autumn birds (117 and 121) was almost the same but 60% of the spring passage passed through in 8 days from Apr 30th to May 7th. **Autumn:** Return passage started on Jul 30th with a single at Combe Gibbet (CDRH) and another at Greenham Com on Aug 3rd (FJC). Highest counts were mostly from QMR, with 5 there on Sep 4th, 7 on Sep 11th, 5 on Sep 21st (all CL) and 5 on Sep 27 (ABT). At Aldworth Down there were 5 on Sep 21st (JOB). Latest records were 1 at Greenham Com on Oct 15th-16th (RAH, GJS) and 1 at QMR on Oct 17 (CL). There was a significant passage of birds exhibiting the characteristics of Greenland Wheatear (*O. o. leucorhoa*) reported from QMR during September, with 1 on 15th, 3 on 21st and 1 on 23rd (CDRH). Elsewhere there was 1 at Inkpen on Sep 24th (CDRH). This was the largest passage of birds considered *Leucorhoa* since 1988. One considered to exhibit these characteristics at Greenham Com on Aug 3rd (GEW) is unlikely to have been of the Greenland race at this early date (Recorder).

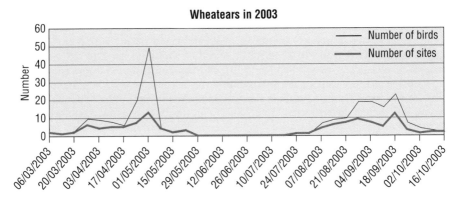

WINTER THRUSHES (FIELDFARE & REDWING)
Turdus pilaris & Turdus iliacus

Common winter visitors

The charts overleaf illustrate the abundance during the first and second winters of the two common species of thrushes that migrate to the UK in winter. The numbers shown in the charts are the sums of the numbers reported throughout the county in each week. Note the difference in scales on the numbers axis when comparing these charts. For more detailed information on the two species reference should be made to the individual species accounts which follow.

In the spring of 2003 the Redwing numbers began reducing earlier than Fieldfare, however, the final sighting for both species was in week ending 27th Apr, usually Redwing depart before Fieldfare. In the autumn of 2003 Fieldfare were reported in small numbers before the arrival of the Redwing, against the usual arrival sequence since Redwing usually arrive before Fieldfare, but the Redwing numbers built up before the Fieldfare numbers built up. Except for Redwing during week ending 5th Jan, which were boosted by a single count of 500 birds at Slough SF, the graphs indicate a reduction in the number of winter thrushes during 2003 compared with 2002. However comparisons are difficult since the reported numbers depend on the efforts of individual uncoordinated observers. The charts indicate that Fieldfare are present in greater numbers than Redwing, but this may be because Fieldfare are more visible and easier to count. Fieldfare tend to form large obvious flocks in open fields whereas Redwing are often found in lightly wooded and suburban habitats as well as in fields, making their total numbers more difficult to count. However the large differences in numbers suggest that there were indeed more Fieldfares.

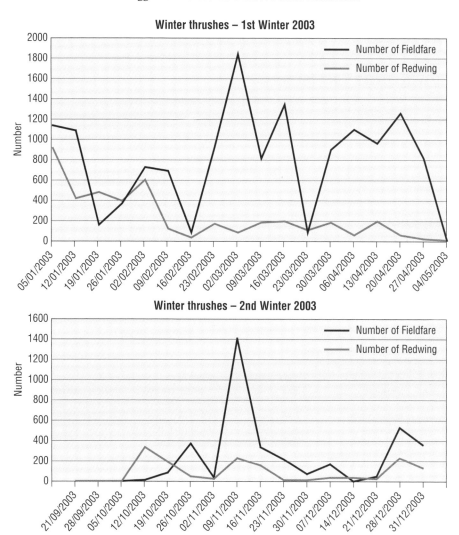

RING OUZEL   *Turdus torquatus*

Scarce passage migrant

Bucking the trend of recent years when records were few and far between, 2003 was the best year for records (7) since at least 1974. All records came during April, this influx being mirrored throughout the Home Counties with a high of 11 at Steps Hill Bucks on Apr 20th. The first Berks record was on Apr 4th when a male was present on Brockhampton Down, Lambourn (JPB). There were no further records until Apr 21st when birds were reported from 3 sites. A popular male was located in the same field at Burnthouse Lane, Pingewood as last year's bird (MO), a female appeared on Greenham Com (RRK; MJD) and an unprecedented spring count of 9 occurred (6m and 3f) at Inkpen Hill (CL) with another male there on Apr 26th (ABT). On Apr 22nd, single males were located at Sheepdrove, Lambourn (JPB) and Sulhamstead (BU) both birds remaining until Apr 25th. The count of 9 at Inkpen Hill is only bettered by a record of at least 30 roosting in Windsor Great Park on Oct 5th 1966.

BLACKBIRD   *Turdus merula*

Abundant resident and common winter visitor

Due to the abundance of this species it was largely overlooked with only 17 observers submitting records. The only counts of note involved 21 in Twyford on Jan 9th (SPA; P Adam) and 15 in a Thatcham garden on Jul 14th (BJE). Only 2 records of confirmed breeding were received, Twyford (SPA) and Cookham (BDC) and there were 2 records of males with partially white plumage, at Sheepdrove (JPB) and Freemans Marsh (RF). Unusually 1 male was in full song at Midgham GP on Dec 7th (RF).

FIELDFARE   *Turdus pilaris*

Common winter visitor, very rare in summer

The graphs above are based on 269 records for 127 sites submitted by 64 Observers, plus an additional 37 Bird Track records for 15 sites. The last reported in the first winter were on Apr 25th when a flock of 300 were seen at Brightwalton flying south (SWi). The first reported in the second winter were at Bowdown Wood, Greenham, where 3 were seen flying over on Sep 26th (RAH). In those weeks where there were counts in excess of 200 the tables show the location of the two highest counts.

First winter

Date W/E	Place	No	Obs	Place	No	Obs
05th–Jan	Englefield	250	RCr	Sheepdrove and at Beenham	200+	ABT/RCr
26th–Jan	Ashampstead	200+	JLe	West Meadows	50+	IW JL
02nd–Feb	Cold Harbour	200+	DJB	Arborfield, Hall Farm	100+	DJB
09th–Feb	Brightwalton	200+	SWi	Ashampstead	c200	JLe
23rd–Feb	Sheepdrove Organic Farm	1000	Birdtrack	Catmore	800	JOB
02nd–Mar	Sheepdrove and Warren Down	650	BDC/BDC	Chapel Green	500	ABT
09th–Mar	Brightwalton	500+	SWi	Sulhamstead	200+	BU
16th–Mar	Brightwalton	1000	SWi	Flocks at Cockmarsh, Binfield and Winnersh	100	DJB/MFW

30th–Mar	Sheepdrove	300	ABT	Streatley (–on–Thames) 134		Birdtrack
06th–Apr	Brimpton	300	GEW	Sheepdrove	200	JPB
13th–Apr	Burnthouse Lane GPs	300	RJB	Woolley Down and at		
				Sheepdrove	100	GDS/JPB
20th–Apr	Burnthouse Lane GPs	330	BU	Pingewood,		
				Burnthouse Lane	300	BMcA
27th–Apr	Brightwalton (In flight)	300	SWi	West Meadows	142	IW JL

Second winter

Date W/E	Place	No	Obs	Place	No	Obs
26th–Oct	Farnborough Down	250	GDS	Burnthouse Lane GPs	35	MGM
09th–Nov	Coombe Hill	500	GDS	Widbrook Common	75	BDC
28th–Dec	Temple	200	DJB	Grazeley, Amner's Farm	100	RJB
to 31st–Dec	Sheepdrove	300	ABT	Boxford	25	JL

SONG THRUSH *Turdus philomelos*
Common resident and winter visitor

A better year for records with birds reported from 89 sites. As usual most counts involved 1-4 birds, higher counts being 5 at Englefield on Jan 5th (JOB), 6 singing at Theale Main GP on Apr 17th (RCr), 6 Ruscombe Floods Apr 19th (DJB), 11 in the Hungerford Newtown area on May 31st (LS), 9 Boxford Com on Jul 7th (JL) and 5-6 dropping into Hawthorns at Thatcham Marsh on Oct 12th (IW; JL). A survey of the East Berks Heaths during Apr-Jun located 43 territories, 20 in Swinley Forest, 12 in Swinley Park, 7 Swinley Brickpits and 4 at Wildmoor Heath (DJB). **Breeding:** Reported from only 5 localities, juveniles were seen at Brimpton on Jun 11th (unfortunately died hitting window) and Jun 29th (GEW), 1 adult feeding young at Cold Harbour on Jun 27th (DJB), 2 ads with 3juvs at Hell Corner Fm Inkpen on Jul 13th (LS), 1 juv at Frogmill on Jul 16th (SJF; FMF) and finally 1 juv at Strand Water on Sep 7th (BDC).

REDWING *Turdus iliacus*
Common winter visitor

Birds were reported frequently in both winter periods (see winter thrushes graphs above). **First winter:** Birds were particularly widespread during Jan with flocks of 200 or more reported from 6 localities. At Slough SF up to 500 were present on 4th (JOB), there followed 200 at Thames Valley Pk on 12th (SH), 200 Frogmill, Hurley on 17th (SJF; FMF), 200+ were seen to go to roost at Lavell's Lake on 17th and 29th (FJC), 250 West Meadows (between Marsh Benham and Kintbury) on 26th (IW; JL) and 2-300 at Arborfield on 29th (DJB). These large flocks had dispersed by Feb with 60+ at West Meadows on 23rd (IW; JL) the only count to exceed 50. Passage was noted in Mar with 91 at Cockmarsh on 11th (DJB) and 100 at Eversley GPs on 29th (IHB) and song was heard at Woolhampton on 18th (JPM). Numbers dwindled in Apr, the last being 4 in fields adjacent to Burnthouse Lane on Apr 21st (BTB). **Second winter:** Return passage began in Oct with 2 over Newbury on Oct 3rd (JL) peaking shortly afterwards when 200+ flew NW over Widbrook Com in 90 minutes on 6th (CDRH). Numbers were lower in Nov-Dec, high counts being 60 at Lavell's Lake on Nov 9th (FJC) and at Grazeley on Dec 28th (RJB).

MISTLE THRUSH *Turdus viscivorus*

Common resident

The status of the Mistle Thrush in Berks is masked by the relatively few records that are received (only 26 known observers submitted records). Nationally this species has undergone a decline, to the extent that it has now been placed on the Amber List and there is no evidence to suggest that this has not been mirrored in Berks. There were six reports of flocks of 10 or greater, all from Jul to Sep. The highest count was 22, reported at Kintbury on Jul 3rd (RRK). Song was reported from Feb 7th (Lower Fm GP: IW; JL). **Breeding:** There were five reports which confirm breeding. On Apr 15th, at King's Meadow Reading, two were seen carrying food to a nest in a poplar tree (AVL); on Apr 23rd, at Brimpton, a juvenile was being fed by 2 adults, while another adult was sitting on a nest in an oak tree (GEW); on Apr 26th a pair were seen collecting food at Hell Corner Fm, Inkpen (LS) and on May 18th one was seen feeding young at Hungerford Marsh (GVW). The aggressive nature of this species enabled a pair to drive 17 Fieldfares from their feeding territory at Midgham GP on Mar 1st (JPM). At Crookham Com two birds noisily defended a berried rowan tree from incomers throughout Nov (JPM) while on 30th Nov, 3 birds were seen trying to gain ownership of a mistletoe laden tree, along with Redwings (SH).

CETTI'S WARBLER *Cettia cetti*

Localised resident in small numbers

Records were received from 15 locations, all but 1 in the Kennet valley. The monthly distribution is shown in the table, these are minimum counts:

	Jan	Feb	Mar	Apr	May	Jun	Jul	Aug	Sep	Oct	Nov	Dec
Thatcham Marsh/Lakes area:												
no of singing males,	6	1	12	13	10	8	2	2	8	9	5	1
+ birds not singing	–	–	+2	+4	–	–	–	+1	–	–	–	–
Other Sites:												
no of singing males,	3	2	1	4	3	12	3	3	2	1	0	1
+ birds not singing	–	+1	+2	+4	+6	+3	+4	+3	+2	-.0	+1	+1
TOTALS NUMBER OF BIRDS	9	4	17	25	19	23	9	9	12	10	6	3

As usual the highest counts all came from the Thatcham Marsh/Lakes area where a maximum of 17 were noted on Apr 6th (JPM). Away from Thatcham no counts of singing males exceeded 3 birds. **Breeding:** This was confirmed at Moatlands GP where a pair reared 2 young (JA). At Thatcham a female with a brood patch was trapped on Jun 14th (IW) and a juv was caught on Jul 5th (IW; JL). For the first time since 1998 birds were reported from East Berks with singles at Wraysbury GPs on Apr 24th (CL) and Nov 6th (CDRH).

GRASSHOPPER WARBLER *Locustella naevia*

Scarce summer visitor and uncommon passage migrant

Records were received from 7 locations. **Spring:** First reported on Apr 21st when there was 1 reeling at Wraysbury (University of London per CDRH) which remained until Apr 24th (MO) and 1 reeling at Hungerford Marsh (Birdtrack) which was heard subsequently on Apr 23rd (JPB), Jun 5th and Jul 22nd (RF). Single reeling birds were also reported from Thatcham Marsh on Apr 23rd and May 7th (RRK), Boxford on Apr 24th (PMC), Stanford Dingley on May 3rd and 31st (BAJC) and Twyford GPs on May 10th (AR). **Autumn:** A f/w was trapped at Thatcham Marsh on Aug 16th (IW; JL) which may have been a product of local breeding. A bird described as a grey morph was located at Brimpton on Aug 17th (GEW).

SEDGE WARBLER   *Acrocephalus schoenobaenus*
Common summer visitor and passage migrant

Records were received from 41 locations. **Spring:** First reported from Dinton Pastures CP on Mar 29th (BTB) and Eversley GPs on Apr 1st (GBr). There were no other records until Apr 12th when the main arrival began and birds were widespread by Apr 17th. Most records involved 1-4 birds with the highest counts of singing males coming from Hosehill Lake with 12 on Apr 17th (RCr), Woolhampton GPs with 10 on May 7th (JPM) and Thatcham Marsh with 15 on May 11th (JPM). **Breeding:** It is likely that breeding occurred at many sites in the county but was only confirmed at Thatcham Marsh where juveniles were regularly caught and ringed from mid June to Sep 7th (IW; JL) and Woolhampton GPs where 5 juvs were ringed on Jul 30th (JPM). A juv at Hosehill Lake on Sep 21st (RCr) as well as some of the later Thatcham birds may have been migrants. **Autumn:** Small numbers were still to be found at several sites in Sep but by Oct singles could only be found at Moatlands GP on 1st (CDRH), Windsor Park on 2nd (CDRH) and finally 1 caught at Thatcham Marsh on 5th (IW;JL).

REED WARBLER   *Acrocephalus scirpaceus*
Locally common summer visitor and passage migrant

Records were received from 28 locations. **Spring/Summer:** The first record for the year was for Thatcham Marsh on Apr 15th (JL). This was the beginning of the main arrival and within the next week birds had been reported from a further 8 sites. High counts at this time included 10+ singing at Brimpton GP on Apr 24th increasing to 16 in song on May 15th (JPM), 22 including 16 in song at Thatcham Marsh on May 3rd (JPM) increasing to 24 singing on May 11th (JPM; IW; JL), 10 Hosehill Lake on May 4th (TGB) and 16 singing at Burghfield Mill GP on May 15th (RCr). High numbers continued to be reported from the main sites with 33 (31 singing) at Thatcham Marsh on Jun 1st (JPM) being the max count. **Breeding:** Reported from 6 sites; at Thatcham Marsh the first juv was seen on Jun 14th (IW; JL) and many more were ringed at this site through the rest of the summer/autumn. Elsewhere 1 ad was feeding a juv at Brimpton GP on Jul 7th (GEW), 12 juvs were ringed at Woolhampton GPs on Jul 30th (JPM), 1ad and 2juvs were located at Widbrook Com on Aug 2nd (BDC), an adult was feeding young at Moatlands GP on Aug 10th (JA) and a pair was feeding juvs at Lower Fm GP from Sep 2nd (SAG). **Autumn:** With most adults having left the breeding grounds by mid Aug, most Sep records involved juvs or f/w birds and reports petered out by the end of the month with only 3 records in Oct. At Thatcham Marsh 5 were caught on Oct 5th and 3 on Oct 12th (IW; JL) the latest date, while at Wraysbury GPs 1 was seen on Oct 11th (CL).

DARTFORD WARBLER   *Sylvia undata*
Resident in small numbers in suitable habitat, rare away from breeding sites

Records were received from 6 locations, all but 1 in East Berks. **W Berks:** All records were for Greenham Com where birds were noted throughout the year. Song was first heard on Mar 2nd (RRK) and high spring counts involved 6 on Mar 31st (AJT) and 5 on Apr 12th (MFW). 2 juvs were located on Aug 3rd (JOB) and a pair with 1 juv on Aug 5th (JPM). **E Berks:** *Jan-Mar:* Reported from 4 sites during the period. In the Swinley Forest birds were present on the MoD heaths of Broadmoor and Wishmoor where high counts of 8 on

Jan 5th (DJB) and 12th (BMA) and 12 on Feb 2nd (DJB) were made and up to 3 (2m, 1f) were present at Caesars Camp (MO). At Wildmoor Heath (probably the best habitat for Dartfords in E Berks), 9 (2prs and 5 singing males) were found on Mar 7th (DJB). *Apr-Jul*: A survey of the East Berks heaths by DJB and PJC located 29-32 territories. In Swinley Forest, 16 territories were found on the MoD lands of Broadmoor and Wishmoor and 2-3 on Crown Estate land in the Caesars Camp area. Elsewhere Wildmoor Heath had 11-13 territories. At least 9 pairs attempted to breed with 7 successful (1 double brooded) including a pair at Caesars camp (rearing 4 young, the first breeding at this site since 1999). Juvs were also seen at Wildmoor and Wishmoor (DJB; PJC). *Aug-Dec*: At Caesars Camp a party of 3-4 birds on Sep 21st included at least 2 juvs (WAN) and were possibly young of a second brood. A high autumn count involved 9 (2 singing) at Broadmoor on Oct 26th (DJB) and a f/w was present at a new site (Swinley Brickpits) on Nov 8th (DJB). Good numbers were still present at Wishmoor in Dec with 10 on Dec 7th (BMA; DJB).

LESSER WHITETHROAT *Sylvia curruca*
Thinly but widely distributed summer visitor and passage migrant

Records were submitted for 56 sites (at least 34 sites holding singing males) for this widespread, but sparse, summer visitor. The earliest records were for Apr 24th when 1 was seen at Wraysbury GPs (CL) and 1 was seen at Hosehill Lake (with 2 there on 26th) (BU). The highest recorded counts were 3 at Twyford GP on Apr 26th (BTB) and 3 at Wraysbury GPs on Sep 19th (DJB); this latter record was also the latest. There were 13 records of 2 birds, the remaining 75 records being of single birds. Indication of breeding success was a juvenile seen at Moatlands GP on Jul 16th (PBT) and a first year bird seen at Kintbury Cress Beds on Aug 17th (RGS). Two immatures seen with a warbler/tit flock on Aug 31st at Dinton Pastures CP (FJC) were probably migrants. A possible indication of the current fortunes of this species comes from Wraysbury GPs where the RRG ringing returns show a 67% decrease in trapped birds on the 2002 figure.

WHITETHROAT *Sylvia communis*
Common summer visitor and passage migrant

Records were received from 75 locations throughout the county. **Spring:** First arrivals occurred on Apr 14th when singles were observed at Dinton Pastures CP (BDC) and Ruscombe (CDRH). Most suitable areas were soon populated with high counts of 17 at Wraysbury GPs on Apr 21st (Birdtrack) and 10 at Southcote Meadows on Apr 22nd (AVL) indicating an influx at this time. By early May the species was clearly widespread and in good numbers with a high of 13 (8s, 2prs +1) noted at Woolhampton GPs May 7th (JPM). **Summer:** On the E Berks heaths 40 territories were located, 32 in Swinley Forest, 2 Swinley Brickpits and 6 on Wildmoor Heath (DJB). At Eversley GPs c13 males held territories (as in 2003) (IHB). **Breeding:** Confirmed at 13 locations most notably in a Farnborough garden where 1pr reared 2 broods of 3y on Jun 15th and Jul 26th (GDS). **Autumn:** Records from Aug onward involved only small numbers, the only double figure count being 10+ at Theale Main GP on Aug 3rd (RCr). By September the species had become scarce with records only coming from 12 sites. Nine at Wraysbury GPs on Sep 5th (RRG) was the highest count and the last report involved 1 at Marsh Meadow, Cookham on Sep 24th (LM) the latest departure date since 1997.

GARDEN WARBLER *Sylvia borin*

Common summer visitor and passage migrant

Birds were reported from 51 locations throughout the county. The earliest record not requiring supporting details was one singing at Theale Main Pit on Apr 13th (DHK) which was followed by a build up of records from Apr 16th from various places including Theale Main Pit, Aldermaston GPs, Dinton Pastures, Gorrick Wood Plantation, Southcote, Eversley GPs, Searle's Lane and Thatcham Marsh. The latest records were for Moatlands GP on Sep 15th (MGM) and Crookham Com on Sep 17th (AJT). The highest count was 8 (6 singing males and a pair at a nest) at Woolhampton GP on May 7th (JPM). It was reported that at least 12 singing males held territory at Eversley GPs, cf 19 last year (IHB). Indication of breeding success was an adult seen with a juvenile at Searle's Lane on Jun 20th (JA) and an adult seen feeding a juvenile at Woolhampton GP on Jul 5th (GEW). The East Berks Heath Survey located 48 territories: 37 in Swinley Forest, 1 in Swinley Park, 5 in Swinley Brickpits and 5 at Wildmoor Heath (DJB).

BLACKCAP *Sylvia atricapilla*

Common summer migrant, and uncommon but regular winter visitor

Winter: As is now expected records were numerous in both winters with a minimum of 87 birds reported from 49 locations, 11 in W Berks, 23 M Berks and 15 in E Berks most from gardens. The table shows the distribution in the winter months (up to Mar 15), broken down into males, females and unsexed birds in the form -/-/-.

Minimum Number of males/females/unsexed	Jan	Feb	Mar	Nov	Dec
W Berks	1/0/0	2/2/1	2/2/1	1/0/0	3/2/0
M Berks	9/3/0	6/3/0	5/3/0	5/3/0	6/2/0
E Berks	6/6/1	3/3/0	4/0/0	3/1/0	6/4/0
TOTAL MINIMUM NO OF BIRDS	26	20	17	13	23

The highest counts during the winter period involved 3f in a Cookham garden on Jan 5th (BDC) and 4 (3m 1f) at the Thames Valley Pk on Nov 30th (SH). **Spring/passage:** Wintering birds remained into March with song heard on Mar 7th at a Finchampstead garden (AFd). What was probably the last wintering record concerned a male that was seen regularly in a Tilehurst garden to Mar 20th (GJSu). A singing male at Horton GPs on Mar 12th (BDC) was probably the first spring migrant and by early April birds were common and widespread with counts of 13m at Burghfield GPs Apr 5th (JA), 14 singing Thatcham Marsh Apr 6th (JPM), 20 Dinton Pastures CP Apr 11th (RRi) and 13 singing at Theale Main GP on Apr 17th (RCr). **Summer:** Survey work in East Berks located 64 territories, 29 in Swinley Forest, 23 in Swinley Park, 10 in Windsor South Forest and 2 at Swinley Brickpits (DJB). Elsewhere at least 8 territories were located on the Moor Green Lakes reserve at Eversley GPs (IHB) and 13 were singing at Moatlands GPs on May 30th (RCr). **Breeding:** Confirmed at Brimpton where 1ad was feeding 2 young on Jun 11th (GEW), a family party was located at Cranes Fm Lambourn on Jun 26th (BDC), 3 juvs at Aldermaston GPs on Jul 18th (JPM) and 1f plus 1juv at Frogmill near Hurley on Jul 27th (SJF; FMF). **Autumn/passage:** Most reports during this period involved 1-10 birds, the only higher counts came from ringing operations. At Wraysbury GPs birds were caught and ringed daily from Aug 30th to Sep 6th and a total of 221 birds were ringed and a further 30 re-trapped, the highest day total being 53/5 on Sep 5th (RRG). Elsewhere 11 were trapped at Woolhampton GPs on Sep 11th (JPM). Passage continued into Nov with 1m at Lavell's

Lake on Nov 13th probably being the last summer bird and with 1m at Caversham on Nov 16th (TGB) probably being the first winter arrival.

YELLOW-BROWED WARBLER   *Phylloscopus inornatus*
Very rare vagrant

Good numbers of this species occurred in SE England during the autumn of 2003 with some birds penetrating inland. This influx was responsible for at least one Berkshire record, a well watched bird at Theale Main GP on Oct 30th (RGB *et al*). [A report of a second bird at Sandhurst on Oct 25th and 27th (TC) was not supported by sufficient detail for acceptance by the Records Committee.] The only previous county record is of one in a garden at Thatcham which was present from Dec 6th 1986 until Jan 7th 1987.

WOOD WARBLER   *Phylloscopus sibilatrix*
Scarce passage migrant and summer visitor

Just two records. The first was on Apr 21st at Upper Basildon where one was singing in young woodland (CMR). The second was of a passage bird seen well (and described) at Dinton Pastures on Aug 9th (J. Tillbrook, Kent).

CHIFFCHAFF   *Phylloscopus collybita*
Common summer visitor and scarce but increasing winter visitor

Winter: Records were received from throughout the county although most reports came from the river valleys. A table showing the winter distribution of birds (with number of sites in brackets) is below:-

Minimum No of Birds	Jan	Feb	Nov	Dec
West Berks	3(3)	5(3)	5(3)	8(4)
Mid Berks	14(7)	10(6)	15(5)	10(4)
East Berks	6(5)	2(2)	14(6)	6(2)
COUNTY MINIMUM	23	17	34	24

First winter: Most counts involved 1-2 birds, the exception being 4 at Sandhurst STW on Jan 3rd (JMC) and 4+ at Bottom Lane Theale on Feb 23rd (IT). A bird probably of the northern race *abietinus* was located at Horton GPs on Jan 7th (CDRH). However, a bird showing characteristics of the Siberian race *tristis* at Bray GP on Jan 12th (CDRH), when heard to call did not give the characteristic sad 'peep' call of *tristis* but the more usual 'hweet' of *P. collybita* showing that the racial identification of Chiffchaffs is far from straight forward. **Spring:** As usual an overlap of wintering birds and new arrivals occurred in early March making it difficult to ascertain when the first spring migrants appeared although 2 singing at Hosehill Lake on Mar 2nd (ABT) and singles at Eversley GPs on Mar 6th (JOB) and Lavell's Lake on Mar 8th (BTB; MFW) would appear to be spring migrants. Birds soon became widespread and very common with high counts of 12 singing at Southcote on Mar 22nd (JLe), 21 singing at Thatcham Marsh on Mar 22nd (DJB) with 14 still singing on May 3rd (JPM), 17 singing at Burghfield GPs on Mar 23rd (RCr) and 15 singing at Dinton Pastures on Apr 15th (RRi). **Summer:** Survey work carried out by DJB located 208 territories; 142 in Swinley Forest, 48 in Swinley Park/Swinley Brickpits area and 18 at Wildmoor Heath. Elsewhere 16 were singing along the K&A canal between Kintbury and Lower Denford on Jun 14th (DR). **Autumn:** Passage commenced during Aug and continued to late Oct- early Nov. There were numerous reports of up to 15 birds, higher counts involved 20+ at Eversley GPs on Aug 23rd (GRa), an astonishing 345 were caught at Wraysbury GPs between Aug 30th and Sep 6th (213 were new birds and 132 were re-traps) (RRG), 20-25 were at Pingewood GPs on Sep 3rd (RCr), 18 Aldermaston GPs on Sep 8th (JPM), 33 caught (plus many others) at Woolhampton GPs on Sep 11th (JPM), 16 ringed at Brimpton GPs on Sep 30th (JPM), 19 Theale Main GP on Oct 5th (RCr) and 30+ at Thames Valley Pk on Oct 13th (SH). **Second winter:** A report of 7 at Burghfield Mill GP on Nov 1st (JPM) was the highest count reported and may have involved both wintering birds and late departing summer visitors. Other counts that exceeded 3 involved 6+ at Wraysbury GPs on Nov 6th with 5+ on Dec 2nd and 14th (CDRH), 4 Bray GP on Nov 25th (DJB) and 5 at the Thames Valley Pk on Dec 14th (ABT). An individual with the characteristics of the northern race *abietinus* was located at Heron Lakes Wraysbury on Nov 9th (CDRH).

WILLOW WARBLER *Phylloscopus trochilus*
Common and widespread summer visitor and passage migrant

Spring: First reported on the slightly earlier than usual date of Mar 23rd with 1 singing at Pingewood GPs (NR) followed by another singing at Twyford GPs on Mar 24th (AR). Birds soon became widespread throughout the county as migrants passed through and residents set up territories. However numbers reported at most sites did not exceed 10 birds at any time the exceptions being 12 singing on Greenham Com on Apr 13th (GDS), 10+ singing at Combe Wood on Apr 18th (IW; JL), 32 singing in Swinley Forest also on Apr 18th (DJB) and 15 singing at Wildmoor Heath on May 13th (DJB). **Summer:** This species was again surveyed on the East Berks heaths and nearby woodlands of the Crown Estate. Results show that a total of 165 territories were located, a decline of 15% on the 2002 total. Additionally 30 territories were located on Wildmoor Heath (DJB). Elsewhere there were no reports that exceeded 5 birds. **Autumn:** Passage began in late July and continued to the end of Sep, but appeared light, high counts being 15+ at Moatlands GP on Aug 7th (RCr), 10+ Dinton Pastures on Aug 10th (BJH) and at Wraysbury GPs, 45 were ringed and 21 re-trapped from Aug 30th to Sep 6th (RRG). Latest departure involved 1 at Eversley GPs on Sep 16th (TC).

GOLDCREST *Regulus regulus*
Common resident and winter visitor

Goldcrests were reported from suitable areas throughout the county although few reports were received for the downland in the NW of the county. For such a familiar bird, it is not surprising that the species was under recorded with only 39 observers submitting records. Most reports involve 1-9 birds with higher counts of 10+ at Wishmoor Bottom on Feb 13th (BMA), 10 Eversley GPs on Mar 1st (BMA), 14 Swinley Forest on May 31st (BMA), 10 Sandhurst STW on Oct 21st (MGM), 20 Burghfield GPs on Nov 13th (RJB) and 15+ at Wishmoor Bottom on Nov 16th and Dec 28th (BMA). **Breeding:** Song was reported from 18 locations and breeding was confirmed at Thatcham Marsh, 1juv on May 31st (ABT); Thatcham, 1 adult was feeding 3 juvs from a garden peanut feeder on Jun 2nd (GJS); Cookham Cemetery, 1 family party on Jun 9th (BDC); South Forest Windsor, 4 family parties numbering 20+ birds on Jun 21st (DJB); Swinley Park, 1 family party on Jun 28th (DJB); Hell Corner Fm Inkpen, 1 family party on Aug 5th (LS) and 1 family party at Strand Water on Aug 29th (BDC). Unfortunately a pair breeding in a fir tree at Frogmill, Hurley failed when the nest was predated and the female killed on May 3rd presumably by a Magpie (SJF; FMF).

FIRECREST *Regulus ignicapilla*

Scarce visitor in all seasons

Although there were fewer reports away from East Berks this year than in 2002, survey results made 2003 the third year in succession that record numbers have been recorded. **First winter:** Just 1 at Eversley GPs on Mar 1st (D J Broadley). **Spring/Summer:** Unusually a female was located on the Ridgeway north of Compton on Mar 29th (ABT) and on the East Berks breeding grounds, 2 males and a female were also located on Mar 29th (DJB). After the success of the 2001-2 surveys, the 2003 Firecrest survey was extended from 3 woodland blocks to 6 and resulted in birds being found in 5 woodland blocks totalling 70 territories of which at least 23 held pairs, the rest singing males. **Breeding:** Confirmed at 4 sites (3 pairs with recently fledged young and 1pr feeding young in a nest c20ft up a Cypress) and was probable at several others where courtship or nest building was observed (DJB). **Autumn/second winter:** Like the first winter, birds were scarce. One was located in Bracknell on Sep 9th (CAW; PJW) and there were 2 reports from Dinton Pastures CP, 1 on Nov 12th (RR) and 1 on Dec 15th (J Barbrook per RR).

SPOTTED FLYCATCHER *Muscicapa striata*

Widespread but thinly distributed summer visitor and passage migrant

Records were received from no less than 68 locations, over half of which were in West Berks. **Spring:** The first record was earlier than the average arrival time with 1 at Dinton Pastures CP on Apr 29th (DNTR) the tenth year there has been an April record since 1974. The main period of arrivals seemed to be between May 3rd and 20th, during which there were counts of 3 at Sulham Woods on May 6th (PMC), 4 singing at Farley Hill on May 8th (DJB) and 3 at Bottom Lane on May 18th (JA). **Summer:** Surveys carried out by DJB revealed 17 territories in Swinley Forest, 7 in Swinley Park, 1 Swinley Brickpits and 4 in South Forest Windsor. **Breeding:** Evidence of breeding came from 14 locations although some later records may have referred to migrant family parties. Confirmed breeding involved 1pr nesting at Bottom Lane Sulhamstead on Jun 9th (TM), 1 nest with 5 eggs on Jun 9th and another with 4 young on Jun 23rd at West Woodhay Lakes (RGS), 1pr feeding young at the nest in South Forest Windsor on Jun 21st (DJB), and 1 nest with 2 young Beech Hill on Jul 14th (JLe). Family parties or juvs were located at Marsh Benham with 2+ juvs on Jul 18th (GDS) and 4+ Jul 19th (IW;JL), 1pr 4juvs near Eversley GPs on Jul 26th (MGLR), 1ad 1juv Brimpton on Jul 27th (GEW) 2ad 6juvs Moor Copse on Aug 5th (JOB), 2ads 3juvs Streatley on Aug 7th (JOB), 1ad 3juvs Crookham Com Aug 12th (GEW), Hosehill Lake Aug 19th (BU), 1 ad + 2 juvs Frogmill Aug 22nd (SJF; FMF). **Autumn:** Passage commenced from late Jul/early Aug and although widespread the only report involving double figures was 10+ at West Woodhay Down on Aug 10th (IW; JL). There were 4 birds at Inkpen Sep 3rd (LS) and 4 birds at Greenham Com on Sep 6th (IW; JL) but the last record was an imm at Woolhampton GP on Sep 24th (GEW)

PIED FLYCATCHER *Ficedula hypoleuca*

Scarce but annual passage migrant and rare summer visitor

As last year, just a single record, of one on return passage at West Woodhay Down Jul 30th, probably an adult, with tit-flock in open woodland (CDRH).

BEARDED TIT   *Panurus biarmicus*

Scarce winter visitor and rare summer visitor

One found at Burghfield Mill GP, Theale by J Holt on Dec 30th was subsequently seen by MO until Dec 31st, by which time it had roamed around other lakes in the immediate area including Moatlands GP and Taxi GP, subsequently remaining in the area until Jan 25th 2004. The second consecutive year for records.

LONG-TAILED TIT   *Aegithalos caudatus*

Widespread and common resident

First Winter Groups: A few small groups were still present early in the first winter season, including 10 at Moor Green Jan 3rd (JOB), 14 at Bray GP Jan 6th, and 22 in three adjacent parties along the Thames towpath at Cliveden Jan 12th (DF).   By Feb birds were more dispersed and several were reported on garden feeding stations, utilising peanuts, fat balls and porridge oats.   **Breeding:** The first record of nesting activity was on Feb 27th at North Street, Theale (RCr), and the last record of breeding activity was of a family party on Jul 18th in Shepherds Meadows (CRW).   An adult was seen gathering feathers from a dead Blackbird in Twyford on May 10th (SPA) whilst a leucistic bird was found at Lakeside Maidenhead Apr 2nd and what was presumed the same bird on Oct 8th (CDRH).   **Ringing:**   RRG ringed a total of 71 at two sites near Windsor, and 122 at Wraysbury GP.   **Second Winter Flocks:**   Autumn post-breeding flocks could be found from Aug 23rd with 20 at Woolhampton (IW, JL), 30 at Cockmarsh Sep 18th (BDC), 50 at Bottom Lane, Theale Oct 5th (DMc, CMc), 30+ Thatcham Marsh Oct 17th (DJB), 63 Theale Main GP Oct 18th (RCr), 150 in four adjacent flocks at Searle's Lane Nov 13th (RJB) and 40 at Eversley GPs on Nov 15th (BMA).

MARSH TIT   *Poecile palustris*

Locally common resident outside E Berks where now uncommon

Records reflected the pattern of recent years with sightings at just over 60 locations, but with 47 of these in West Berks.   Ironically, the number of reports has been significantly higher since it became evident that the species may be declining in the county, with typically only a third as many records being received as a decade ago.   **First winter:**   Half of all records submitted for 2003 came from the first three months of the year, and included 15 sites in West Berks, 4 sites in Mid Berks and 3 in the East which were not subsequently referred to during the breeding season.   This may indicate a greater level of breeding than recorded, or that birds disperse to other sites during winter.   **Breeding:** First indications of breeding came from Woolhampton with a pair observed carrying nest material Apr 7th whilst another was observed collecting food at Crookham May 9th (JPM).   On May 17th a pair were feeding young in a nest in metal gate post near Woolley Fm, somewhat removed from woodland cover (GDS).   Family parties were reported from Hamstead Lock Jun 7th (IW, JL), Bowdown Woods Jun 7th (SAG) and Bowsey Hill (the only East Berks breeding record) on Jun 17th (BDC). Whilst there was only 1 account of birds on garden feeders for Jan-Mar, there were 7 such records for Oct-Dec.   **Ringing:**   Ringing operations included 5 caught at Bagnor Cress Beds Dec 7th (IW, JL) and 3 in Windsor Great Park (RRG).

WILLOW TIT *Poecile montanus*
Uncommon and local resident now confined largely to W Berks

Just 46 records covering 18 locations (of which only 2 were outside West Berks). Although the number of sites was similar to a decade ago, they include 10 locations not recorded from in 1993, so an element of under-recording may be occurring. The Combe Wood area (from where all 6 species of Tit were recorded this year) is generally regarded as one of the strongholds for Willow Tit and indeed 5 males were singing there Apr 18th (IW, JL). Song was also heard at Bagnor Cress Beds Mar 16th (NRGp), at Hamstead Lock Apr 24th (IW, JL) and at Marsh Benham on May 4th (DJB). Most reports were of one's or two's but groups of 4 were noted at Inkpen in March (MJT) and West Woodhay Down Jul 30th (CDRH). There were no confirmed breeding records received and no capture reports from ringing operations (compared to 26 ringed by NRGp in 1982 and 36 in 1983).

COAL TIT *Periparus ater*
Common resident

Of the 37 locations noted, 14 were in East Berks, just 5 in Mid Berks and 18 in West Berks, which reflects the distribution of woodland. **Breeding:** There were no reports of nest box use this year, but breeding was confirmed from 6 sites, including observed mating at Wishmoor Bottom Mar 28th (KC). Food sources utilised at feeding stations included peanuts and fat balls. **Groups:** The only significant counts were of 11 in Crowthorne Woods May 31st (BMA) and 25 at Sulham Woods Oct 28th (JLe). In E Berks, surveys by DJB showed Coal Tits to be easily the commonest tit in Swinley Forest and to be abundant in Windsor Forest and Swinley Park where they were found in all areas of conifer woodland and less commonly in deciduous.

BLUE TIT *Cyanistes caeruleus*
Abundant resident

Records were numerous and widespread, the higher counts including 24 at Swallowfield Apr 26th (BMA), 18 Boxford Com Jun 7th (JL), 25 Sulham Woods Oct 28th (JLe) and 20 at Mount Hill Dec 31st (JL). No nest box accounts were received, the nearest equivalent being a bird seemingly using the 'End of Motorway' sign at J6 of the M4! (MFW). **Ringing:** RRG processed 468 ads, 792 pulli and had 625 re-traps at their Berkshire ringing sites.

GREAT TIT *Parus major*
Abundant resident

Just 9 observers submitted records, but in sufficient numbers to confirm the species, though less numerous than Blue Tits, remains common, at least at the 42 locations covered. The highest counts were of 11 Shurlock Row Feb 18th with 22 there Mar 1st (Birdtrack) and 12 at Boxford Com April 29th (JL). **Breeding:** The only breeding records came from a Twyford garden where a pair produced 3 young (SPA), Quarry Woods, Cookham where a pair had taken over a Tawny owl nest box (BDC) and a similar case on Cockmarsh where a Little Owl box had been commandeered (BDC). **Ringing:** 235 were caught at Berkshire sites, plus 157 re-traps (RRG).

NUTHATCH   *Sitta europaea*

Widespread common resident

Although this species tends to be more obvious and voluble in spring, the 207 records were fairly evenly distributed across both the county and the calendar, with most coming from woodland and perhaps surprisingly, just 8 from gardens. **Groups:** Counts included 10 across Windsor Great Park in January (ABT), whilst 16 territories were located by DJB in Swinley Park between March and June. **Breeding:** Evidence of breeding included a male feeding his mate at a nest hole in Shurlock Row (RAll), mating observed at Combe (BMA), 2 pairs in nest boxes on Snelsmore Com (IW, JL), and an adult feeding young at the nest at Park Wood, Tidmarsh (MDB). Family parties were also noted at Bowsey Hill (BDC), Swinley Park and 2 in Windsor South Forest (DJB). **Ringing:** A bird was ringed at Bangor Cress Beds in Jan with 2 more being caught there in Dec (IW, JL). In E Berks RRG ringed 27 new birds and had 23 re-traps.

TREECREEPER   *Certhia familiaris*

Common resident

Forty two observers submitted 157 records from 59 locations, an increase on last year. **Groups**: Most sightings were of one's or two's but 6 were found in Combe Wood Apr 18th (IW, JL) and also in Crowthorne Woods Jun 1st (PBT). There were also 3 reports of birds found in mixed tit flocks. **Breeding:** Nest-building was observed at Bottom Lane, Theale May 6th (RCr) and a nest was discovered at Wishmoor Bottom in Jul (BMA). A family party was found in Windsor South Forest Jun 7th (DJB). **Ringing:** Activities of NRGp resulted in 1 being re-trapped at Brimpton GP Sep 30th and 1 caught at Thatcham Marsh Oct 12th (IW, JPM, JL). 33 were caught and 3 re-trapped by RRG at 2 E Berks ringing sites.

RED-BACKED SHRIKE   *Lanius collurio*

Former summer visitor, now a rare passage migrant

An adult female on Greenham Com on Aug 3rd-6th (JC *et al*) was the third record for the county in the last 5 years. Typically it showed well for its steady stream of admirers and is the first for West Berks since May 17th 1978 when a male was found at Woolhampton.

GREAT GREY SHRIKE   *Lanius excubitor*

Scarce winter visitor

With birds in each of '98, '99 and the millennium year, a two year gap was at last closed with an adult bird at Brightwalton Feb 17th (SWi); also observed by PBT before dusk.

JAY   *Garrulus glandarius*

Common resident and uncommon passage migrant

Counts of up to 4 birds reported from many sites across the county, with higher counts of 4 together at Lavell's Lake Feb 24th (MFW); 4 at Virginia Water Mar 19th (DF); 6 at Cookham, Strand Water Mar 31st, with 4 there Sep 7th and 3 Oct 9th (BDC); 4 at Hungerford, Newtown May 31st (LS); 4 at Beedon Oct 1st (SAG) and 7 on the north side of Inkpen Hill on Oct 10th (RGS). A party of 5 at the Jubilee River Jun 30th consisted of 2 ad and 3 juv (BDC).

MAGPIE *Pica pica*
Abundant resident

Widespread and common across the county and probably under reported as a result. Flocks of up to 10 were widely reported with higher counts being 12 (comprising 2 family parties) at Thatcham Marsh Jun 1st (JPM); 14 at Ravenswood Oct 10th (BMA); 18 together at Odney Island Cookham Nov 16th (DF) and 25 on the paddocks at Ravenswood Dec 16th (BMA). ABT was "unlucky" to see 13 at QMR Mar 24th and MSFW also counted 13 together in the same tree at Wick Hill Dec 9th. A family party of 2 ads and 2 juvs was observed pursuing a Song Thrush which collided with a window at Hell Corner Fm Inkpen on Jun 14th (LS). While the thrush was dazed the Magpies attacked and killed it before carrying off the corpse.

JACKDAW *Corvus monedula*
Abundant resident

Counts of up to 300 came from several sites, with many records of smaller numbers. Larger flocks seen throughout the year were 500 at Long Lane, Cookham Jan 10th (BDC); 400+ east at Frogmill Jan 14th (SJF, FMF); 500 at Moss End Jan 21st (BDC); c300 near Lower Culham Fm Feb 4th (SJF, FMF); c1500 at Lower Fm GP Feb 16th (JL); 500 with other crows at Shurlock Row Apr 7th (BDC); 600 among sheep at Grazeley Jul 6th (SAG) and 1200+ at Englefield Aug 1st (RCr). The outstanding report was of the spectacular sight of some 5000 birds at the roost by the Kennet Canal at Thatcham Jan 25th (ABT).

ROOK *Corvus frugilegus*
Abundant resident

Reported from relatively few locations, with records from only just over 30 sites. Large flock counts included 250 at Long Lane, Cookham Jan 10th (BDC); 300 at Bury Down Feb 27th (BMA); c400 at Aldworth June 24th (BMA); c150 on the gallops at Compton July 7th (BMA) and the largest flock of 700+ at Englefield Aug 1st (RCr). Records from rookeries reported 12 nests at Kintbury Park (LS), 39 nests near Farnborough (GDS) and 42 active nests in Hungerford Newtown (LS).

CARRION CROW *Corvus corone*
Abundant resident

Reported widely across the county, with counts up to 30 birds. Larger flocks included 200 at Eversley GP Jan 2nd feeding by Longwater Lane (BMA); 250+ at Sandhurst SF Jan 3rd (JMC); c200 at Aldworth Jun 24th (BMA); c110 at QMR Oct 19th (MMc), with 120 there Oct 21st (MMc) and then 256 feeding on exposed banks there Nov 10th (CDRH); c100 at Coley Meadows, Reading Nov 25th (JLe) and 80 at Long Lane, Cookham Dec 25th (BDC). A leucistic bird, the individual seen in 2002 was on the Compton Downs on Feb 25th and what was possibly the same bird on the Lambourn Downs on May 14th (CDRH).

RAVEN *Corvus corax*

Scarce but increasing visitor (breeds in Wiltshire)

2002 Correction – The Walbury Hill and Combe Hill records for Jul 26th refer to the same family party.

2003 Records of this species continue to increase especially in W Berks where neighbouring county populations have consolidated their numbers to such an extent that the first apparent breeding attempt was recorded in Berks for 143 years (see 'Attempt by Ravens to breed in Berkshire' by Bruce Archer). The table shows the increase in records during the previous 10 years.

Year	1994	1995	1996	1997	1998	1999	2000	2001	2002	2003
Number of records	2	0	3	0	2	1	2	5	8	25

First winter: Most reports came from the SW of the county with records from the Combe, Inkpen and Walbury Hills area involving 2 on Jan 24th (DJB) and 25th (ABT), 2 Feb 16th (MFW) 3 on Feb 19th (DDC; G Newport), 2 Feb 21st (BMc; RMc), 1 heard Feb 23rd (FJC) and 1 on Mar 15th (MSt), Mar 16th (BTB) and Mar 30th (CDRH). Elsewhere 1 was noted at Bury Down on Jan 26th (RRi), 1 flew E over Thurle Down on Feb 25th (CDRH) and 2 flew E over Catmore on Feb 26th (CDRH). **Spring/Summer:** Records were more widespread with 1 over Combe Gibbet on Apr 11th (PMC), 2 over Brightwalton Com on Apr 12th (GDS), 1 Greenham Com on May 1st (SWi), 1 Woolley Down on May 17th (GDS) and 1 flying N over Snelsmore Com on Jun 6th (KT). **Autumn/Second winter:** Two were seen over West Woodhay Down on Aug 30th (IW; JL) and a juvenile was located at Combe Bottom the same day (IW; JL) possibly indicating local breeding. There were a further 3 reports from the Combe area in Sep with 2 over Walbury Hill on Sep 20th (AJP), 2 at Inkpen Hill with possibly a third bird present on Sep 24th (CDRH) and 2 in Combe Bottom on Sep 28th (IW; JL). Elsewhere 1 flew NE over Kintbury Cressbeds on Oct 12th (RGS) and 2 were in Hamstead Pk on Dec 25th (DR).

CORVIDS SP.

Mixed flocks of corvids (mostly rooks and jackdaws) were reported from a few locations, including c50 (mostly jackdaws) at Kintbury Cress Beds Mar 3rd, 100 there Jul 31st and 200 Aug 9th (RGS); 600 in a field at Binfield Sep 7th (NA) and 400 at Aldworth Sep 29th (BDC).

STARLING *Sturnus vulgaris*

Common resident and winter visitor, formerly abundant

Widespread reports from over 50 sites around the county. Flocks of over 100 included up to 600 over Reading STW Feb 10th (NA); c300 in flocks around compost at Sheepdrove Organic Fm Feb 14th (JPB); 200 at Dorney Wetlands Aug 17th (JOB); 400 at Lower Fm GP Aug 21st (SAG); 600 at Dorney Wetlands Sep 29th (JOB); at least 200 feeding on stubble north of Maidenhead Oct 6th (BMA); 200 at Strand Water, Cookham Oct 6th (BDC); over 100 at Lavell's Lake Oct 8th (GRa) and c500 disturbed by a peregrine at White Waltham Airfield Nov 5th (DF, BDC). The largest gathering was an impressive flock of c8000 birds going to roost at Brimpton GPs Oct 26th (GEW).

HOUSE SPARROW   *Passer domesticus*

Common but declining resident

Reported from about 50 sites around the county, many close to human habitation including garden sightings. Most counts were in single figures with a few larger flocks. The highest counts included 20 at Beenham Jan 2nd (BMc; RMc); several smaller flocks totalling 50 birds at Cookham Rise Jan 10th (BDC); at least 20 at Sheepdrove Organic Fm Feb 12th (JPB); 25 in a Pinkneys Green garden Jun 22nd increasing to 30 Jun 26th (MJF, LJF); 40 at Cookham Rise Jun 25th (BDC); c15 at Lower Fm GP Aug 9th (IW, JL, SAG), increasing to 35 there Aug 25th (SAG); 22 in a Thatcham garden Aug 31st (BJE) and 20 in the Pinkneys Green garden for the month Sep (LJF).

TREE SPARROW   *Passer montanus*

Formerly a not uncommon resident, now a rare and declining visitor.

There were no summer records and only reports from one location. In the same private area as in 2002 at Cookham Rise 3 were present on Jan 24th, 1 on Nov 27th and 2 there on Dec 10th (CDRH).

CHAFFINCH   *Fringilla coelebs*

Abundant resident and winter visitor

High first winter counts included 200 at Eversley GP Jan 3rd (JOB) and c100 at Hall Fm, Arborfield Jan 15th (DJB). In March the usual influx of migrant finches to Swinley Forest and surrounding areas bought larger than usual numbers of Chaffinches to the area and were reported as being abundant by Mar 16th (DJB) before numbers decreased to more usual totals by early Apr. Second winter flocks included 120 at Long Lane, Cookham Oct 25th (BDC); c60 increasing to 150+ at Coldharbour from Nov 13th to 18th (DJB) and 175+ at Hall Fm, Arborfield Nov 25th (DJB). Elsewhere counts of up to 100 birds come from around 80 sites across the county.

BRAMBLING *Fringilla montifringilla*

Winter visitor commoner in some years than in others

First winter/Spring passage: The year began quietly with only small groups reported during Jan-Feb, the largest being 15+ in Swinley Forest on Jan 12th (A Jupp). One of the largest influxes in recent years occurred during March and was centred on the Swinley Forest and surrounding woodlands. Several flocks of 100-200 birds adding up to c1000 birds were located on Mar 15th (DJB). Further large counts from this area involved 100+ around the Devil's Highway Mar 21st (DJB); a noisy flock of 100 birds at Caesar's Camp Mar 21st (PBT); 100 with Chaffinch and Crossbill at Caesar's Camp Mar 28th (BMA); 350+ in Swinley Park Mar 29th (DJB), with 100+ in the Wishmoor area on same day (PJC), 200+ there the next day (DJB). Birds were noted as being abundant in the Surrey Hill area on Apr 4th and Caesars Camp on Apr 5th (DJB) and remained common in the area to mid Apr (DJB). Elsewhere in the county numbers remained low, 20+ at Gorrick Wood on Apr 15th (PJC) being the highest count. There were no records from Mid Berks and only 2 from West Berks; 3 at Snelsmore Com on Jan 9th (IW; JL), a bird heard from woodland at Walbury Hill on Jan 24th (DJB) and 16 at Ashampstead Common on Mar 15th (CDRH). Latest first winter records were on Apr 21st when 50 were at Swinley Park (DJB), c50 at Hut Hill (DJB) and 2 at Wishmoor (JEM). **Second winter:** Counts included 10 at Searle's Lane GPs Nov 9th (RJB); 50+ near the roost at Remenham Nov 26th (CDRH) and 16 birds in two groups at Long Lane, Cookham (BDC). The earliest second winter record came from Widbrook Com where 2 were seen with Chaffinches Oct 11th (CDRH).

GREENFINCH *Carduelis chloris*

Common, widespread resident and winter visitor

Widely reported throughout the year at locations across the county. **First winter:** The highest counts were c40 at Snelsmore Com on Jan 1st (JW); 20 at West Ilsley Jan 19th (SAG) and 20 in Windsor Great Park Feb 18th (JOB). **Autumn/Second winter:** More widely reported and in higher numbers than in the first winter. Up to 30 were present in SPA's Twyford garden in Sep and 23 in Nov (SPA), 40+ feeding with Goldfinches on a seeded field at Woolhampton GPs Oct 23rd (JPM); 68 at Long Lane, Cookham Oct 25th (BDC); c20 at Woolhampton GPs Nov 10th (JPM); 150+ (much the largest flock reported) at Lowbury Hill Nov 15th (DJB); c50 in Maidenhead Nov 20th (LJF); c30 in a rowan tree at Crookham Com Dec 4th (JPM) and c50 at Brimpton GPs Dec 27th (GEW).

GOLDFINCH *Carduelis carduelis*

Common and widespread resident

First winter: The only flock of note involved 50 in a Crowthorne garden during Jan (BMA). **Breeding:** There were few records confirming breeding although it can be assumed that breeding occurred throughout the county. Juveniles were reported from 5 sites. **Autumn/Second winter:** Post breeding flocks began to appear in Aug. There were about 60 at Dorney Wetlands on Aug 1st (BDC) and 50 still present on Aug 29th (JOB); 50 at Greenham Com Aug 7th (JOB) and c60 there on Sep 26th (RAH). At Woolhampton GPs, 120 were present on Aug 24th (RRK) increasing to 300 on Sep 8th (CDRH) and still c200 (mostly juvs) on Sep 29th (GEW) and Oct 5 (MFW); 60+ at Wigmore Lane GP Aug 28th (JLe) and 50+ nearby at Burnthouse Lane Pingewood on the same date (TABCG); 50+ at Eversley GPs Sep 8th (DJB) and 150+ at Sonning Meadows Sep 20th (ABT).

In December flocks were located at Broadcommon Hurst, 50+ on Dec 11th (DJB); Thatcham, 55 on Dec 19th (GJS) and Thatcham Marsh, 50 on Dec 30th (ABT).

SISKIN   *Carduelis spinus*
Common winter visitor and passage migrant, scarce summer visitor
First winter: Birds were common and fairly widespread throughout the county during this period. Flocks of 50 or more included a max count of 100 at Burghfield GPs (Searle's Lane) on Jan 1st (MFW), c100 Eversley GPs Jan 2nd (BMA), 80 Wraysbury GPs Jan 7th (per Birdguides), 100+ Bottom Lane Theale Jan 11th (RCr), c50 Marsh Benham Jan 24th (DJB), c100 Cranbourne Chase Windsor Jan 31st (CDRH), 80+ Pingewood GPs Feb 1st (JA; RPo), 60 Combe Wood Feb 16th (MFW) and 100 Moatlands GP also on Feb 16th (RJB). Large numbers were noted in Swinley Forest on Feb 24th with several males singing (DJB). **Spring passage:** Although occurring throughout the county, it was in SE Berks where passage was most evident. In Swinley Forest many flocks of varying sizes were reported from early March into April with DJB stating that Siskins were abundant in the area during much of this time. Nearby several hundreds were noted at Swinley Park on Mar 15th (DJB). Numbers declined from early April, the last report outside of SE Berks being 1 at Kintbury on Apr 25th (NRB). **Summer:** Small numbers persisted in Swinley Forest, notable reports being 1 singing at Rapley Lake on May 6th (DJB), 4 Caesars Camp on May 18th (BDC) with 1 over on Jun 13th (DJB), 4 Surrey Hill on May 27th (DJB) and 1 juv near to the Lookout (indicating local breeding) on Jun 2nd (BMA). Elsewhere a female was located at Swinley Park on May 9th with 3 there on May 28th (DJB) and 1 flew over Swinley Brickpits also on May 28th (DJB). An intriguing report concerned a juv that visited a Twyford garden from Jun 9th-16th (SPA). Evidence that a number of pairs bred near Bracknell came from the garden of Mrs J. Cooper near South Hill Park who reported that Siskins came continuously to bird feeders throughout June and July with often 10 or more present including juvs (see inside back cover for illustration by Andrew Cowdell). They finally dispersed in Sept and were replaced by wintering birds from December (Recorder). **Autumn/Second winter:** An early f/juv at a Crowthorne garden on Aug 18th (BMA) was possibly a local bird. Definite migrants were noted from Sep 6th when 10 were located at Hungerford (RGS). Reports increased into Oct but numbers did not reach the same levels as in the first winter, the largest flocks being c70 over the Obelisk Pond Windsor Gt Pk that flew from the direction of Berks on Nov 1st (FJC), c50 at Warfield on Nov 17th (KC), c80 Arborfield Mill on Nov 25th (DJB) and 50 at Thatcham Marsh on Dec 30th (ABT).

LINNET   *Carduelis cannabina*

Locally and thinly distributed resident more widespread and common on passage and in winter
Widely reported, from some 75 sites around the county, spread throughout the year. First winter records included a large flock at Bury Down numbering c250 Jan 10th (DJB), 200 on Jan 11th/12th (JOB, TGB) and 100 on Jan 13th/18th (SWi,: JOB);c100 East Ilsley Jan 10th (DJB); c100 were at Cold Harbour Jan 21st (DJB) and c180 at West Woodhay Jan 22nd (LS). A roost at Lower Fm GPs held c180 Jan 22nd, c300 Jan 24th and peaked at c500 Feb 16th (JL), while there were c130 at Ashampstead Feb 24th (JLe). In the second winter period a flock of 100+ were feeding on rape stubble near Farnborough Down Sep 12th building up to 128 on Sep 17th and c150 Sep 25th (GDS). Elsewhere a flock at Cold Harbour increased from c150 Oct 4th (MSFW) to c200 Oct 6th (DJB); there were 100 at Strand Water, Cookham Oct 6th increasing to 150 Oct 9th (BDC); 160+ at Englefield Oct

15th decreasing to 51 by Nov 15th (RCr) and 100 at Bury Down Nov 14th (GJS). Evidence of breeding came from Greenham Com, nest building on Apr 18th and juvs in Aug (JPM), Twyford where a juv presumably of local origin visited a garden on Jun 24th-28th (SPA) and Brimpton GP, a pr feeding young on Jul 21st (GEW).

LESSER REDPOLL   *Carduelis cabaret*

Locally common passage migrant and winter visitor formerly a sporadic breeder

Reported from about 50 sites where suitable habitat is to be found. **First winter:** Numbers were low with double figure counts only reported from Eversley GPs with 10 on Jan 8th (RR), c15 Bottom Lane Theale on Jan 11th (RCr) and 12+ there on Feb 2nd (JA; RPo), 10 Twyford GPs Jan 16th (MFW) and 10 Wishmoor Bottom Feb 27th (KC). **Spring passage:** The first report of what was probably passage occurred at Greenham Com where c30 were present on Mar 13th (JPM). Like the Siskin, passage was most evident in the woodlands of SE Berks where numbers gradually built up in Swinley Forest from mid Mar with flocks in excess of 100 birds regularly encountered throughout the forest by late Mar/early Apr and noted as abundant on Apr 4th (DJB). Elsewhere there were 200+ at Swinley Brickpits and 150+ at Swinley Pk on Mar 29th (DJB), 50+ Windsor South Forest Apr 12th (DJB) and 50+ at Gorrick Wood plantation Apr 15th (PJC). Numbers declined during April, the only May reports being 7 Wishmoor Cross on 7th (DJB), 1-2 over Wildmoor Heath on 13th (DJB), 3 over Emmer Green on 24th (ABT) and 1 over Wishmoor Bottom on 30th (DJB). **Autumn/Second winter:** Passage commenced on Oct 5th when singles were reported at Eversley GPs (RJG) and Thatcham Marsh (IW; JL). Birds were slightly more numerous than in the first winter, largest flocks being c30 Kintbury Cressbeds Oct 26th (RGS), 20 Lavell's Lake Nov 8th (FJC) and 15 at Sandford Lake Dinton Pastures Nov 19th (MFW) probably belong to the Lavell's flock.

MEALY REDPOLL   *Carduelis flammea*

Rare winter visitor

Three birds at Thatcham Marsh Oct 25th with the characteristics of Mealy Redpoll were watched at close range for a good period (ABT).

CROSSBILL   *Loxia curvirostra*

Regular winter visitor in variable numbers and occasionally breeds

Sightings reported throughout the year, with the majority being in the first winter period, but continuing through May and in smaller numbers through the summer, when juvenile birds were seen in the flocks. Most sightings came from the woodland areas around Bracknell and Ascot, with flocks numbering well over 100 birds. Specific reports included 130+ at Swinley Brickpits Mar 1st, Mar 15th and similar number Mar 29th (DJB); 150+ at Devil's Highway Mar 21st (DJB); 100+ in Wishmoor Bottom area Mar 29th (PJC), with 165+ in same area the next day (DJB).In April breeding was confirmed within the Swinley Forest when a male was observed feeding a recently fledged juv on Apr 17th (DJB). Sightings continued through May with c175 at Swinley Park (including 2 juv) May 4th (DJB) and c200 birds reported in Swinley Forest at Caesar's Camp and Devil's Highway May 10th (DKP; MFW). In the same area juv birds were present among flocks of 60+ and 55+ on May 27th and 29th and on Jun 13th a party of 32 birds included 12 juv (DJB). A flock of 20 in High Standinghill Woods Windsor May 31st included two family parties, 5 juvs seen begging for food (DJB).

Elsewhere in the county 2 were at Simons Wood, Finchampstead Mar 17th (TGB); 50+ at Gorrick Wood Plantation Mar 21st (KCr); 11 over Burnthouse Lane GP Apr 1st (MGM); 4 at Snelsmore Com Apr 12th (ABT) and 7 at Walbury Hill Jul 1st (ABT). There were many fewer sightings from second winter period with largest count being a total of c50 birds in Wishmoor area Nov 16th (WAN).

BULLFINCH *Pyrrhula pyrrhula*

Common and widespread resident, occasional passage migrant

Widely reported throughout the year, normally single birds or small parties of up to 5 birds, both male and female. Higher counts included 7 at Theale Main Pit Jan 5th (JOB); 6 at Shurlock Row Jan 5th (RAll); 7 together on Compton Downs Jan 6th (ABT); 6 at Thatcham Marsh Jan 10th (DJB); 6 at feeding station Hosehill Lake Apr 1st (BU); 6 at Lavell's Lake May 6th (TOA); 5 at Theale Main Pit Aug 5th including 1 juv (RCr) with 12 (the highest count) there Oct 18th (RCr). Evidence of breeding came from 7 locations, 6 involved sightings of juvs and 1 of nest building.

HAWFINCH *Coccothraustes coccothraustes*

Now a scarce winter visitor which may no longer be resident

The individual located in Windsor Great Park on Dec 31st 2002 remained into 2003 being seen intermittently feeding on Hornbeam seeds by MO until Feb 18th (JOB). The only record for the year.

LAPLAND BUNTING
Calcarius lapponicus

Rare winter visitor and passage migrant

One of this species (a juv or f/w) was located at QMR Oct 4th (ABT *et al*) (interestingly at the same site and similar date as 1 reported in 2002, when a f/w bird was at QMR Oct 2nd). A second bird was found on stubble near to Widbrook Com, Cookham on Oct 6th (CDRH *et al*).

SNOW BUNTING
Plectrophenax nivalis

Rare winter visitor

1 f/w female was found at QMR Dec 2nd (CDRH *et al*). The first record since 1999 it proved to be a popular diversion for observers visiting the site to see the Storm Petrel.

Hawfinch by Tony Keene

YELLOWHAMMER   *Emberiza citrinella*

Common resident and winter visitor

Reported from over 70 sites around the county throughout the year, mainly from the downland areas, including a flock of c50 at Bury Down from mid Jan until into Feb at least (MO); 30+ at Ashampstead Jan 21st (JLe); 50 at West Ilsley Mar 2nd (JOB); 65 at Sheepdrove Mar 18th (BDC); 14 near Aldworth Aug 25th (TGB) with 20+ in same area Nov 1st (DJB). Highest counts away from the downs were 30 with Chaffinches feeding on stubble at Ufton Nervet Jan 18th (KEM) and c85 at Long Lane, Cookham Dec 27th (BDC). **Breeding:** Birds were reported from 33 locations during May/June with at least 22 holding singing males. However the only confirmed breeding record came from Brimpton where a female was feeding young on Jul 12th and 1pr with 4 juvs on Sep 15th (GEW).

REED BUNTING   *Emberiza schoeniclus*

Locally common but contracting resident and locally common passage migrant

Widely distributed where there is suitable wetland habitat, with reports from some 80 sites mainly of 1 or 2 birds. Outside the breeding season larger counts were reported. **First winter:** A flock of 18 was at Colnbrook Meadows Jan 18th (DR); a flock at the feeding station at Woolhampton GPs numbered 25+ Jan 18th and peaked at c30 Feb 24th (JPM); 20+ were reported at Hosehill Lake Feb 28th (BU) with 15+ there Apr 1st (BU) and 20 in a mixed flock with Yellowhammers at a Wokingham site Apr 2nd (KCr). **Summer:** Singing males were reported from several sites and 7 territories were identified at Wildmoor Heath (DJB). In the Searles Lane, Moatlands and Southcote area a nationally significant total of 92 pairs were located (TABCG). **Second winter:** 32 were feeding in a set-aside strip at Engelfield Oct 5th where numbers up to 18 were recorded on several dates until Dec 27th (RCr); 11 (mostly fem) were ringed at Brimpton GP Reedbed Nov 13th and 20+ were at Remenham Nov 26th (CDRH).

CORN BUNTING   *Emberiza calandra*

Common but increasingly local resident and locally common winter visitor

Given the view that this bird is in decline nationally it is encouraging to report sightings in the county from around 30 sites, primarily downland areas with a number of singing males in evidence. Outside of the breeding season, the year started and ended with some of large counts. The year started with 130 at Bury Down Jan 12th (CDRH); 60+ (in two flocks) at Compton Downs Feb 21st (DJB); 56 on wires near Farnborough Down Feb 23rd (GDS); 60+ at Bury Down Feb 27th (BMA); 35 over the observer's house at Farnborough Down Mar 1st (GDS); 30 at Sheepdrove Mar 18th (BDC) and breeding season reports of 20 at Weathercock Hill May 4th (ABT) and 15 at Sheepdrove Jun 25th (BDC). The year ended with reports of 50 in a mixed flock at Bury Down Dec 8th (BMA) and a high count of c200 at Sheepdrove Fm Dec 31st (ABT) the largest reported flock in Berks since 260+ were located at Slough SF on Jan 20th 1979. Away from the Downs, birds were recorded at only 6 locations with all but 2 referring to single individuals seen on just 1 date. The exceptions were Engelfield where one sang from May 1st-4th (RCr) and the Cold Harbour area between White Waltham and the A4 where this species holds on in decreasing numbers and although present all year the highest counts reported were 7 on Jan 26th (BAJC) and 5 singing during Apr/May (DJB). There were no confirmed breeding records anywhere in Berks.

ESCAPES AND HYBRIDS

ESCAPES

Black Swan *Cygnus atratus*
Records were received from 12 locations throughout the county. Most records involved 1-2 birds, higher counts being 4 at Wraysbury GPs on Jul 27th and 3 there on Sep 27th (CDRH), 3 Windsor Park on Oct 2nd (CDRH) and at the aptly named Black Swan Lake, Dinton Pastures, numbers built up during the autumn and peaked at 5 in Nov (LM *et al*) before declining during Dec.

Lesser White-fronted Goose *Anser erythropus*
One adult Theale GPs on Aug 29th (DKP) to at least Oct 16th (RCr).

Chinese Swan Goose *Anser cygnoides*
Three were reported from Mill Pond Bracknell (a regular site for this species) on Jan 3rd (MFW) and 1 was paired with a Canada Goose at Padworth Lane GP from Feb 15th to at least Mar 29th (MFW)

Bar-headed Goose *Anser indicus*
Records were received from 20 locations, mostly in NE Berks. The table shows the monthly site distribution:-

	Jan	Feb	Mar	Apr	May	Jun	Jul	Aug	Sep	Oct	Nov	Dec
Number of sites	4	3	2	3	0	1	3	5	5	3	3	3
Maximum no of birds	12	9	4	4	0	6	3	9	17	*17	10	*18

* Involves a group of 8-9 birds that were seen at 2 locations during the month.
Most reports involved 1-4 birds, but there were 6 at Bisham on Jan 31st (CDRH) and Feb 11th (LM), 6 Lower Fm GP on Jun 6th (RF). Between Maidenhead and Cookham, 10 were located at Summerleaze GP on Sep 26th (CDRH), of which 8 were relocated nearby on fields adjacent to the R Thames on Oct 1st (LM) and seen on several dates in Nov-Dec (DF) before moving to Odney Island Cookham where 9 were present on Dec 24th (DF). Where aged all birds were adults.

Ross's Goose *Anser rossii*
The 2002 adult remained in the NE of the county, being reported from Cockmarsh on Jan 6th (CDRH), Bisham on Feb 10th (CDRH), the R. Thames at Spade Oak on Feb 11th (LM) and Summerleaze GP on Mar 23rd (BDC). Further sightings occurred in the Summerleaze GP/Cookham Rise area in late summer into early autumn with the bird being seen on several dates from Jul 31st (CDRH) to Sep 28th (BDC).

Ruddy-headed Goose *Chloephaga rubidiceps*
Two of this rare South American species were located at Twyford GPs on Dec 5th (CDRH).

Muscovy Duck   *Cairina moschata*
One was present on the Spade Oak reach of the Thames on Mar 22nd (LM).

Wood Duck   *Aix sponsa*
At Whiteknights Lake 5 were reported on Jan 11th (MBu) then 6 on Jan 26th (JJW) and 4 (2m, 2f) on Feb 11th (MBu). A drake was seen on the R. Dunn at Hungerford on Mar 6th (RGS) and Apr 18th (MSt) and a female visited Lavell's Lake briefly on Apr 16th (BMc; RMc). Four drakes were on Whiteknights Lake on May 20th (MBu) and what may have been the one female made an extended visit to Lavell's Lake from Aug 1st (MFW; LM) to Oct 1st (MBu; MFW). A pair was located at Maiden Erleigh Lake on Aug 2nd (I D Paine), 1 was reported from Lower Fm on Aug 30th (JLS) and finally 5 (3m, 2f) were on Maiden Erleigh Lake on Nov 14th (LM).

Chiloe Wigeon   *Anas sibilatrix*
A drake at Brayfield Farm on Mar 9th (CDRH)

White-cheeked Pintail (Bahama Pintail)   *Anas bahamensis*
One was reported from Twyford GPs on Aug 25th (MFW).

Rosy-billed Pochard   *Netta peposaca*
A male and female on Muddy Lane GP on Jan 14th (GJS)

HYBRIDS

Bar-headed x Greylag Goose
One Windsor Great Park on Aug 14th (CDRH).

Emperor x Canada Goose
One Cockmarsh on Jan 6th (CDRH).

Emperor x Snow Goose
One Bisham on Mar 28th (CDRH)

Canada x Greylag Goose
One Pingewood GPs on Apr 25th (MFW) was followed by 1 at Dinton Pastures CP on Apr 26th to May 19th and again on Sep 3rd (MFW) and 6 juvs (with parents) on the Thames at Frogmill Hurley on Sep 16th to Oct 31st (SJF; FMF).

Canada x Farmyard Goose
Two on the Thames at Frogmill on Jul 15th and Oct 21 (SJF; FMF).

Mallard x Gadwall
The 2002 male returned to Wraysbury GPs, being reported on Nov 10th and 23rd (CDRH).

Teal x ?
A male was located at Lower Fm GP on Oct 16th (LM).

Pochard x Ferruginous *Aythya Hybrid*
A female first reported as a Ferruginous Duck was located at Bray GPs from Oct 14th into 2004 (MO). Another, this time a male appeared at Burghfield Mill GP on Oct 31st (CDRH) and Nov 1st (JPH).

Pochard x Tufted *Aythya Hybrid*
A female was present at Burghfield GPs on Feb 7th (PBT) and Mar 16th (PBT; MFW). What may have been this bird returned to the Theale area in the second winter with sightings at Moatlands GP from Oct 19th to Dec 17th (PBT *et al*). Further east 2 birds were located at Wraysbury GPs on Nov 10th, a male on Silverwings Lake and a female on Heron Lake (CDRH). Single males of the 'Lesser Scaup-type' were found at Brimpton GPs on Jan 28th (GEW) and Heron Lake Wraysbury on Apr 1st and 8th (CDRH).

Tufted x ?
A male was located at Moor Green Lakes, Eversley GPs on Feb 3rd (BMA).

Peregrine Hybrid
An escaped juvenile (wearing Jesses and aireal) appeared at QMR on Nov 25th (CDRH).

Glaucous x Herring Gull
In the QMR gull roost a 1st summer was located on Apr 16th and there were two 1st summers (siblings?) present on Apr 17th (CDRH).

Garganey, Moor Green Lakes – Gary Randall

Pectoral Sandpiper, Moor Green Lakes – Mike McKee

Caspian Gull, Queen Mother Reservoir – Mike McKee

Knot, Queen Mother Reservoir – Dave Rimes

Earliest and Latest Dates of Summer Migrants

SPECIES	ARRIVALS			DEPARTURES		
Hobby	Apr 13	Cookham Rise	BDC			
		Thatcham Marsh	JPM	Oct 7	Brimpton GPs	GEW
Little Ringed Plover	Mar 3	Eversley GPs	KBB	Sep 25	Greenham Common	GEW
Common Tern	Mar 26	Eversley GPs	BMA			
		Dinton Pastures	PBT	Oct 8	Searle's Lane GPs	JA,RCr
Turtle Dove	Apr 29	Ruscombe	CDRH,DJB			
		Theale GPs	RCr	Sep 24	Brimpton GPs	GEW
		Woolhampton GPs	JPM			
Cuckoo	Apr 12	Inkpen	LS	Aug 19	Queen Mother Res	CL
Nightjar	May 7	Wishmoor Bottom	DJB	Aug 8	Caesar's Camp	BMA
		Snelsmore Com	CDRH			
Swift	Apr 18	Pingewood GPs	JA	Sep 11	Slough SF	CDRH
Sand Martin	Mar 8	Lower Farm GP	DCr,JC	Oct 24	Dinton Pastures	PBT
Swallow	Mar 30	Woolhampton GP	GRa	Nov 16	Searle's Lane GPs	JA
House Martin	Mar 21	Reading	SHa	Oct 19	Thatcham Marsh	IW,JL
Tree Pipit	Mar 16	Swinley Forest	JOB	Aug 23	Eversley GP	IHB
Yellow Wagtail	Mar 25	Queen Mother Res	JAS	Dec 17	Wokingham SF	DJB
Nightingale	Apr 5	Searle's Lane GPs	JA	Aug 20	Burghfield GPs	KBW
Redstart	Apr 12	Lavells Lake	MO	Oct 10	Wraysbury GPs	CDRH
Whinchat	Apr 18	Lower Farm GP	MJD,RRK	Sep 26	Greenham Common	RAH
						SCC
Wheatear	Mar 6	Queen Mother Res	JAS	Oct 17	Queen Mother Res	CL
Grasshopper Wblr	Apr 21	Wraysbury GPs	CDRH			
		Hungerford Msh	Birdtrack	Aug 17	Brimpton	GEW
Sedge Warbler	Mar 29	Dinton Pastures	BTB	Oct 5	Thatcham Marsh	IW JL
Reed Warbler	Apr 15	Thatcham Marsh	JL	Oct 12	Thatcham Marsh	IW JL
Lesser Whitethroat	Apr 24	Wraysbury GPs	CL			
		Hosehill Lake	BU	Sep 19	Wraysbury GPs	DJB
Whitethroat	Apr 14	Dinton Pastures	BDC			
		Ruscombe	CDRH	Sep 24	Cookham	LM
Garden Warbler	Apr 13	Theale	DHK	Sep 17	Crookham Common	AJT
Wood Warbler	Apr 21	Upper Basildon	CMR	Aug 9	Dinton Pastures	JT
Willow Warbler	Mar 23	Pingewood GP	NR	Sep 16	Eversley GPs	TC
Spotted Flycatcher	Apr 29	Dinton Pastures	DNTR	Sep 24	Woolhampton GP	GEW

Latest and Earliest Dates of Winter Migrants

SPECIES	DEPARTURES			ARRIVALS		
Golden Plover	Apr 26	Hungerford	RSm	Aug 10	Lower Farm GP	JCh,RRK
Rock Pipit	Mar 14	Queen Mother Res	JAS	Sep 26	Queen Mother Res	CDRH
Fieldfare	Apr 25	Brightwalton	SWi	Sep 26	Bowdown Wood	RAH
Redwing	Apr 21	Burnthouse Lane GP	BTB	Oct 3	Newbury	JL
Brambling	Apr 21	Swinley Park	DJB			
		Wishmoor area	DJB,JEM	Oct 11	Widbrook Common	CDRH
Lesser Redpoll	May 30	Wishmoor Bottom	DJB	Oct 5	Thatcham Marsh	IW,JL
					Eversley GP	RJG

CONTRIBUTORS TO THE SYSTEMATIC LIST

AA	A Absolum	DF	D Fuller	JCh	J Chivers
ABT	A B Tomczynski	DHK	D H Kelway	JD	J Dellow
ACo	A Cox	DHu	D Hunt	JEM	J E Mitchell
AD	A Donaldson	DJB	D J Barker	JEW	J E Warren
ADB	A D Bassett	DJW	D J White	JG	J Goodey
AFd	A Ford	DKP	D K Parker	JH	J Haseler
AG	Anstace Gladstone	DL	D Long	JJW	J J Walling
AHo	A Horscroft	DMc	D McEwan	JK	J Knibbs
AJ	A Jupp	DNTR	D N T Rimes	JL	J Legg
AJM	A J Murray	DR	D Rear	JLa	J Langham
AJP	A J Parkes	DRH	D R Hobley	JLe	J Lerpiniere
AJT	A J Thomas	DTu	D Tulley	JLS	J L Swallow
AM	A Male	ED	E Dudley	JMC	J M Clark
ANS	A N Stow	EW	E Weyman	JO	J Overall
AR	A Rymer	FJC	F J Cottington	JOB	J O'Brien
ARE	A R Evans	FMF	F M Farnsworth	JPB	J P Ball
ARo	A Roberts	GBe	G Berry	JPH	J P Holt
AVL	A V Lawson	GBr	G Brookes	JPM	J P Martin
BAJC	B A J Clark	GDS	G D Scholey	JSte	J Stewart
BB	B Beglow	GEW	G E Wilson	JStr	J Stratton
BCu	B Curtis	GG	G Grey	JTi	J Tilbrook
BDC	B D Clews	GGl	G Glomber	JW	J Wilding
BF	B Fitzpatrick	GJS	G J Stewart	JWi	J Winter
BJE	B J Emms	GJSu	G J Sumner	KBW	K B Wills
BJH	B J Hollands	GLa	G Langsbury	KC	K Chard
BMA	B M Archer	GM	G Mundy	KCr	K Creed
BMc	B McCartney	GRa	G Randall	KEM	K E Moore
BTB	B T Bennett	GRW	G R Webb	KIT	K I Tubb
BU	B Uttley	GS	G Selman	KJ	K Jenks
BUp	B Upton	GU	G Ugland	KL	K Langton
CAB	C A Briggs	GVW	G V Wordley	KPa	K Panchen
CAW	C A White	HE	H Edwards	KS	K Spring
CC	C Clark	HFM	H F Matthews	KT	K Tomey
CCH	C C Humphrey	HMC	H M Clews	LCo	L Cooper
CDRH	C D R Heard	HMG	H M Goodship	LFor	L Forster
CL	C Lamsdell	HRN	H R Netley	LGa	L Gabrielson
CMc	C McEwan	ICB	I C Bell	LJF	L J Finch
CMR	C M Robinson	IDP	I D Paine	LM	L Matthews
CN	C Nock	IF	I Farquhar	LRB	L R Blundell
CRe	C Reeve	IT	I Twyford	LRL	L R Lewis
CRP	C R Poole	IW	I Weston	LS	L Staves
CRW	C R Wilson	JA	J Andrews	MASa	M A Sales
DBM	D B Marsh	JAns	J Anstis	MBa	M Batchelor
DBo	D Bowtell	JAS	J A Simpson	MBo	M Booth
DBra	D Brazier	JAtk	J Atkinson	MBu	M D Budden
DCr	D Crispin	JBr	J Brown	MC	M Collings
DDC	D D Callam	JBu	J Buchanan	MCo	M Coon
DE	D Edwards	JC	J Crispin	MDD	M D Dowty

122

MDL	M D Lenney	PMC	P M Cropper	RSJ	R S Jacobs
MES	M E Stacey	PML	P M Lamsdale	SAG	S A Graham
MFW	M F Walford	PMO	P M Olive	SCC	S C Coulson
MGM	M G McCarthy	PRai	P Raisey	SCol	S Colgate
MHo	M Holmes	PRB	P R Blackford	SDi	S Dimond
MHu	M Hunt	PSk	P Skinner	SdT	S de Tute
MJ	M James	PWr	P Wright	SE	S Edwards
MJD	M J Dear	RAd	R Addison	SFu	S Furey
MJF	M J Finch	RAdn	R Adnams	SGa	S Gabrielson
MJM	M J Mitchell	RAH	R A Haynes	SH	S Hughes
MJS	M J Smith	RAL	R A Lyle	SHa	S Harney
MJT	M J Taylor	RAll	R Alliss	SHe	S Heffer
MM	M McQuaid	RAn	R Andrews	SJF	S J Farnsworth
MMc	M J McKee	RAns	R Anstis	SJo	S Jones
MMcM	M McManus	RB	R Bayton	SMe	S Meads
MR	M Raper	RBal	R Baldock	SP	S Pavlou
MRa	M Railton	RCl	R Clark	SPA	S P Adam
MSFW	M S F Whitaker	RCr	R Crawford	SPo	S Poole
MSi	M Simmons	RCW	R C Watts	SR	S Runnacles
MSt	M Stuttard	RDa	R Dawson	SRi	S Ricks
MTu	M Turton	RDi	R Dinnadge	SRo	S Roby
MTuc	M Tucker	RDr	R Dryden	SW	S Weeks
NA	N Adam	RF	R Frankum	SWe	S Welch
NCh	N Charles	RFu	R Fuller	SWh	S Whyte
NJD	N J Dalton	RFug	R Fuge	SWi	S Wilson
NJMo	N J Montegriffo	RG	R Gibbs	TAl	T Allerton
NR	N Rampton	RH	R Hutchins	TBa	T Barnes
NRB	N R Blissett	RHo	R Howe	TC	T Crompton
NRG	N R Godden	RHS	R H Stansfield	TF	T Finnegan
NS	N Stow	RIn	R Innes	TGB	T G Ball
PA	P Adam	RJ	R Jakubowski	TH	T Hemmett
PB	P Burton	RJB	R J Burness	TM	T Marlow
PBa	P Bamford	RJG	R J Godden	TOA	T O Alexander
PBT	P Bright-Thomas	RJH	R J Hardie	TPo	T Powell
PBy	P Bysshe	RJS	R Smith	TS	T Sweetland
PDT	P D Tilbury	RLe	R Lee	VFo	V Forster
PG	P Gipson	RMc	R McCartney	VH	V Hassel
PGr	P Green	RMH	R M Hand	WAN	W A Nicoll
PH	P Hickman	RMu	R Murfitt	WAS	W A Stacey
PIn	P Ind	RPo	R Povey	WG	W Gordon
PJC	P J Crowley	RR	R Reedman	WM	W Miles
PJO	P J Orr	RRi	R Righelato	WP	W Pope
PJSi	P J Simpson	RRK	R R Keel		
PJW	P J White	RRo	R Royle		

Where few records were supplied by some observers their names appear in full in the relevant species accounts. Where several observers report the same bird(s) the letters (MO) are used. Records were also received from the following sources for which we are very grateful: Birdguides (BG), Bird Line South East (BLSE), Bird Track, Newbury Ringing Group (NRGp), Moor Green Lakes Report, (MGLR), Rare Bird Alert (RBA), Theale Area Bird Conservation Group (TABCG).

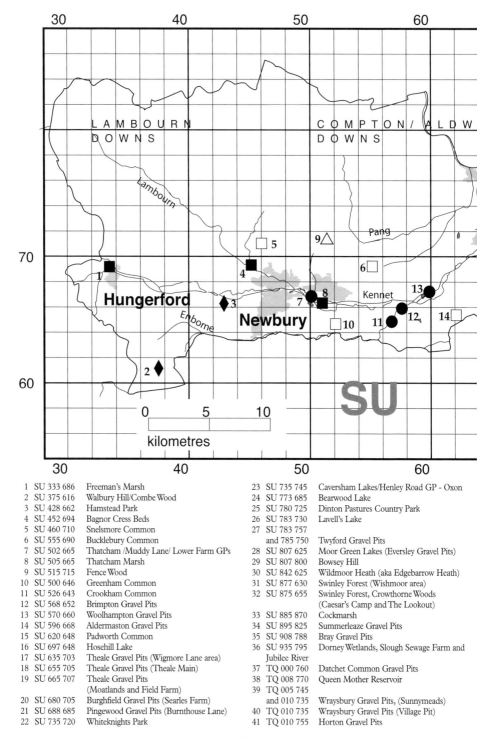

1	SU 333 686	Freeman's Marsh
2	SU 375 616	Walbury Hill/Combe Wood
3	SU 428 662	Hamstead Park
4	SU 452 694	Bagnor Cress Beds
5	SU 460 710	Snelsmore Common
6	SU 555 690	Bucklebury Common
7	SU 502 665	Thatcham /Muddy Lane/ Lower Farm GPs
8	SU 505 665	Thatcham Marsh
9	SU 515 715	Fence Wood
10	SU 500 646	Greenham Common
11	SU 526 643	Crookham Common
12	SU 568 652	Brimpton Gravel Pits
13	SU 570 660	Woolhampton Gravel Pits
14	SU 596 668	Aldermaston Gravel Pits
15	SU 620 648	Padworth Common
16	SU 697 648	Hosehill Lake
17	SU 635 703	Theale Gravel Pits (Wigmore Lane area)
18	SU 655 705	Theale Gravel Pits (Theale Main)
19	SU 665 707	Theale Gravel Pits (Moatlands and Field Farm)
20	SU 680 705	Burghfield Gravel Pits (Searles Farm)
21	SU 688 685	Pingewood Gravel Pits (Burnthouse Lane)
22	SU 735 720	Whiteknights Park

23	SU 735 745	Caversham Lakes/Henley Road GP - Oxon
24	SU 773 685	Bearwood Lake
25	SU 780 725	Dinton Pastures Country Park
26	SU 783 730	Lavell's Lake
27	SU 783 757 and 785 750	Twyford Gravel Pits
28	SU 807 625	Moor Green Lakes (Eversley Gravel Pits)
29	SU 807 800	Bowsey Hill
30	SU 842 625	Wildmoor Heath (aka Edgebarrow Heath)
31	SU 877 630	Swinley Forest (Wishmoor area)
32	SU 875 655	Swinley Forest, Crowthorne Woods (Caesar's Camp and The Lookout)
33	SU 885 870	Cockmarsh
34	SU 895 825	Summerleaze Gravel Pits
35	SU 908 788	Bray Gravel Pits
36	SU 935 795	Dorney Wetlands, Slough Sewage Farm and Jubilee River
37	TQ 000 760	Datchet Common Gravel Pits
38	TQ 008 770	Queen Mother Reservoir
39	TQ 005 745 and 010 735	Wraysbury Gravel Pits, (Sunnymeads)
40	TQ 010 735	Wraysbury Gravel Pits (Village Pit)
41	TQ 010 755	Horton Gravel Pits

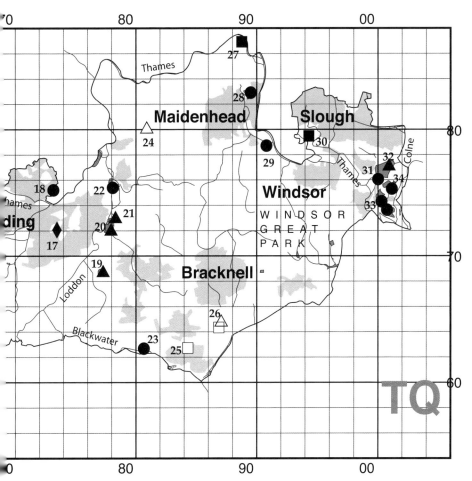

The main areas for birdwatching in Berkshire are the river valleys of the Kennet, Lambourn, Loddon, Blackwater and the Thames, the areas of downland around Walbury Hill, Lambourn, Compton and Aldworth and the forests and heathlands in the south and east of the county.

This map shows the general area of the Lambourn, Compton and Aldworth Downs and Windsor Great Park but includes most other frequently mentioned sites visited regularly by birdwatchers. For further detailed site information try www.berksbirds.co.uk or www.birdsofberkshire.co.uk where maps and site descriptions can often be found. Sites on this map have been given a number, a map reference (approximate centre) and one of the following symbols:

●	Gravel Pits	▲	Lakes and Reservoirs
□	Commons and Heaths	△	Downland and Parkland
■	Marshes and Sewage Farms	◆	Woodland

Please note that inclusion of a site does not guarantee free or safe access.

SPECIES FOR WHICH NOTES OR DESCRIPTIONS ARE REQUIRED

For the purposes of considering the acceptability of records of locally rare or scarce species the Berkshire Records Committee divides sightings into three categories:

1. Nationally rare species for which records first have to be accepted by British Birds Rarities Committee;

2. Locally rare species for which a full description is required on an " Unusual Record Form";

3. Locally scarce species (or less scarce species seen in unusual circumstances eg exceptional date) for which a short supporting note is required.

The species for which supporting notes or a full description are required are as follows:

Category 2: Full description needed

Fulmar; Storm Petrel; Purple Heron; White Stork; Spoonbill; Bean Goose; Pink-footed Goose; American Wigeon; Ferruginous Duck; Velvet Scoter; Honey Buzzard; Goshawk; Rough-legged Buzzard; Spotted Crake; Corncrake; Crane; Kentish Plover; Dotterel; Pectoral Sandpiper; Purple Sandpiper; Buff-breasted Sandpiper; All Phalarope species; all Skua species; Sabine's Gull; Ring-billed Gull; "Caspian" Gull; Iceland Gull; Roseate Tern; Bee-eater; Shore Lark; Richard's Pipit; Tawny Pipit; Bluethroat; Savi's, Aquatic, Marsh, Icterine, Melodious and Yellow-browed Warblers; Golden Oriole; Woodchat Shrike; Serin; Twite; Mealy Redpoll; Common Rosefinch; Lapland and Ortolan Buntings.

Category 3: Short note required indicating grounds for identification

All Divers; Red-necked, Slavonian and Black-necked Grebes; Manx Shearwater; Leach's Petrel; Gannet; Whooper Swan (unless feral); White-fronted Goose; Brent Goose; Scaup; Eider; Long-tailed Duck; Marsh Harrier; Hen Harrier (away from Downs); Montagu's Harrier; Osprey; Knot; Temminck's Stint; Curlew Sandpiper; Black-tailed and Bar-tailed Godwit; Spotted Redshank; Mediterranean Gull; Glaucous Gull; all Auk species: Long-eared Owl; Hoopoe; Wryneck; Water Pipit; Dipper; Wood Warbler; Firecrest; Pied Flycatcher; Bearded Tit; Red-backed Shrike; Great Grey Shrike; Hooded Crow; Raven; Tree Sparrow; Snow Bunting; and all exceptionally early or late dates for migrants where confusion with another species is possible.

Where a Category 2 species is identified by a large number of observers of like mind a description or detailed supporting notes is usually unnecessary and where a record is supported by a photograph adequate for identification purposes a short supporting note will usually be sufficient. The Berkshire Records Committee may call for additional information or supporting notes for species other than those listed above, where this is considered appropriate to properly adjudicate an observation.

Anyone in doubt about the level of detail needed should contact the County Recorder from whom copies of the " Unusual Record Form" can be obtained. Observers with access to the Internet can find a copy of this Record Form at **www.berksbirds.co.uk**.

Grovelands Garden Centre

166 Hyde End Road, Shinfield, Reading

Bird food, bird boxes and feeders
Outdoor clothing for all weather protection
Unusual specialist plants, shrubs and Roses
Herbaceous plants & bulbs, Climbers and Conifers
2 year guarantee on hardy plants
Composts & Peats, Grits & Gravels
Pet food & accessories
Bedding plants
House & Conservatory Plants and hanging baskets
Barbecues & Patio Heaters and Garden Ornaments
Outdoor Garden Furniture (large selection)
Christmas Trees & Tree Decorations
(decorating service available)

Coffee Shop

Open 7 days a week
For seasonal offers and more information visit **www.grovelands.com**
Freephone **0800 0747195**
Located just south of Reading on the B3349 between Shinfield and Spencers Wood

130